IMAGES
of America

UNIVERSITY PLACE

I0806444

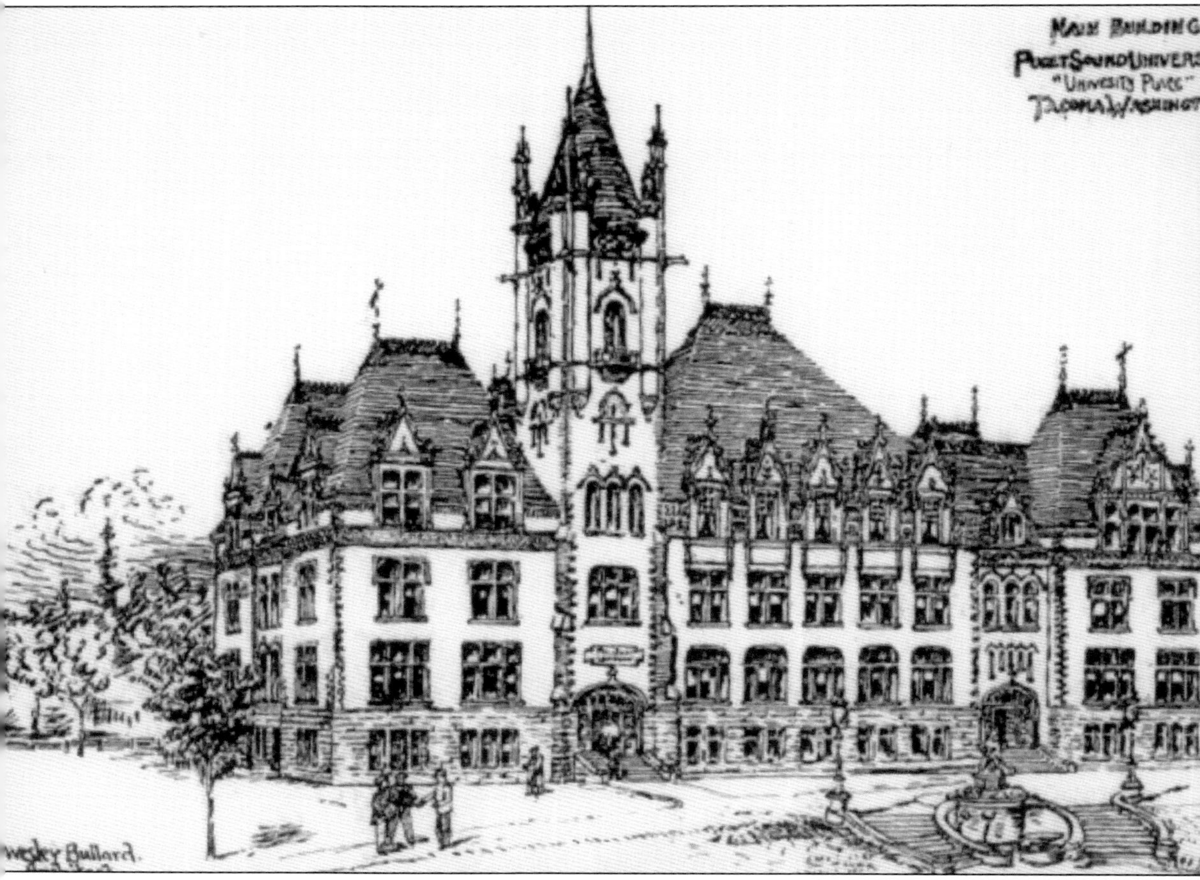

This sketch is a rendering of the Main Building of the proposed Puget Sound University, which was to be constructed in the mid-1890s. The university never came to fruition, but the name "University Place," which appears in the upper right-hand corner of the sketch, survived. (Sketch courtesy of the University of Puget Sound Library.)

ON THE COVER: Members of the newly formed University Place Volunteer Fire Department pose with their first fire truck in December 1941. The truck was purchased with donations from residents of the community. The photograph was taken in front of the University Place School, located on the corner of Twenty-seventh Street West and Grandview Drive. The school serviced all students in the district, from kindergarten through eighth grade. (Courtesy of the UP Historical Society via the UP Fire Department.)

IMAGES
of America

UNIVERSITY PLACE

Arne Handeland

ARCADIA
PUBLISHING

ISBN 978-0-7385-9515-3

Published by Arcadia Publishing
Charleston, South Carolina

Printed in the United States of America

Library of Congress Control Number: 2012932891

For all general information, please contact Arcadia Publishing:
Telephone 843-853-2070
Fax 843-853-0044
E-mail sales@arcadiapublishing.com
For customer service and orders:
Toll-Free 1-888-313-2665

Visit us on the Internet at www.arcadiapublishing.com

This book is dedicated to my family: to Andee, for her encouragement and support in all my endeavors; to our children, Karina and Brent, who grew up living and experiencing the opportunities that University Place had to offer and inspired me to do this book for them and for everyone else in University Place; to the memory of my mother, Martha, who was born in University Place in 1910; and, finally, to all the other Leland and Tweiten family members who contributed to the growth of this wonderful community.

Contents

ACKNOWLEDGMENTS

University Place Historical Society; Cindy Bonaro, UP librarian and president of the historical society; City of University Place; UP Fire Department; Tacoma Public Library, Northwest Collection; Joe Scorcio, Danny Marshall, Joe and Sally Thomas, UP School District; George Luscombe, for his history of UP schools; Pat Mercero and Vi White, early preservers of UP history; Inez Leland Glass; Steve Anderson; Laurent Jarvis; Sally Barrett; Lorna and Elmer Smith; Joe Stortino; Joseph Gouednik; Burleigh Cubert; Deborah Nicholas; Junita Fowler Bjork; Andee Handeland; Rick Gamas; Jack Harding; Bob Lucey; Jamie Fay; Sherylee Ceccanti; Linda Grimsey; Andy Ward; Bill Bush; Neil Holden; Don Larsen; Brooke Judge; John Tollefson; Art Broback; Nancy Archer; Carolyn Rzesutek; Joan Curtis; Sue Kaelin; and many others for their input and advice.

Unless otherwise noted, photographs and images used in this book are from the archives of the University Place Historical Society and my own personal collection.

INTRODUCTION

> Any attempt to describe the charming beauty and magnificent grandeur of the water and mountain scenery surrounding University Place will always fall short of making an adequate impression upon the mind of the reader or listener. Even those familiar with the picturesque landscapes of Western Washington will be compelled to visit the grounds or combine, in their imagination, many of the most impressive scenes of the far-famed Puget Sound country in order to realize the never ending pleasure of the inhabitants of University Place with their location and surroundings. On the western horizon stand the majestic Olympic Mountains on whose serrated crest, like a silhouette against the sky, perpetual snows rest as a mantle of purity. Eastward stands the majestic Mount Tahoma (now Mount Rainier), monarch of the Cascade Range, lifting its regal head far above the clouds nearly three miles above the shores of Puget Sound, snow-capped and ice-girdled throughout the centuries.

With such a description, who wouldn't entertain the desire to own a slice of this idyllic paradise? This is how University Place was advertised by the University Land Company in 1895, when it was promoting the sale of lots surrounding the proposed Puget Sound University, along the shores of the Sound just south and west of Tacoma. When the college outgrew its location at South Tenth Street and Yakima Avenue, this Methodist Episcopal Church–run school began looking for a more spacious location. A tract of land of about 420 acres was acquired partly through donation (100 acres) and the rest by purchase at $300 per acre. This tract was called "the University Place." The university would occupy approximately 60 acres, and the remaining land would be subdivided and sold in lots 25 feet by 100 feet at $125 each. This would raise the $500,000 needed to construct the university buildings. With a great deal of excitement, plans were drawn and ground was broken in 1894 near present-day Thirty-first Street and Grandview Drive. Then economic disaster struck. The Panic of 1893 gradually moved its way west, and by 1895, all plans to finish the university died. Only the name, University Place, survived as a reminder of the university that never got built at this location. (The college did move from Tenth Street and Yakima Avenue to South Ninth Street and G Street in 1894, and then to Sixth Avenue and Sprague Street in 1903, and finally to its present site at 1500 North Warner Street in Tacoma in 1924.)

However, the few residents of University Place at the time did not relent on educating their own children. In 1894, the first University Place school, with an enrollment of seven students, was started in a rented house on the southwest corner of Twenty-seventh Street and Crystal Springs Road. On October 5, 1895, residents petitioned for the formation of School District No. 83, encompassing about eight square miles (the approximate boundaries of the current city of University Place). Despite building a new school at Twenty-seventh Street and Elwood Drive and naming it Lemon's Beach School (after early University Place pioneers John and Mary Lemon), the district decided to retain the name University Place School District. The rest is history.

Prior to the 1890s, University Place was largely unoccupied. Even Native Americans of the region (the Puyallups, Nisquallies, and Steilacoom tribes) did not have settlements in the area. The Steilacooms probably had seasonal encampments along the shores of Puget Sound extending to Day Island, and the upland areas were used for hunting and foraging but not for habitation. The eventual occupation of University Place came about after Europeans arrived in the region, beginning with British explorer George Vancouver's expedition into Puget Sound in 1792 while looking for the Northwest Passage through North America. This formed the basis for British claims to the region and the establishment of British settlements north of the Columbia River, including the Hudson Bay Company's Fort Nisqually near Dupont and the Puget Sound Agricultural Company near Steilacoom and Lakewood. In 1841, Lt. Charles Wilkes of the United States Exploring Expedition came to Puget Sound, thoroughly charting it and establishing American claims to the region. Most Americans coming to the Oregon country, however, continued to settle south of the Columbia River. Tensions grew between Britain and the United States over the Oregon country, and threats of war were openly expressed (such as James K. Polk's campaign promise of "54-40 or fight" in the 1844 presidential election). But the land claims and boundary dispute were settled short of war in 1846, with the United States compromising with Britain. The existing border between British Canada and the United States was extended along the 49th parallel, from the Rocky Mountains to the Pacific Ocean, with the exception that all of Vancouver Island would remain within Canada. Following this treaty, Americans began moving in to the Puget Sound area, displacing the British who were already there, not always without rancor. The United States established Fort Steilacoom to protect its interests in the region from both the British and the Native Americans. Eventually, the British were forced to leave or become Americans, and the Native Americans signed treaties relegating them to reservations and giving them defined fishing rights.

In the midst of this transition, the British ship *Albion* was confiscated by US Customs in 1850 for illegally cutting timber for spars near Port Angeles. The ship was taken to Steilacoom, where the crew was taken off the ship and told not to return until the *Albion*'s fate was determined. This took several months, and most of the crew left, making their way to the goldfields of California. However, a few stayed put. One of these, William Bolton, the *Albion*'s shipwright, remained in Steilacoom; his British heritage and rather crude language and behavior was not always welcomed by the Americans. So, he, along with his young apprentice William Elders, partner Fredrick Rapjohns, and crew member Dick Gibbs, moved to unoccupied land north of Steilacoom along Puget Sound. Bolton quickly became a US citizen and was granted a land claim of 640 acres that became known as Bolton's Plain or Bolton's Prairie. He and his companions were the first residents of what has become University Place. Bill Bolton created a successful shipbuilding and ship-repair business near present-day Sunset Beach, got married, and eventually died in University Place on January 5, 1904.

So, that is the story behind the beginnings of University Place. This book will touch on only a few of the many personal stories and memories of the thousands of people who have lived and are living here and who have made an impact on the growth and destiny of this vibrant community. I can only hope that this Images of America book will broaden your knowledge of University Place and perhaps inspire you to want to learn more and share and record your own histories.

One

The Early Years and Pioneers

Where to start? The human habitation of University Place is no more than the blink of an eye in historical terms, but earlier events certainly had an impact on the region's development. From the Ice Age, to the Crusades, to national rivalries, all of these leave their footprint on University Place.

First, during the last Ice Age some 12,000 years ago, the Vashon Glacier covered the Puget Sound basin, between the Olympic and Cascade Mountains to just south of Olympia, with a sheet of ice at places miles thick. Where it covered University Place, the ice was about half-a-mile thick. As the glacier melted and retreated, it carved out Puget Sound, leaving behind all the inlets, passages, bays, and islands that are so familiar to us. The region that would become known as University Place inherited a pretty rocky topography with little topsoil and a sand-and-gravel deposit that would be the basis for the main industry in UP for over 100 years.

The onset of the Crusades in the 1200s set in motion an age of exploration, with the aim of discovering and controlling newfound riches in the Middle East and Asia. Finding a water route through the Americas was the goal of many early explorers, including Capt. George Vancouver, who came into Puget Sound in 1792. In many instances, more than one nation claimed the same area. Puget Sound was claimed by Great Britain and the United States and, to a lesser extent, by Spain and Russia. Eventually, the United States prevailed, and Washington became the nation's 42nd state.

This chapter will explore some of this early history and will touch on the pioneers who came and settled in University Place.

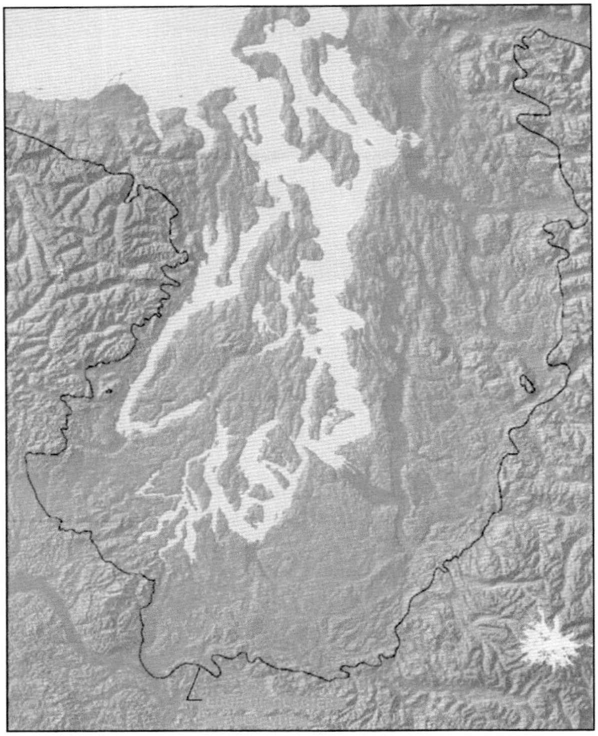

A sheet of ice, known as the Vashon Glacier, covered the Puget Sound basin some 12,000 years ago. At University Place, the ice was about one half of a mile thick. As it retreated, it left the region with a pretty rocky environment and a huge sand-and-gravel deposit. The dark black line shows the extent of the glacier through the Puget Sound region.

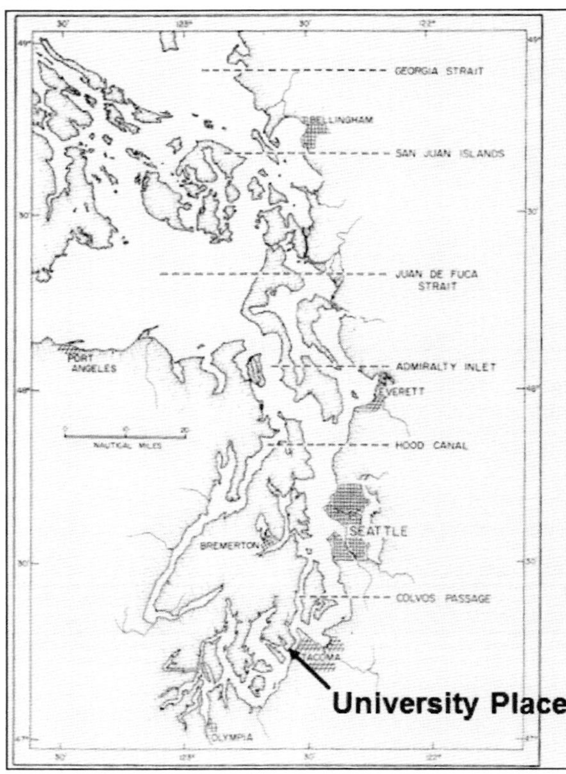

As the glacier melted, Puget Sound with its many islands, inlets, bays, and passages was left in its wake. University Place is located on the Sound, just south and west of Tacoma.

Capt. George Vancouver explored the Washington and British Columbia coasts in 1792, searching for the Northwest Passage through North America. Lt. Peter Puget of the Vancouver expedition sailed into and mapped much of Puget Sound, establishing many of the place names as well as British claims to the region.

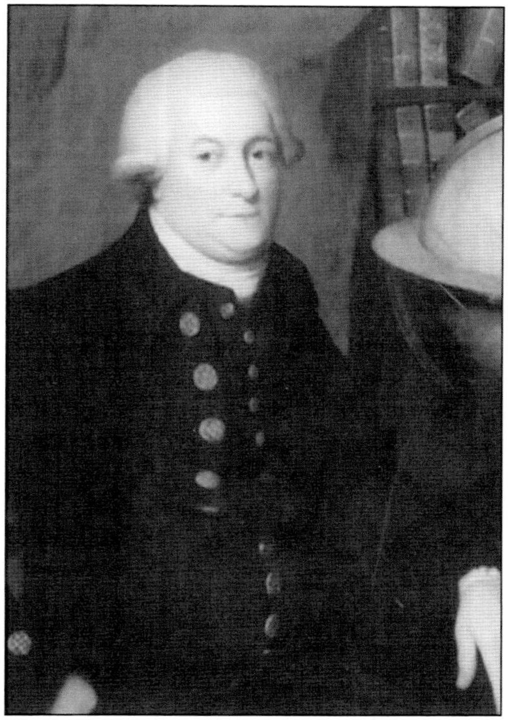

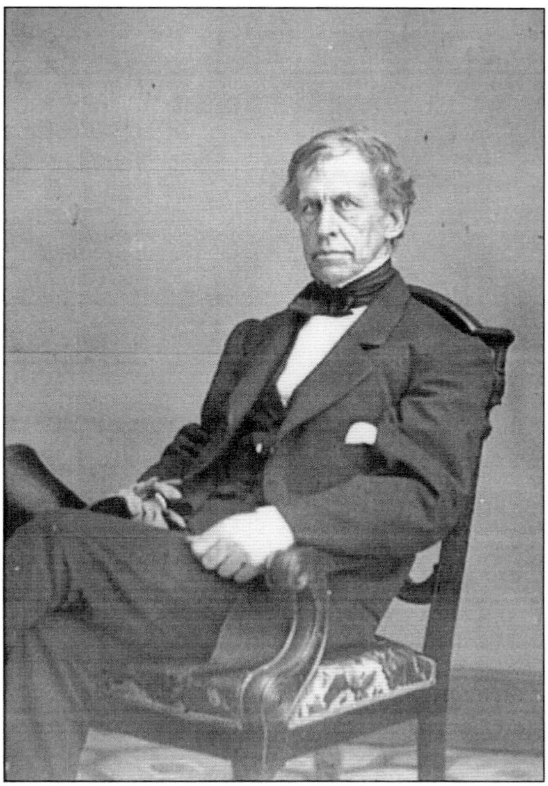

Lt. Charles Wilkes of the United States Exploring Expedition came to Puget Sound in 1841, produced detailed charts of the southern Sound, and gave names to many of the islands and bays. Wilkes established US claims north of the Columbia River.

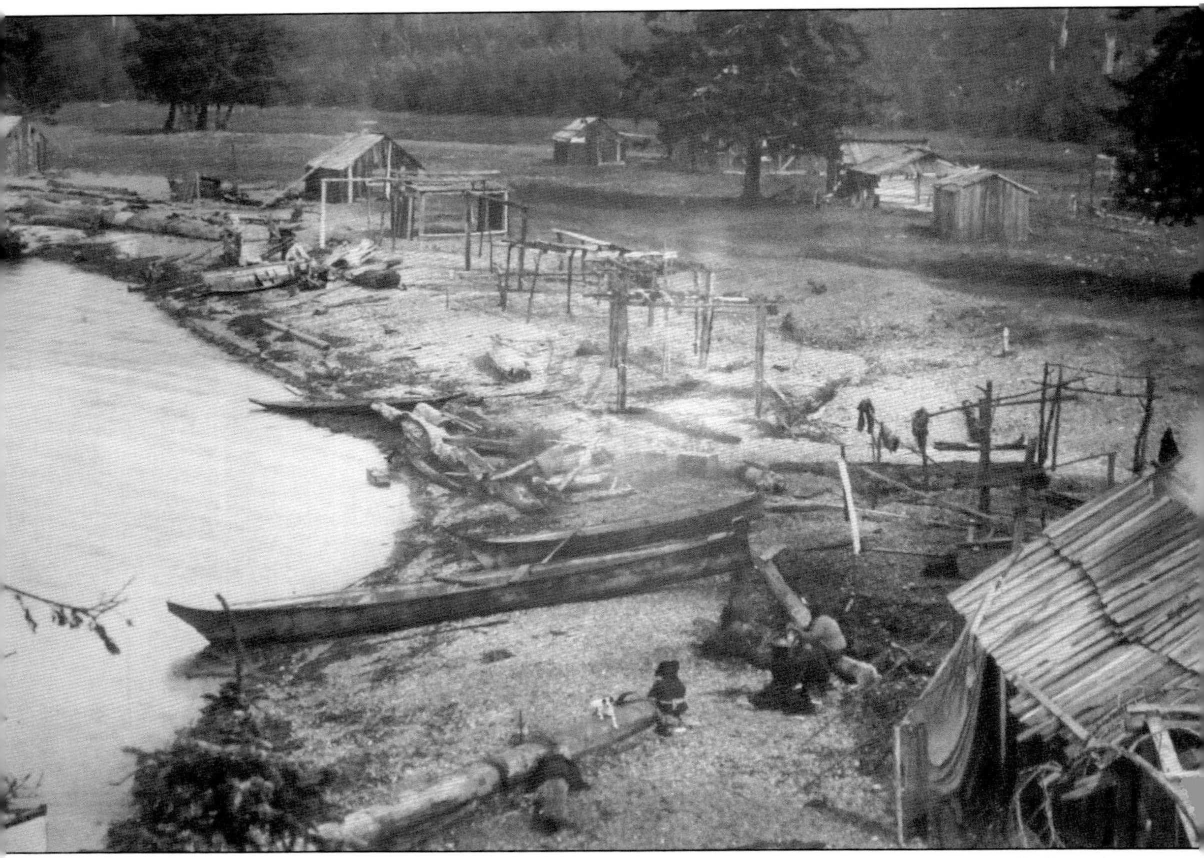

The Steilacoom Indians are the indigenous inhabitants south of Chambers Creek, but they also had a permanent camp on the north side of the creek that is now part of University Place. However, most of the tribe's activities and living were confined to south and west of the creek because this region was much more geographically accessible than going up the steep hill on the north side of the creek. Seasonal camps probably extended along the Puget Sound shoreline to Day Island, the northern extent of University Place, and perhaps some hunting and gathering occurred on the uplands. (Courtesy of the Steilacoom Tribal Museum.)

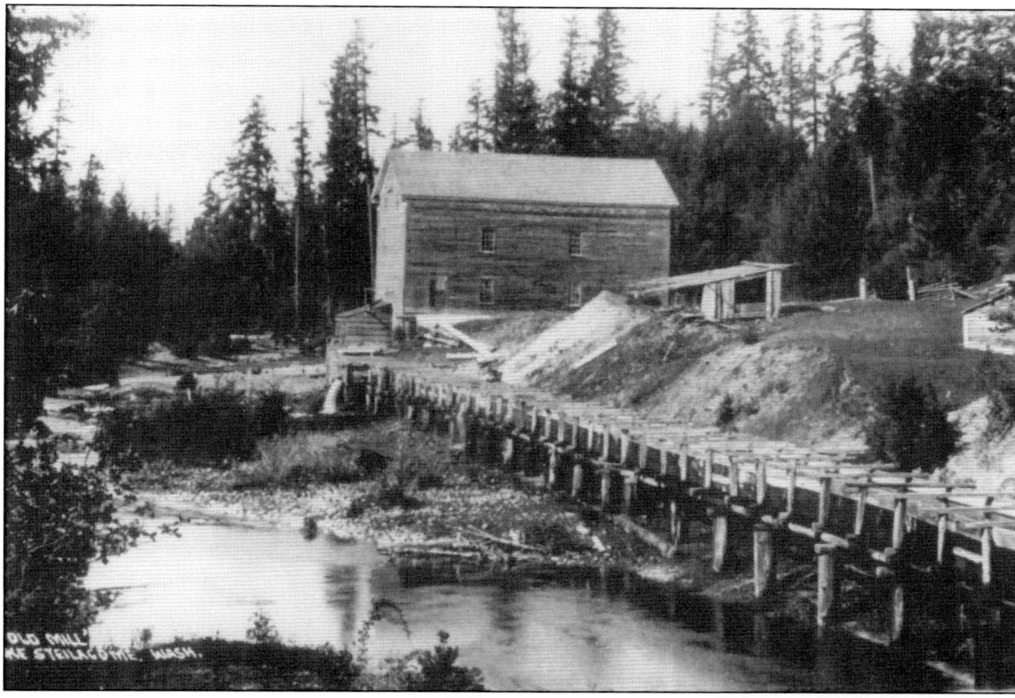

Although Thomas Chambers settled in Steilacoom, he is the namesake of the creek that separates University Place from Steilacoom and of a primary school in the UP School District. Chambers came to Steilacoom with his wife in 1847 and settled on land once owned by J.T. Heath of the Hudson Bay Company. In 1848, he was appointed justice of the peace and county commissioner and was known as Judge Chambers from that time on. He was elected as a probate judge in 1854. Chambers was a businessman who built and operated a gristmill, a flour mill, and a lumber mill on Chambers Creek. He died on December 28, 1876, and is buried in the Masonic Cemetery near Steilacoom. Chambers Primary School (right) is one of several UP locations bearing his name.

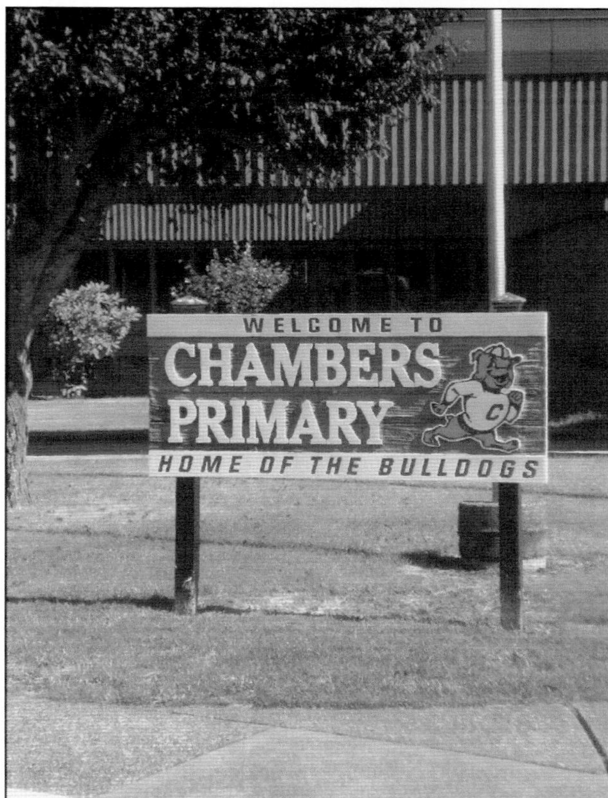

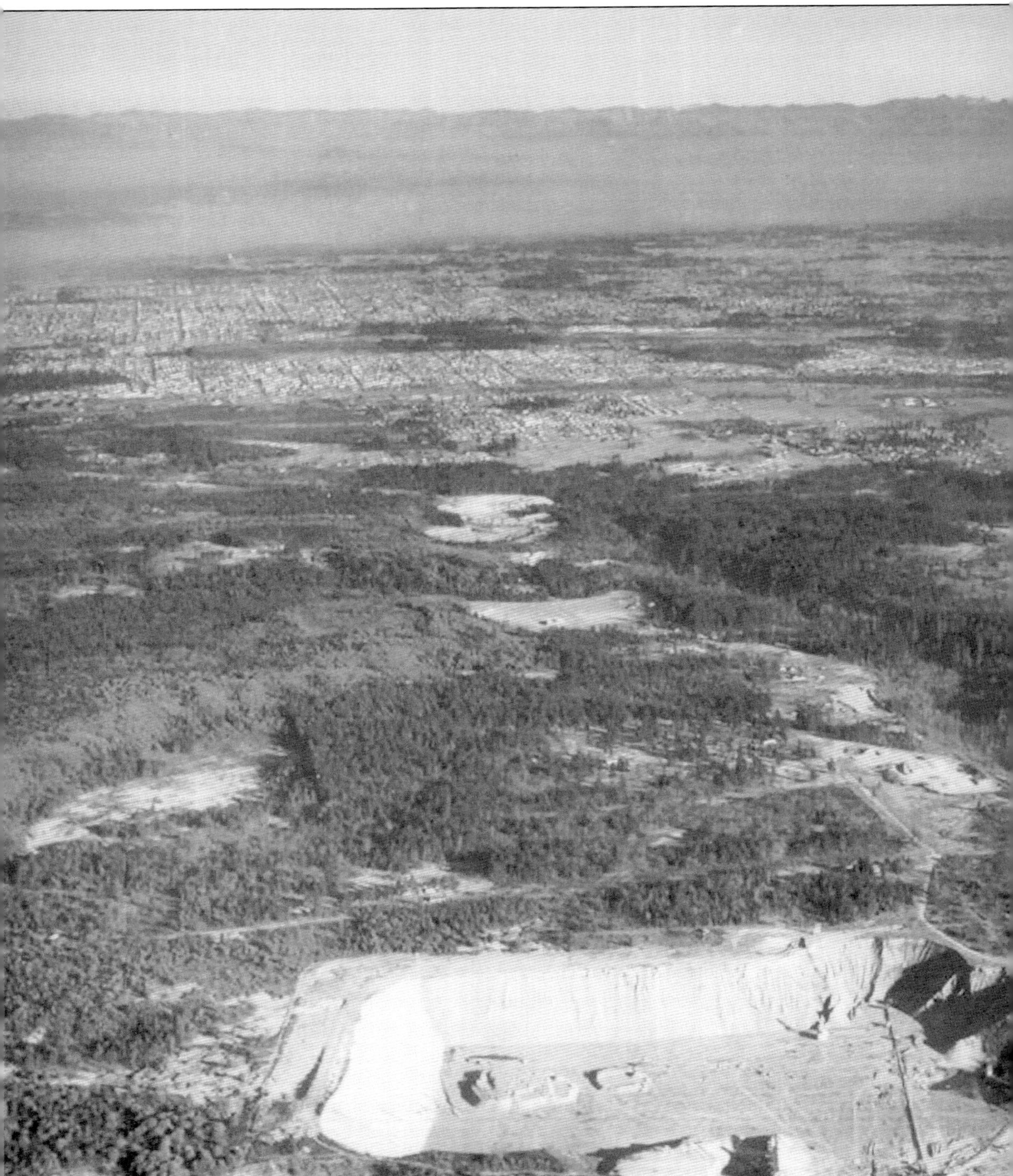

This aerial photograph of University Place predates most current development. It centers on the area of the gravel pits near where John S. Baker built the Sunset Beach hotel in the mid-1890s. William Bolton settled near this area in the 1850s. The gravel pits of the Glacier and Pioneer

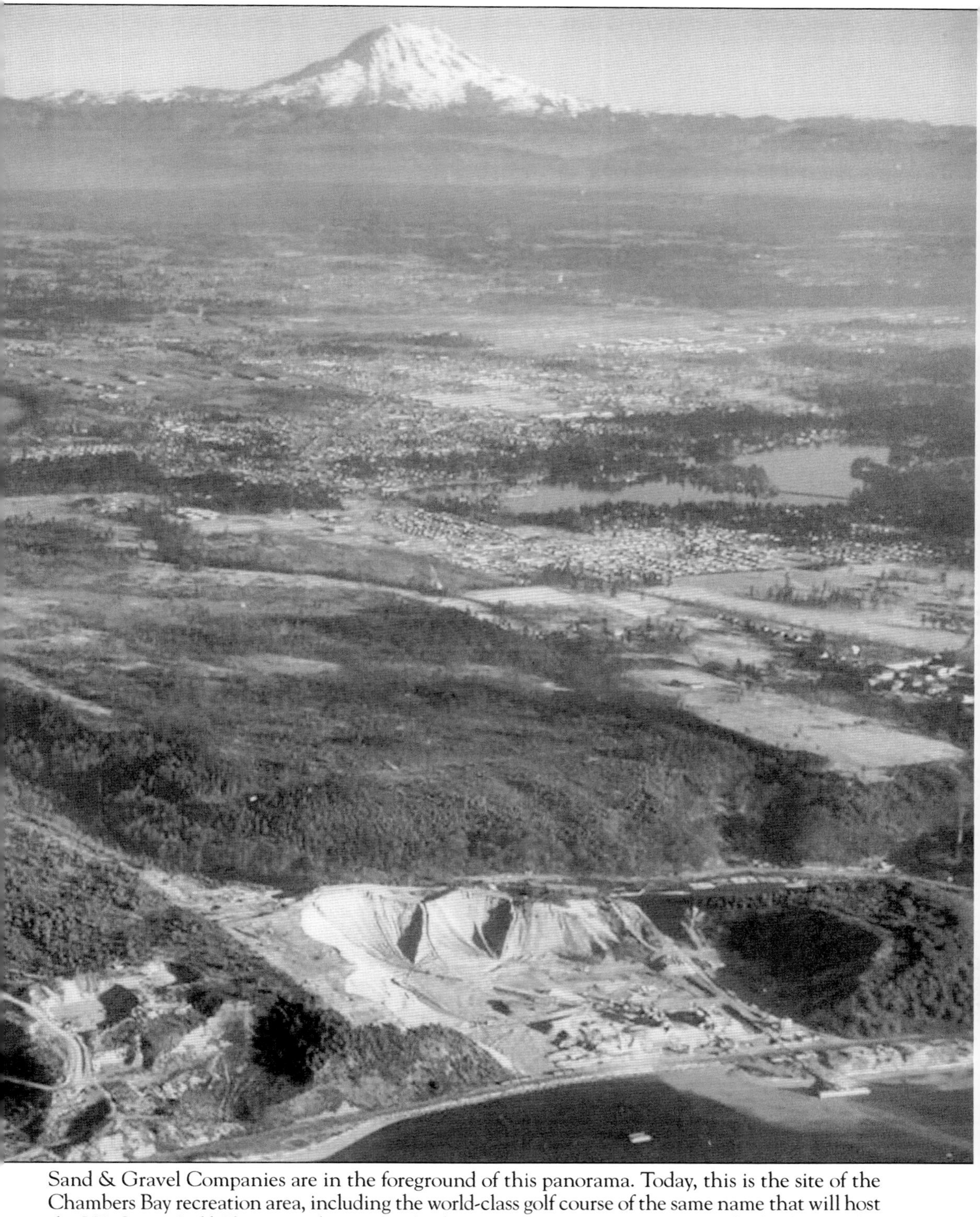

Sand & Gravel Companies are in the foreground of this panorama. Today, this is the site of the Chambers Bay recreation area, including the world-class golf course of the same name that will host the US Open Golf Championship in 2015. The majestic Mount Rainier is in the background.

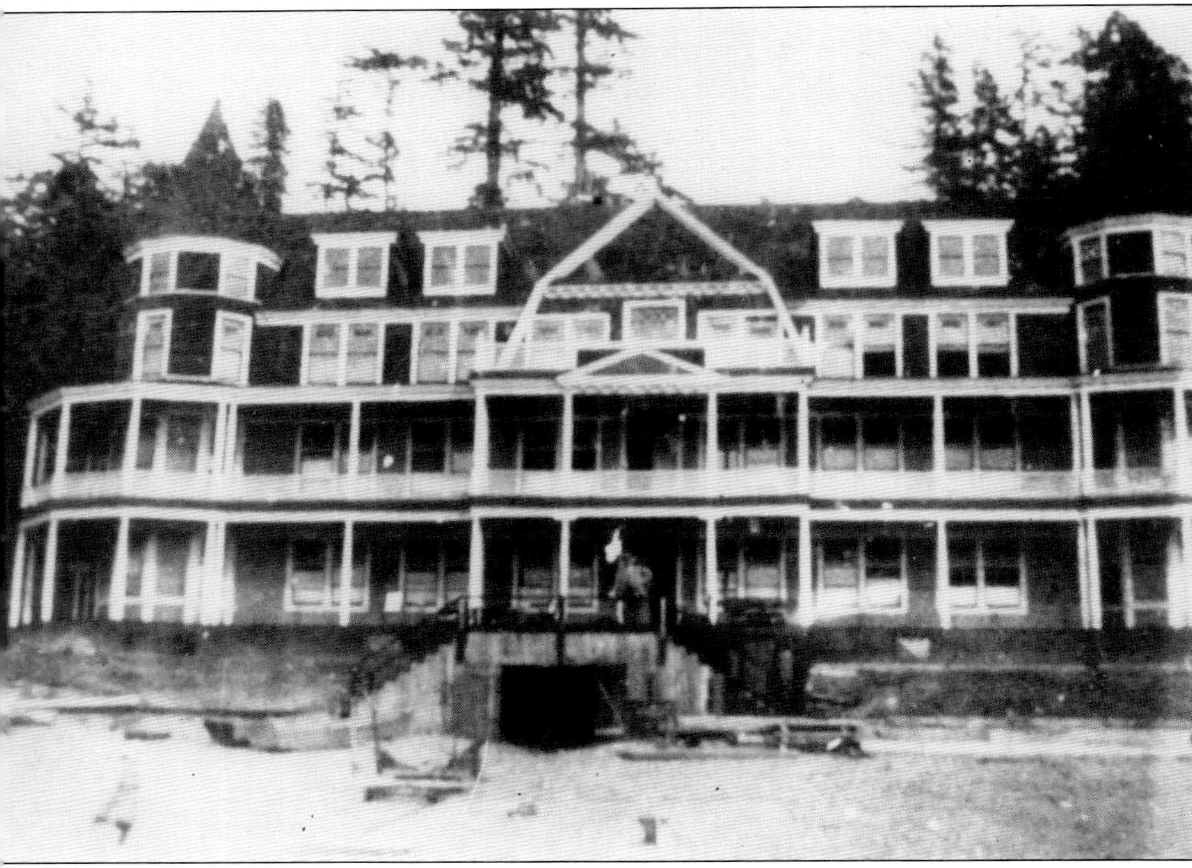

In the late 1890s, John S. Baker bought a seven-and-a-half-acre plot known as Sunset Beach and proceeded to build a four-story lodge on the hill overlooking Puget Sound. It could be reached by a wagon road winding through University Place but was mainly accessed by small steamers reaching its dock. It serviced sailors of the Mosquito Fleet that plied the waters of the Sound and weekend revelers from Seattle, Tacoma, and Olympia. The lodge provided saddle horses, swimming, boating, hiking, clamming, and, by some accounts, "ladies of the night." The hotel burned to the ground in 1904 and was never rebuilt. The land was eventually platted and placed on the market for residential development in 1933.

In March 1888, John and Mary Lemon, along with Chester Higbe and Phillip Buckner, purchased a 167.5-acre tract of land on the Puget Sound from Rudolphus Weston and his wife, Nancy, for $30,000. The Lemons (shown at right and below) later bought out Higbe and Buckner. The Lemons came west from Minnesota. John had served in the Ohio infantry during the Civil War and published a newspaper for many years in Ohio and then Minnesota. The Lemons were very interested in education and were instrumental in encouraging the Methodist Church to build a college near their homestead, then known as Lemon's Beach. Due to the depression starting in 1893, the college was never built, but the area became known as University Place. In addition, the Pierce County directory of 1915 lists School District No. 82 as Lemon's Beach School District. University Place School District is No. 83 and was formed in 1895. (Both, courtesy of the Tacoma Public Library, Northwest Room, Richards Studio Collection.)

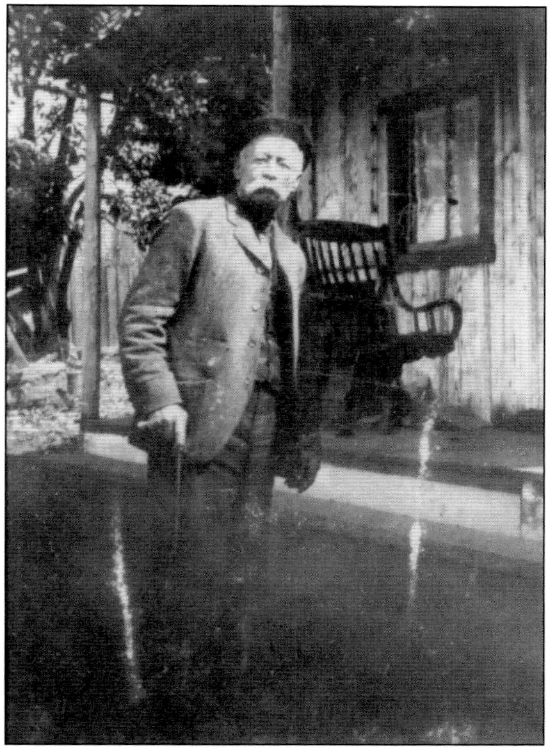

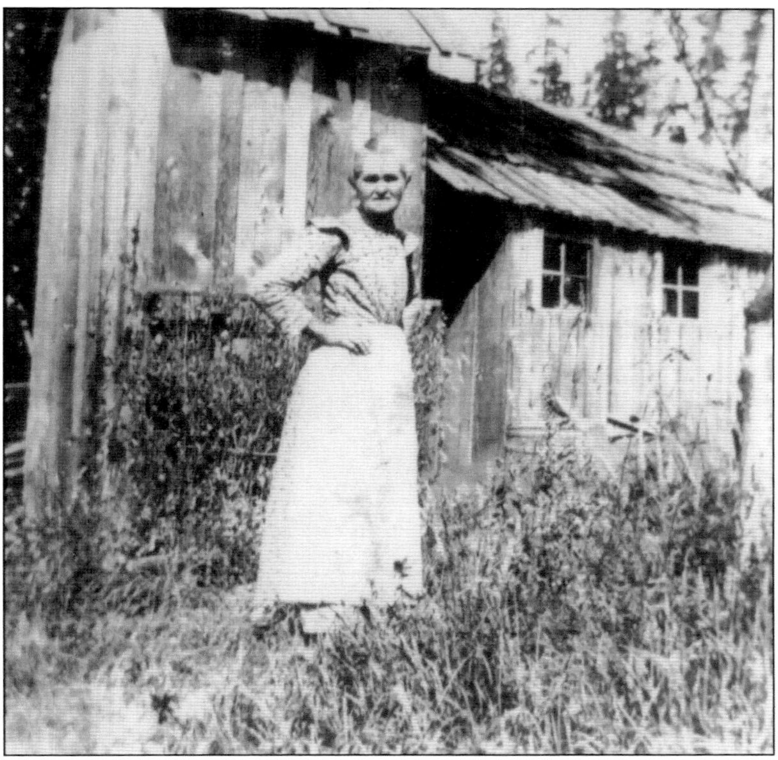

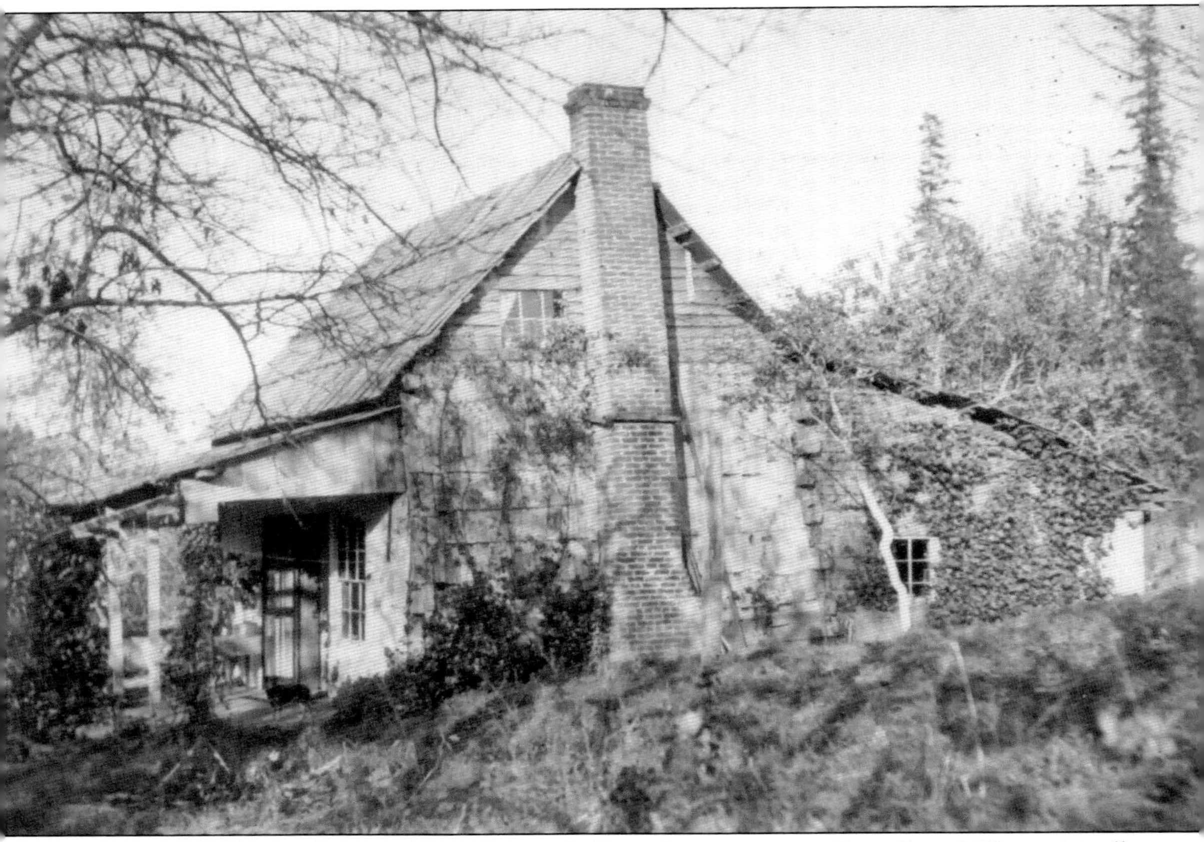

This is the home of John and Mary Lemon, built on their property on Puget Sound. They originally lived in the cabin/barn built by Reverend Weston when they moved onto the property in 1888. The cabin can be seen in the background of the photograph of Mary on the preceding page. The Lemons had four children: Charles, who became a Tacoma firefighter and shipyard worker; Bertha; Minnesota, who was called Minnie; and Anna. The Lemon property evolved into an orchard and cattle ranch, worked by John, and a holiday retreat and picnic area along the beach, run by Mary. In 1912, they sold a swath of land along the beachfront to Northern Pacific Railroad for $25,000. The railroad was securing property for the right-of-way to build its new route, which would effectively cut off access to the beach in University Place for the next 100 years. (Courtesy of the Tacoma Public Library, Northwest Room, Richards Studio Collection.)

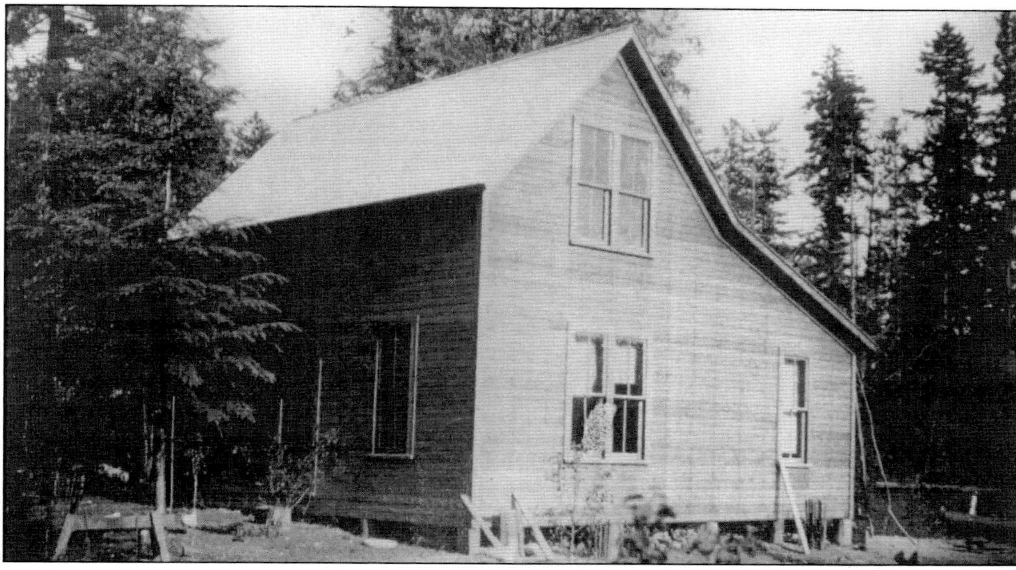

Andrew Jackson Drum was an Illinois farmer who came to this area in 1884, long before it was known as University Place. Somewhat discouraged by all of the tall trees, he returned to Illinois for eight years and then decided in 1892 to return and give the region another try. He cleared 10 acres by hand, bought more land and cleared it, and kept going until he owned most of the property from Cirque Drive to Fifty-fifth Street West and from Seventy-eighth Avenue West to Bridgeport Way. The above photograph shows the home he built for his family; it stood for 102 years before being demolished. The Drums made their living farming the land and raising chickens. They had a 150-foot chicken coop, where Cirque Drive now is, and stocked it with over 3,000 chickens. A portion of the property was exchanged with the school district in the 1980s and now houses an intermediate school bearing the Drum family name. The photograph below shows Truman Drum, Andrew's son, standing in front of the Drum Station along the Tacoma-Steilacoom trolley line. The trolley line survived until the late 1920s.

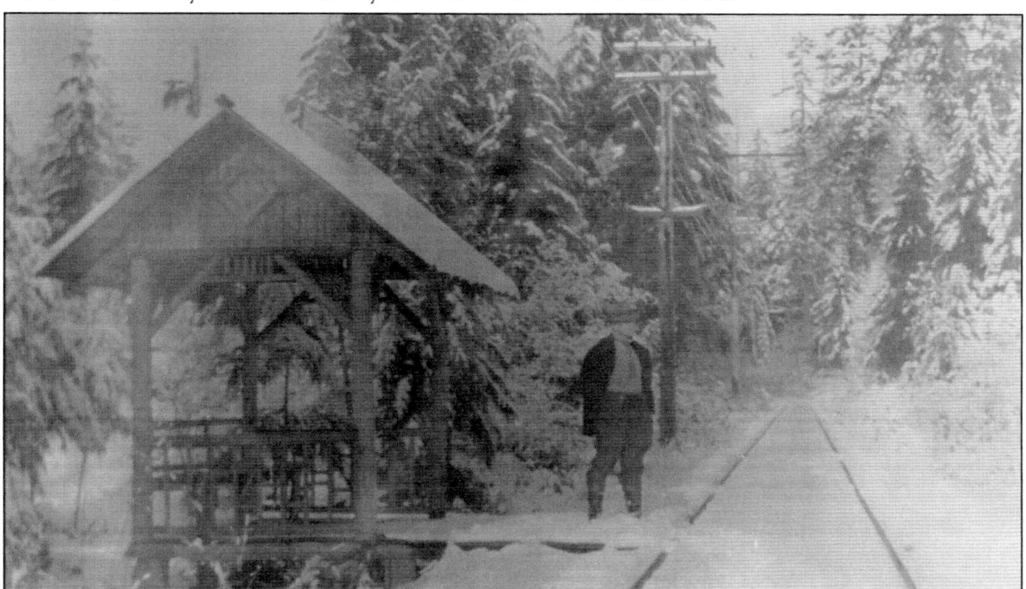

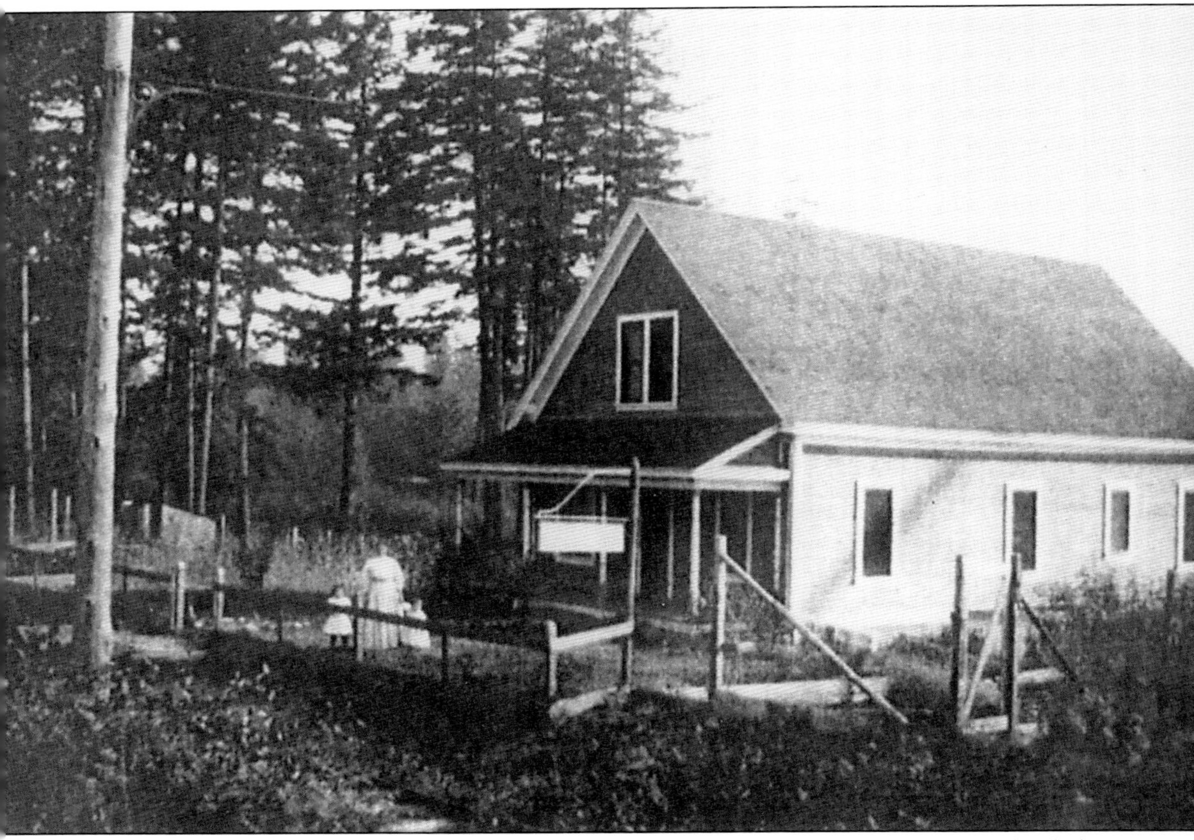

This photograph shows the home of L.F. Drexler and his family. Located on the east side of Thirty-fifth Street West and Bridgeport Way, the structure was also known as the Ferndale Station for the trolley line between K Street (now Martin Luther King Way) in Tacoma and Steilacoom. The operators of the trolley line brought groceries, lumber, water (at 25¢ a barrel), and other supplies on the freight run at the end of the day and dropped them at the Ferndale Station for UP residents. Drexler came to University Place in 1901 at the age of 25 and stayed for the rest of his life. He was an integral part of the development of University Place as a community. He predicted that UP would one day be the biggest residential area in Pierce County, but most people just laughed.

Two

A UNIVERSITY TRIES, A COMMUNITY SURVIVES

As stated in the introduction, University Place had its origins in the 1890s, with the dream of building Puget Sound University on a 400-acre parcel of undeveloped land overlooking Puget Sound southwest of Tacoma. Ground was broken for the college in 1894, and surrounding property was platted and put up for sale, but the ongoing depression that had begun on the East Coast in 1893 stopped any further development. By the early 1900s, all plans for a university were abandoned and much of the land became available for payment of back taxes. J.W. Murphy bought almost 600 acres for around $15,000. The university had paid around $300 an acre less than 10 years earlier. With the opportunity for cheap land, new settlers began arriving in the early 1900s. When electricity became available in 1910, the first University Place Improvement Club consisted of 42 families. Some of those early families are known and documented—the Thomases, Drexlers, Lelands, Elders, Stephans, Lemons, and Tollefsons—but many are not.

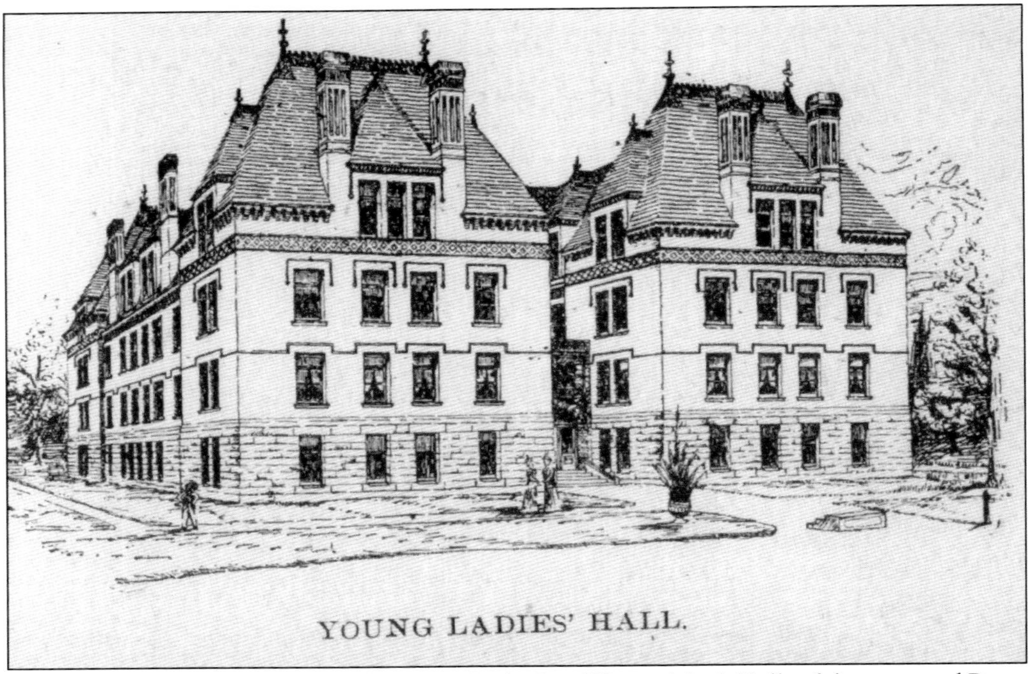

The sketches on this page depict the Young Ladies' and Young Men's Halls of the proposed Puget Sound University. These buildings were conspicuously separated by the Main Building shown on page 2. Although construction was started in 1894, it was soon halted as the depression of 1893 worked its way west. Only the name "University Place" survived. (Both, courtesy of the University of Puget Sound Library.)

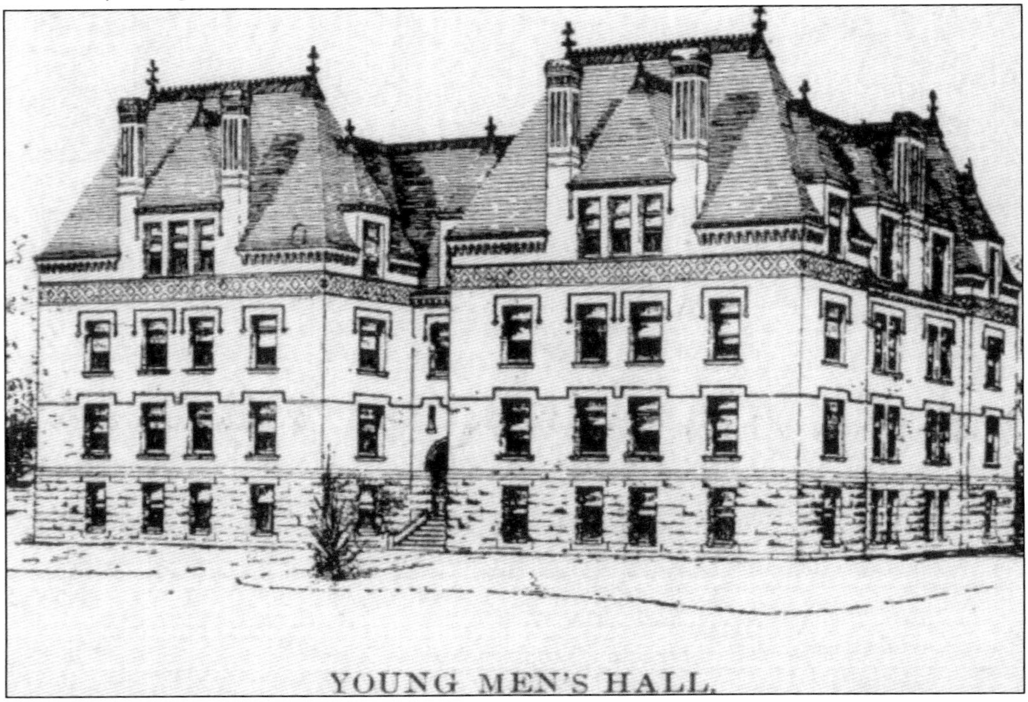

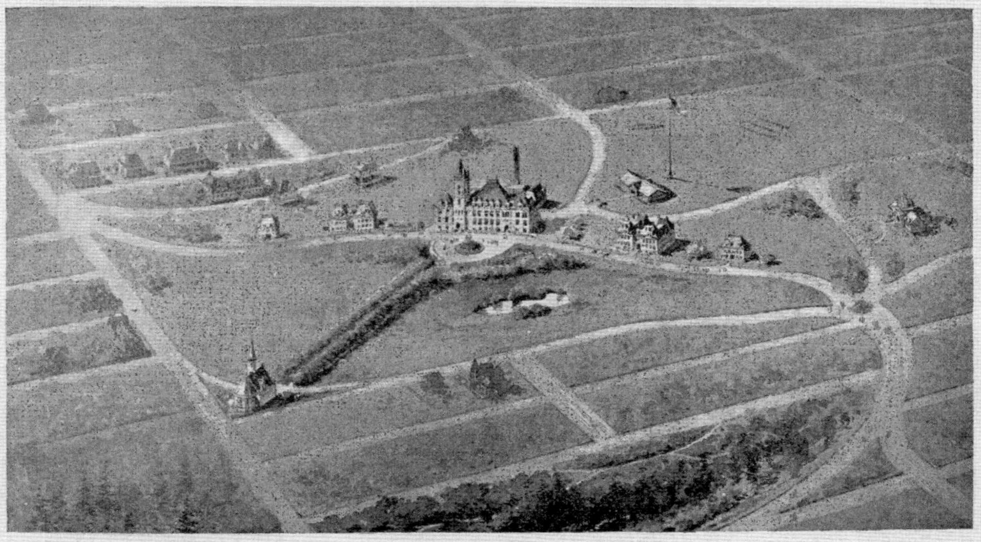

BIRDS-EYE VIEW OF CAMPUS AS PROPOSED.

This sketch shows a bird's-eye view of the 60-acre campus that was intended to become Puget Sound University. (Courtesy of the University of Puget Sound Library.)

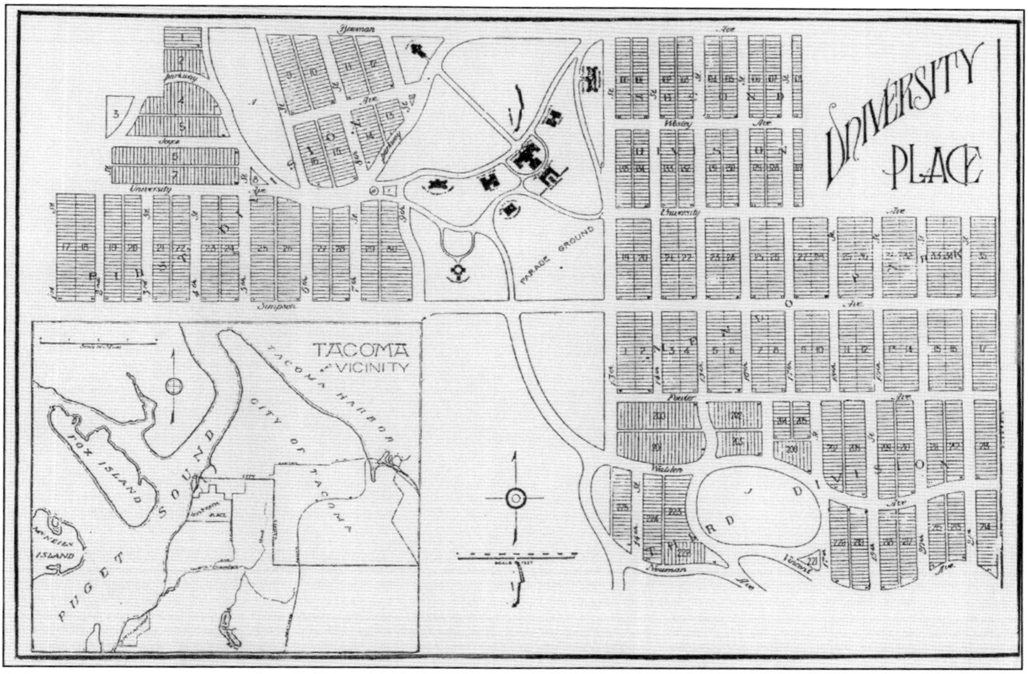

The properties surrounding the university that were put up for sale can be seen in this plan. Lots 25 feet by 100 feet were being offered for $125 each. Anyone buying land had to sign a pledge to never allow alcohol on the premises. (Courtesy of the University of Puget Sound Library.)

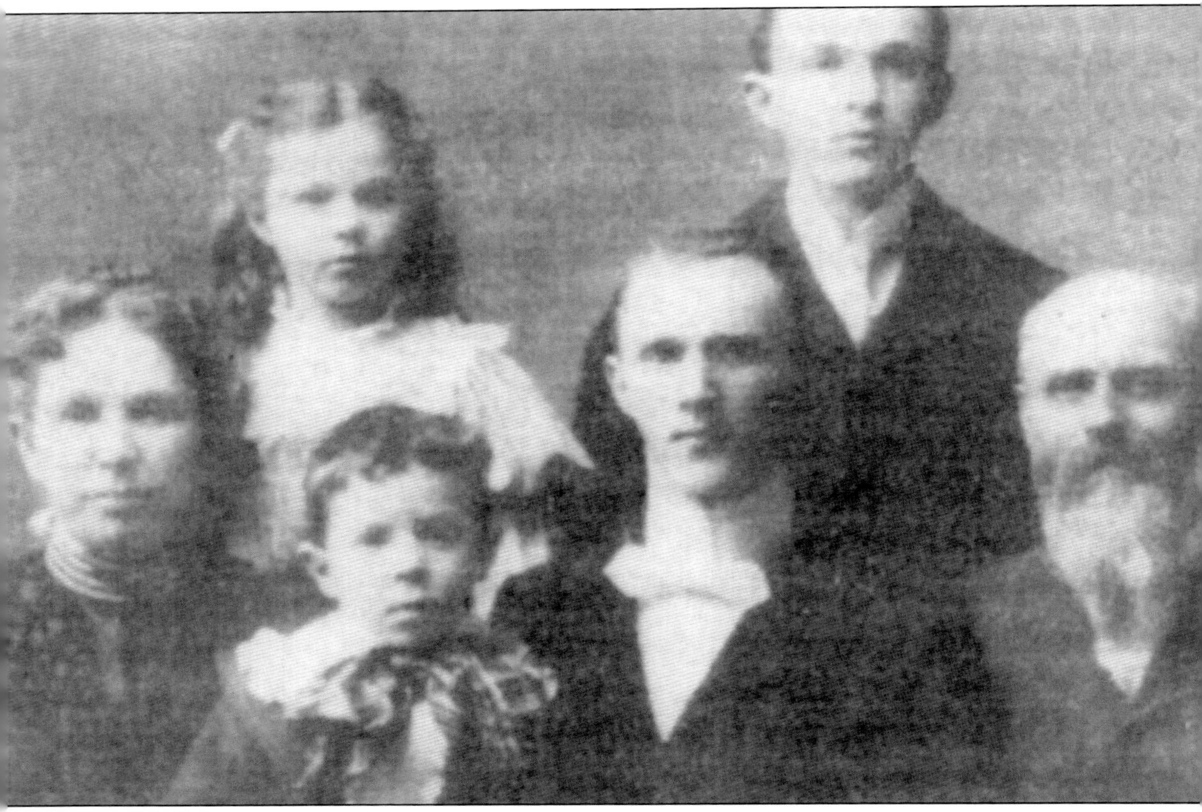

The Elder family moved to University Place from Tacoma in 1893 when F.A. Elder was appointed by Puget Sound University to handle property matters. After the university failed, the Elders remained and were instrumental in forming the University Place School District. F.A.'s brother Sam was named the first district director in November 1895. Members of the Elder family are, from left to right, as follows: (first row) Carrie E., Roger, Dwight, and F.A.; (second row) Edna and Clifford.

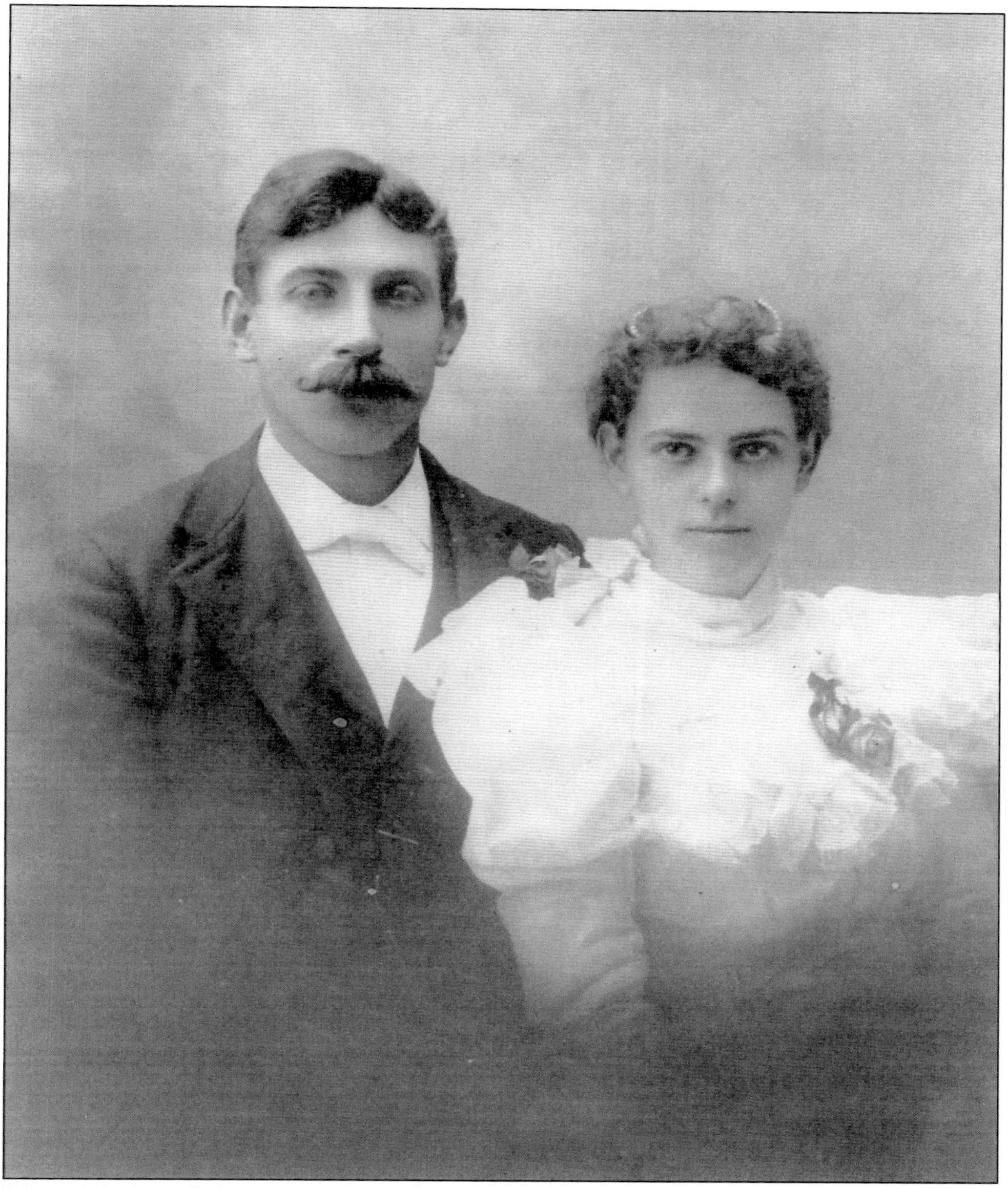

Lily and Richard Colegate were married in New York City in 1897 and came west to University Place in the early 1900s. They owned property along Sunset Drive and raised seven children of their own as well as taking in other boys who needed help. Lily was called "Grandma Colegate" by all of the neighbors and helped everyone in the community any way she could. Richard was injured working at the Clear Firs Lumber Mill and lost a hand. After that, he became the custodian at University Place School and knew all the children who attended there in the early years.

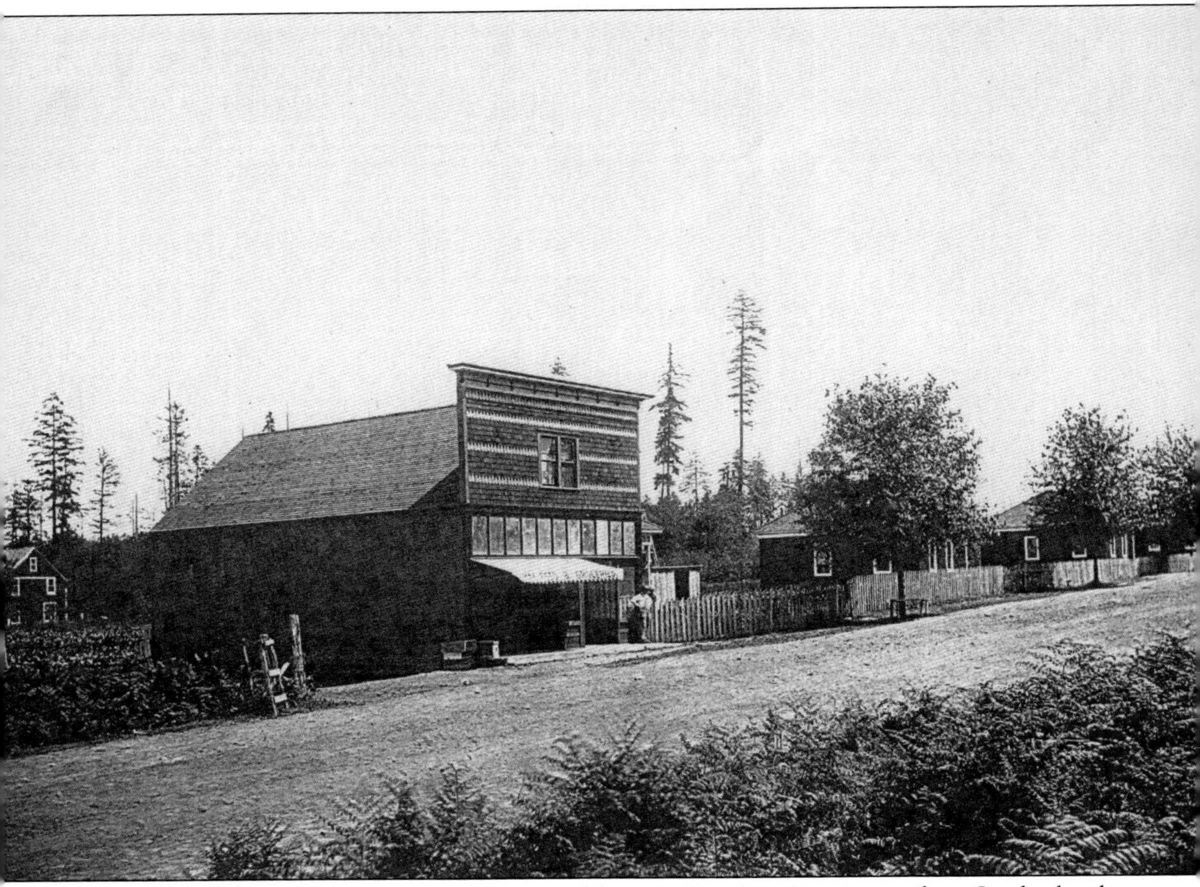

Frank and Agnes Thomas came to University Place via Aberdeen. Immigrants from Czechoslovakia, the couple purchased a hotel on the main street of Aberdeen and pursued the American dream. Unfortunately, the hotel was destroyed when the entire business district of Aberdeen went up in flames around 1900. When they heard of the opportunity to get a good deal on land in University Place, they made the move. This photograph is of the grocery store and some of the rental houses they built near Twenty-seventh Street and Grandview Drive. Agnes ran the store, and Frank had a shoe repair shop in downtown Tacoma. Their sons, Al, Joe, and Frank Jr., played a big role in the development of UP.

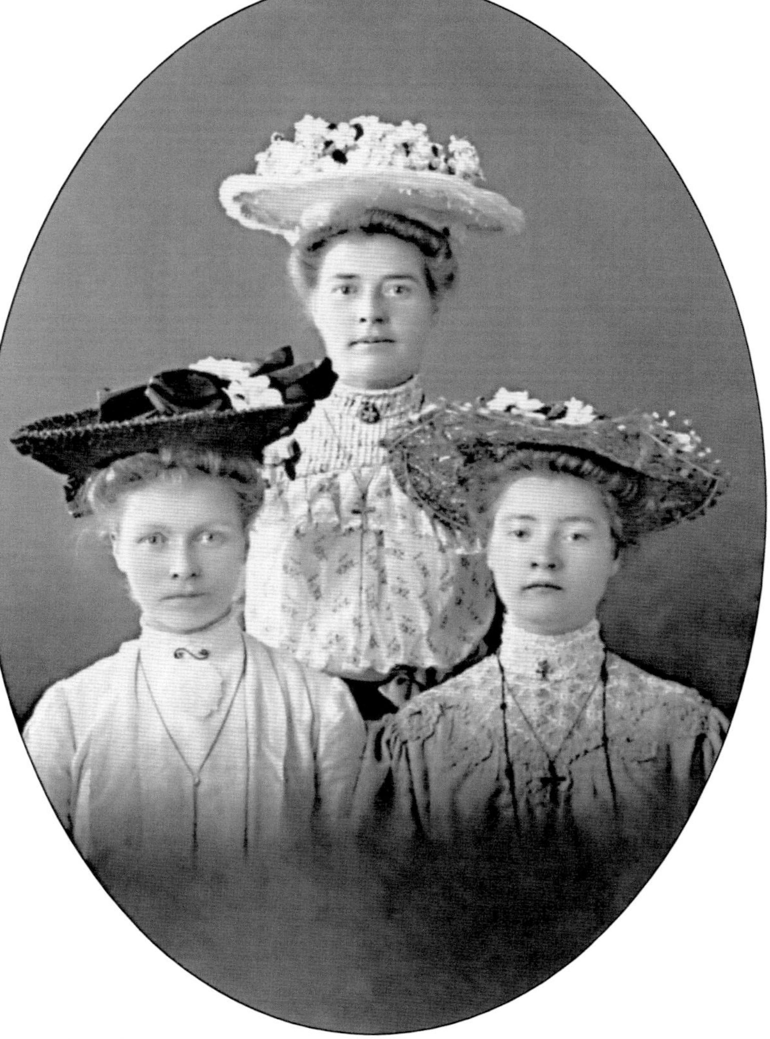

The Leland sisters, Bertha, Inger, and Pauline, left Sirdal, Norway, and arrived to join relatives and friends already in the Tacoma and University Place area in 1904. All three sisters married men in University Place—Bertha wed Tom Olson, Inger married Oscar Leland, and Pauline (the author's grandmother) joined with Ommund Tweiten. Bertha and Tom had no children and lived out their lives in UP. Tom died in an accident at the Clear Firs Lumber Mill in 1936, and Bertha passed on in 1946. Oscar and Inger had a large family that was well known and very involved in the growing University Place. The Leland home, built in 1910, is still occupied by family members. The Tweiten family returned to Norway in 1920 but came back to Tacoma by 1930. Pauline moved back to UP in 1946, into a house built by her son-in-law Torvald Handeland, the author's father, and remained there until she died in 1969.

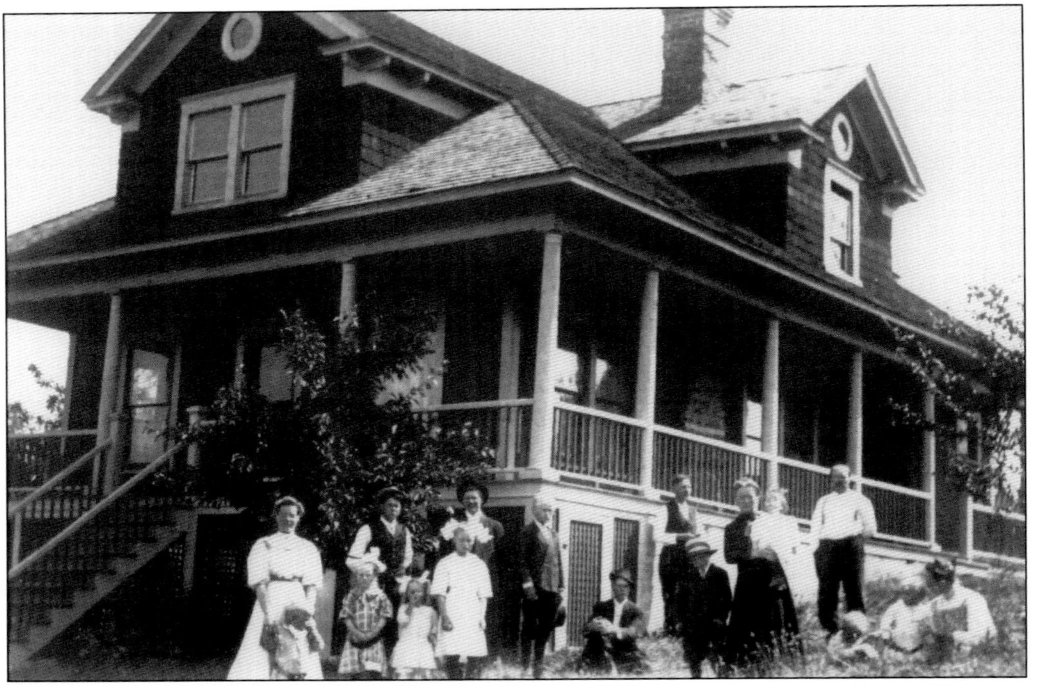

Shown here is one of two almost identical homes built by Oscar Leland on Sunset Drive in the early 1900s. In this 1913 photograph are, from left to right, (first row) Carl Tweiten, Anna Leland, Martha Tweiten (author's mother), Sara Leland, Ommund Tweiten, Inger Leland (holding Amanda Leland), Gunder Leland, Oscar Tweiten, and Pauline Tweiten; (second row) Bertha Olson, Isak Leland, Tom Olson, Gerhard Leland, Alex Leland (seated), Oscar Leland (by porch), and Ommund Tweiten.

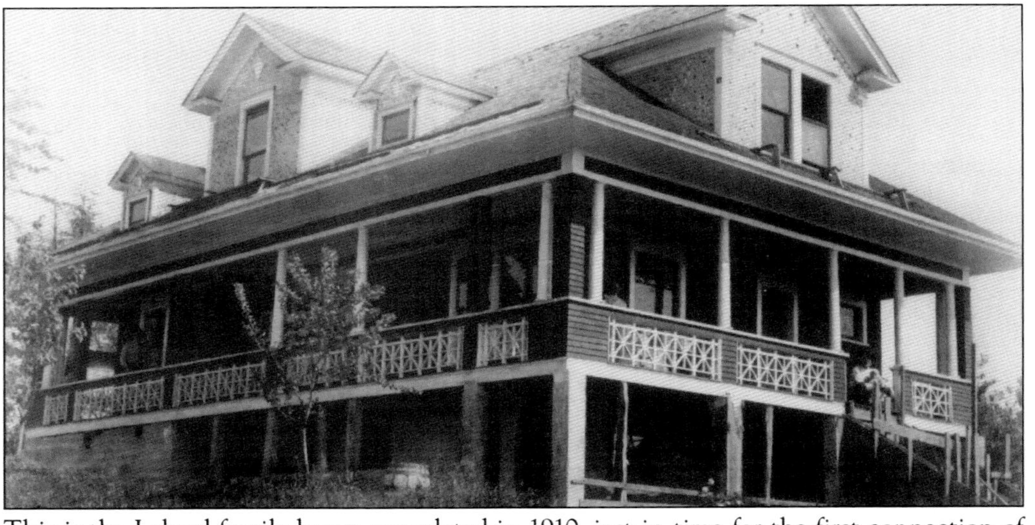

This is the Leland family home, completed in 1910, just in time for the first connection of electricity to University Place on Christmas Eve of that year. Oscar and Inger Leland raised their entire family in this home and often shared it with other relatives. This house is located on Sunset Drive and is still occupied by the granddaughter of Oscar and Inger, Kathy Stewart, and her husband, Jim.

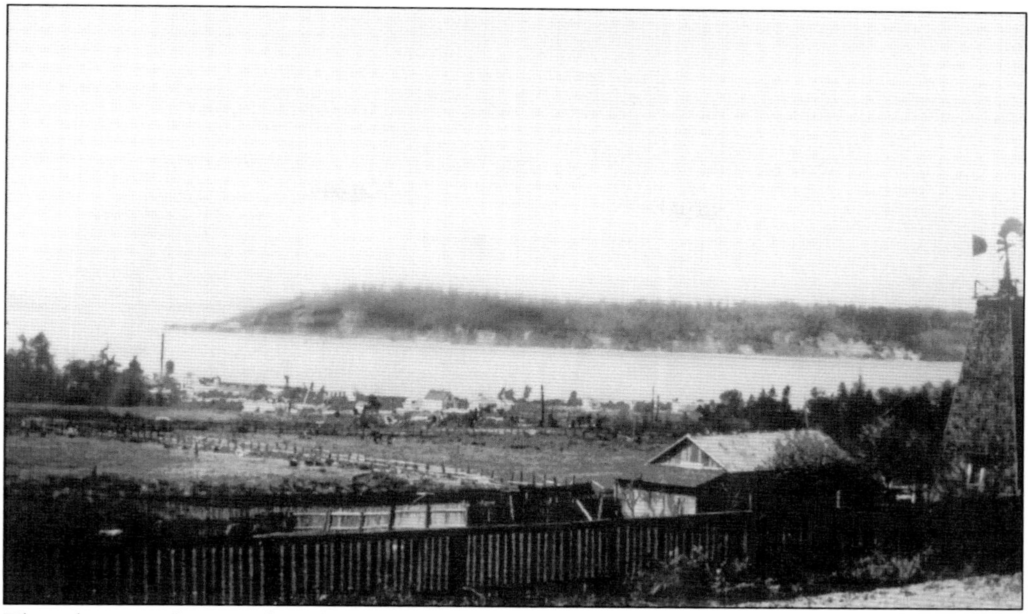

This photograph was taken from the Leland property, between Mountain View Avenue and Sunset Drive. Note that most of the land has been cleared all the way to Puget Sound. On the left, the smokestack of the Clear Firs Lumber Mill can be seen.

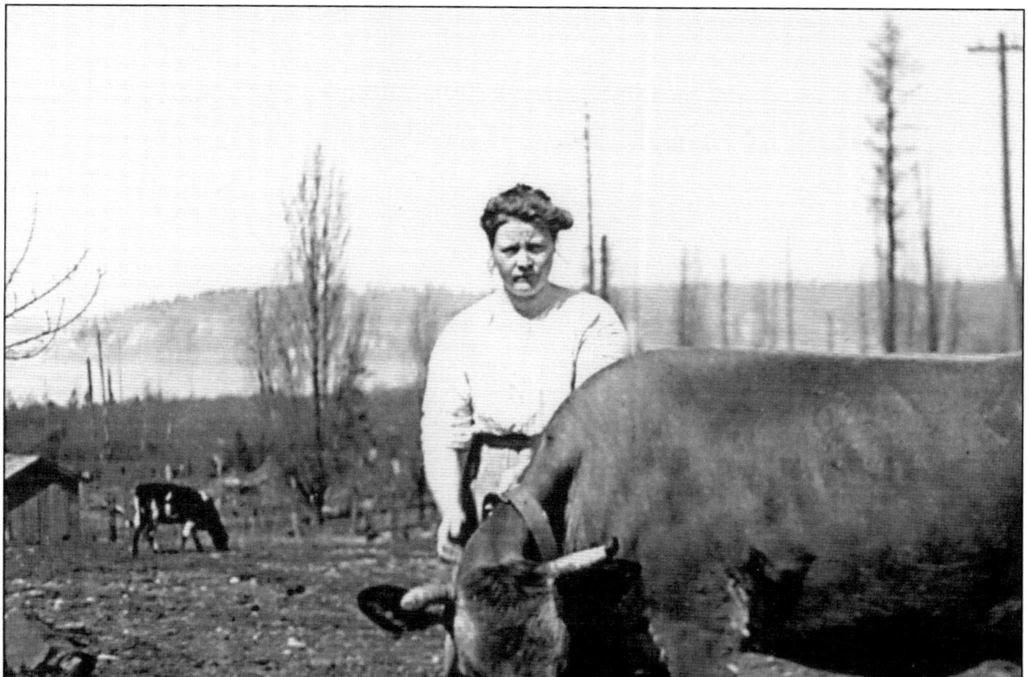

Pauline Tweiten poses with her cow, Lucky, on the Leland property in the mid-1910s. The Tweiten family moved back to Norway in the 1920s to try to make a living there but returned to the Tacoma area by 1930.

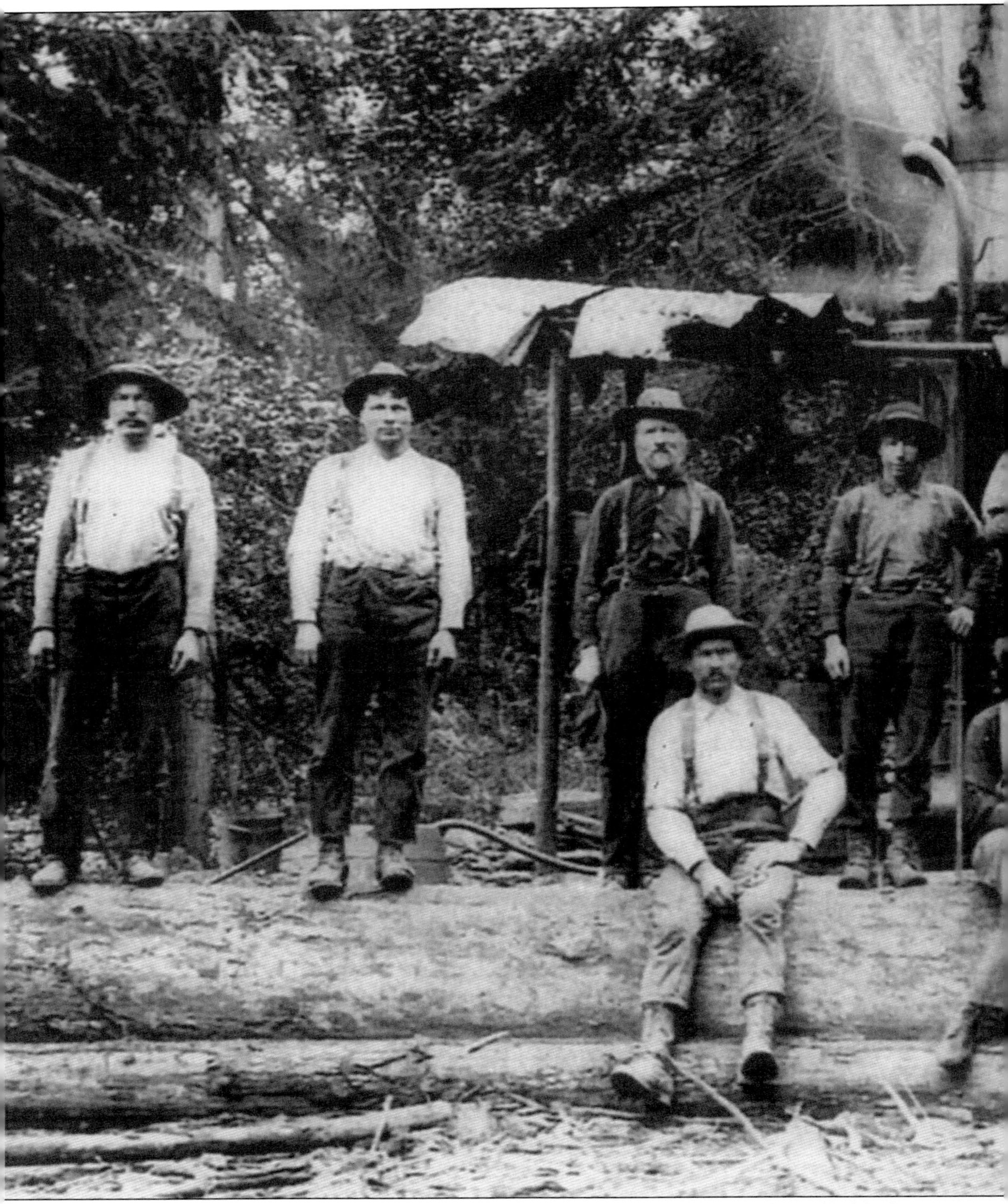

When the first settlers came to University Place, it was heavily forested. This called for logging operations to clear the land for farms and businesses. A sawmill, Snyder Brothers (later Clear Firs Lumber Mill), was located on the water at the end of Nineteenth Street. Thomas Chambers

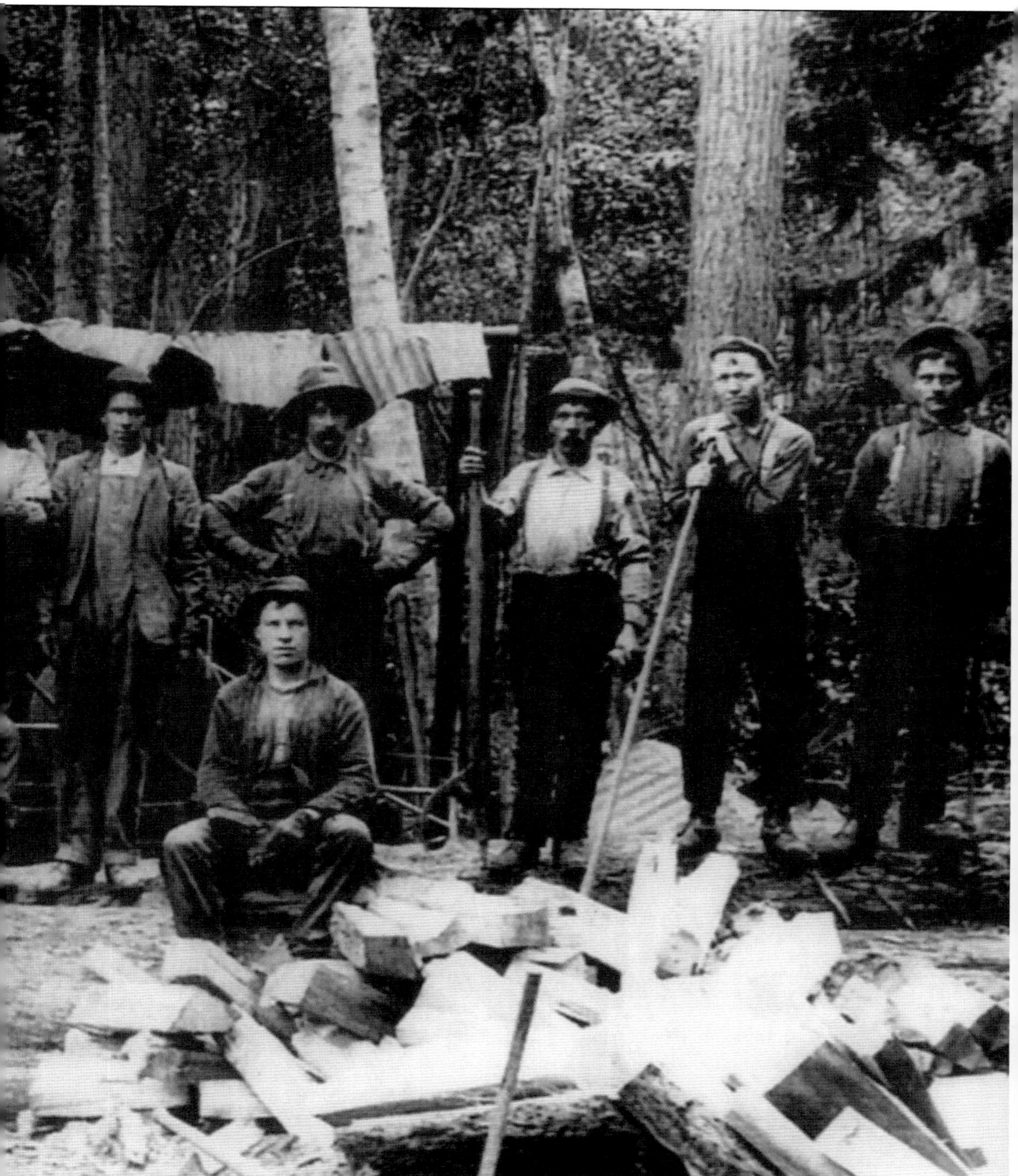

operated another mill in Steilacoom. The logging enterprise shown here was operated by Oscar Leland near Nineteenth Street around 1910. Oscar probably took this photograph, as he was also an amateur photographer. Ommund Tweiten is on the far left, and Tom Olson is on the far right.

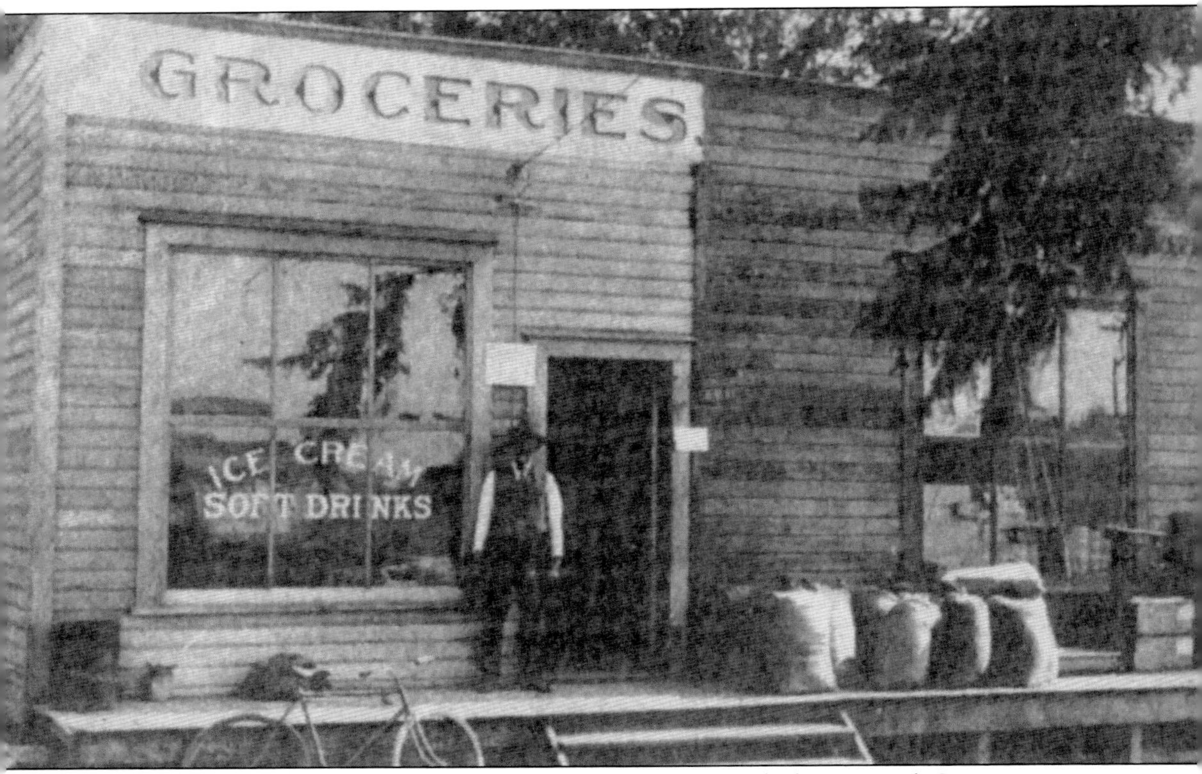

In 1909, the Stephans Grocery Store opened at the west end of Nineteenth Street, on property known as the Belmarlow Addition. It served the people living in that corner of UP, the residents of Day Island, and others in the Titlow Beach area. The store remained a family operation until 1960. The building still remains as Crystal Springs Pottery, but it is no longer open for business.

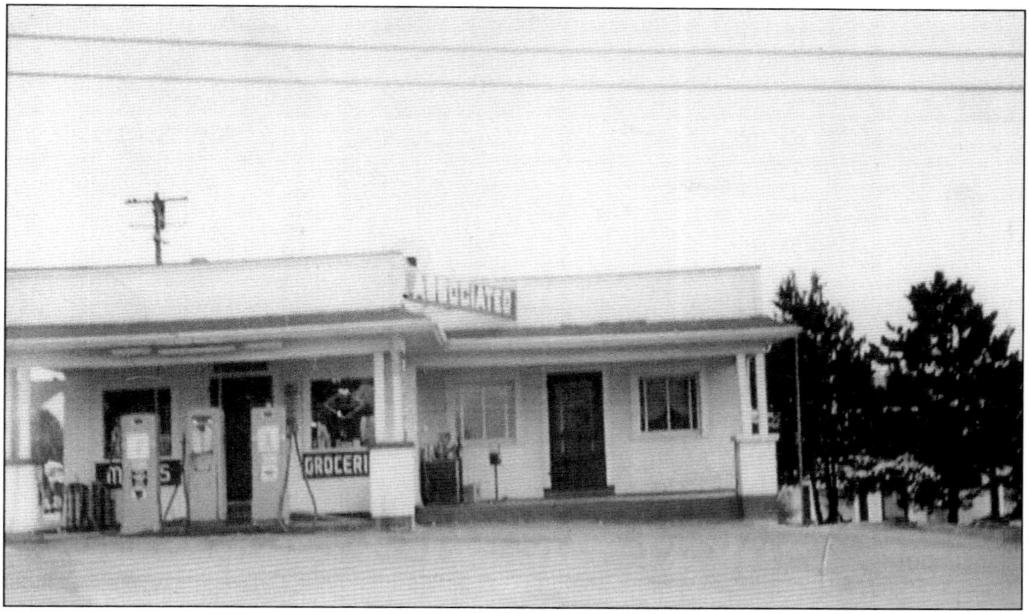

The Coffman Grocery Store and Gas Station, located on the corner of Twenty-seventh Street and Locust Avenue, was the third to arrive in University Place. Miles and Marian Coffman came to UP in 1925 and opened the store in 1928. After Marion died, Miles married Nina Trosper, who had been their housekeeper and babysitter. Together, they ran the store and meat market until the early 1960s. The above photograph shows the store and gas station in 1956. The interior of the store is seen at right. Note the price for 10 pounds of Smothie spuds: 79¢. (Both, courtesy of Linda Grimsey.)

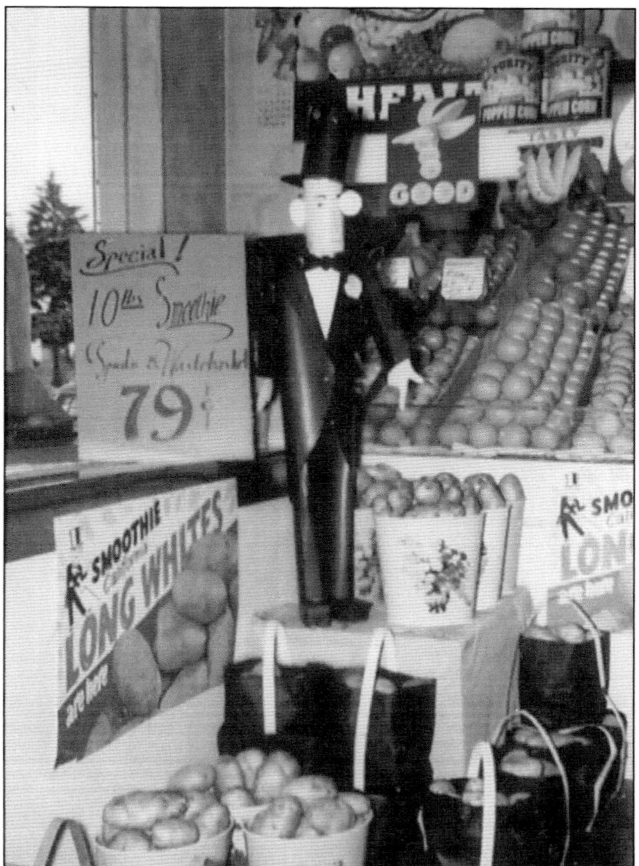

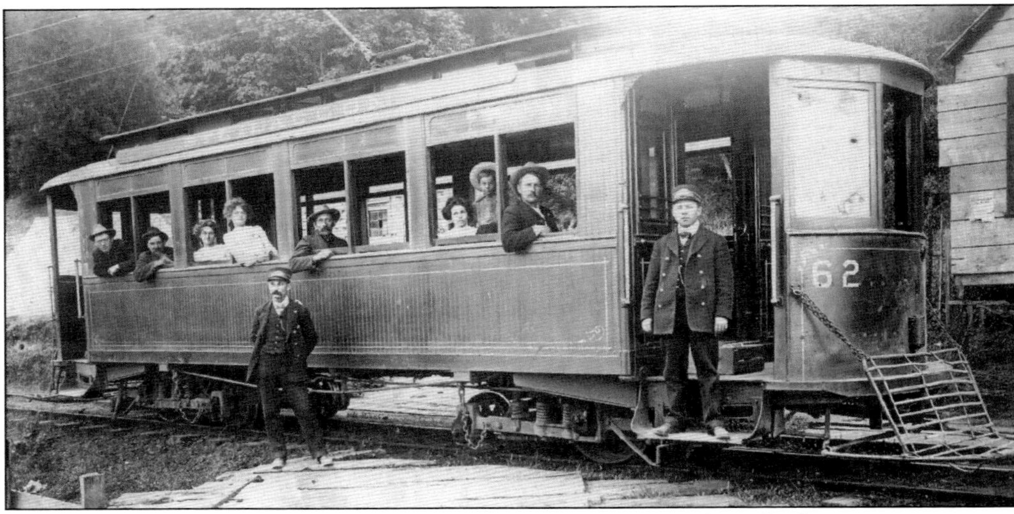

The Tacoma & Steilacoom Railway Company started in 1890. When the first transcontinental railroad to the northwest chose Tacoma as its terminus, Steilacoom was still hopeful that it would become a metropolis on Puget Sound. A railway line linking Tacoma and Steilacoom was constructed, running through University Place and down Chambers Creek, with early stops at Nineteenth Street and Mildred Avenue (Sixty-seventh Street today) and Thirty-fifth Street and Bridgeport Way. More stops would be added as University Place grew. At the time, it was the world's first interurban streetcar system, running 12 miles from downtown Tacoma to Steilacoom. In the early days of University Place, the streetcar provided vital transportation for residents to get to jobs and brought groceries and supplies to the community. The line was abandoned in 1916 when it started losing money due to the advent of the automobile and the building of more roads. The tracks were torn out in the late 1920s. (Courtesy of the Tacoma Public Library, Northwest Room, Richards Studio Collection.)

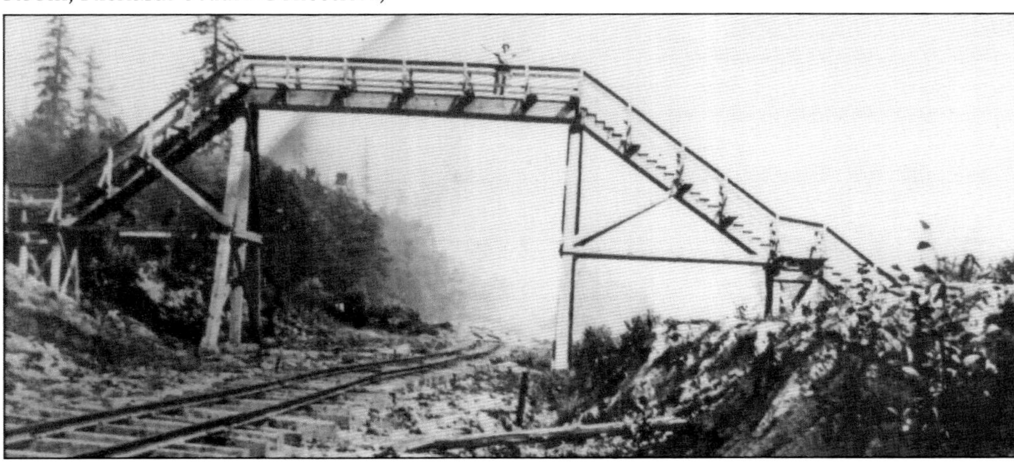

Beginning in 1910, the Northern Pacific Railway started acquiring the right-of-way along the waterfront in order to construct a north-south line on the Pacific coast. A 1,250-foot strip of land was bought from the Lemon family for $25,000 in 1912. With few exceptions, the completion of the tracks effectively cut off beach access to Puget Sound in University Place for the next 100 years. This lone bridge across the tracks was near Nineteenth Street. It was a favorite play area for kids before it was demolished by the railroad. (Courtesy of the Tacoma Public Library, Northwest Room, Richards Studio Collection.)

Julius Tollefson (right) emigrated from Norway in 1907. After working for eight years for Simpson Lumber Company's Camp 7, near Elma, he returned to Norway to marry his wife, Inga, and then settled in University Place on property he bought from Oscar Leland on Twenty-third Street and Mountain View Avenue. In 1924, he was contracted by the University Place School District to provide and drive the school bus and to serve as custodian and maintenance person. He held this position until 1940, when he got involved in a plywood co-op on D Street in Tacoma. He soon left that business to become superintendent of properties for Tacoma School District until his retirement in 1954. (Courtesy of John Tollefson.)

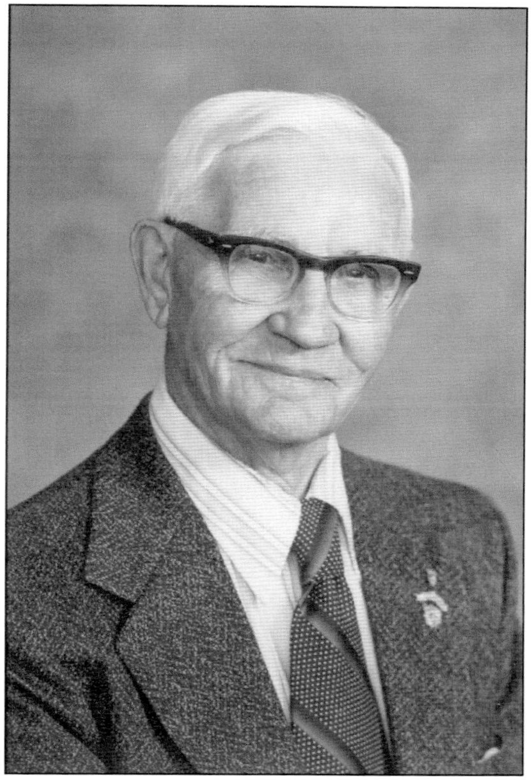

Below, posing with their new 1926 Chandler—which would serve as the school district's bus—in front of their home is the Tollefson family. From left to right are Mildred, Thelma, John, Inga, Emma, and Irene. (Courtesy of John Tollefson.)

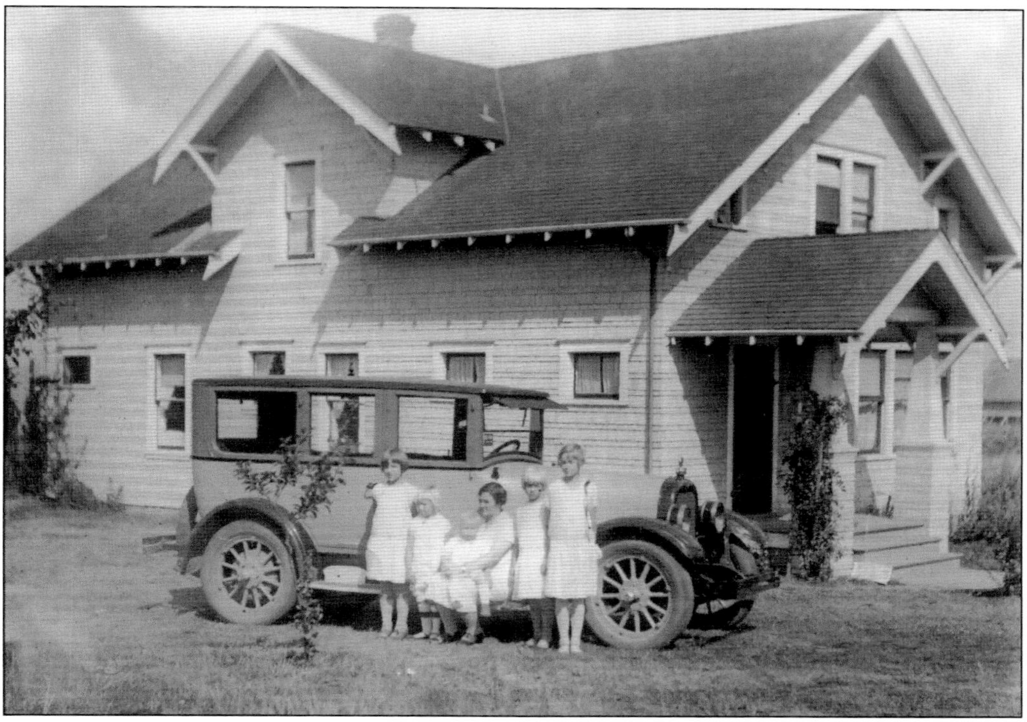

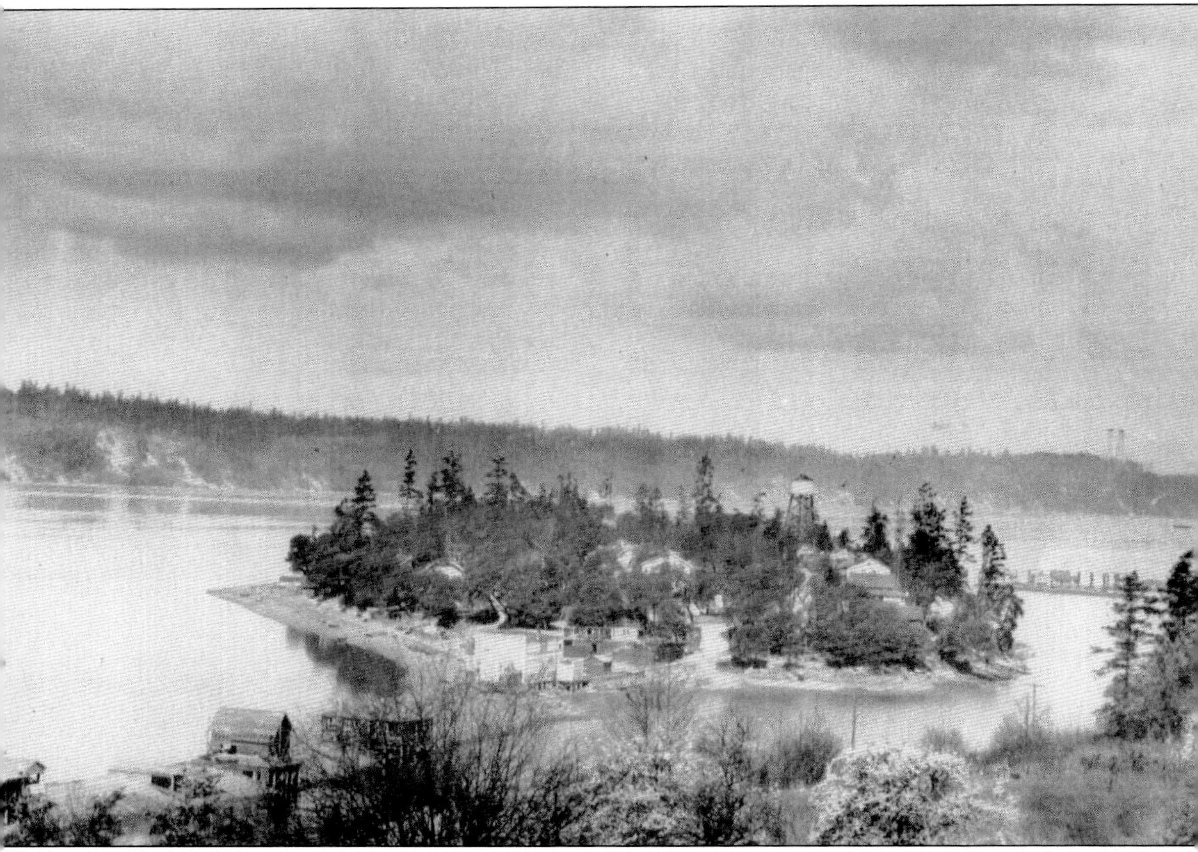

Day Island is located at the very northwestern corner of University Place, off Nineteenth Street. It was deeded to Anthony Williamson by Pres. U.S. Grant in the late 1860s. Williamson sold the island to Gen. August Kaust, and Dixon Kaust, a nephew of August, built the first house on the island in 1897. As can be seen by the presence of power poles, this photograph of the island was taken sometime after 1910, when electricity first came to University Place. Although definitely a part of University Place, Day Island has long had its own improvement club, identity, and history. An excellent history of Day Island has been written by Marcia Willoughby Tucker, *Day Island: A Glimpse of the Past.*

Three
University Place School District No. 83

When the building of Puget Sound University in University Place failed in the mid-1890s, it did not mean an end to education in the community. Residents already here (the Lemons) and those that came because of the university (the Elders) wanted an education for their own children. In 1894, a two-room house on the corner of Twenty-seventh Street and Crystal Springs Road was rented for this purpose, a teacher was hired, and school began in UP. Seven students were enrolled that first year. On November 5, 1895, a petition for the formation of School District No. 83 was granted. The next year, a one-room, wood-framed structure was built on a half-acre site at Twenty-seventh Street and Elwood Drive, given to the district by the Elder family. A second room was added, but it too was soon outgrown. On July 1, 1915, a special election was held, and by a vote of 34 to 2, the district was authorized to issue bonds for $15,000 to purchase a five-acre plot of land on the corner of Twenty-seventh Street and Grandview Drive and to build a new four-room school. It opened its doors to grades one through eight in February 1916, with 54 students enrolled. With electricity coming to homes in 1910, telephone and rural mail service in 1912, and two grocery stores before 1915, University Place continued to grow, and new classrooms were added in 1923–1924. In April 1927, George R. Curtis was hired by the board of directors as principal of UP School. Little did they know they were hiring not only the new face of University Place schools but the new face of the entire community. He was often referred to as "Mr. University Place," as the school district and community became virtually synonymous. Through Curtis's wisdom and guidance, the district continued to flourish and grow. New schools and facilities were built as needed, with full community support. Finally, George's dream of having a complete K-12 school system for University Place children came to fruition when a new junior/senior high school was constructed in 1957. The only name considered for the school was George R. Curtis Junior/Senior High School. The first Curtis High School class graduated in June 1962. Today (2012), University Place School District has four primary schools (grades K–4), two middle schools (grades 5–7), one junior high (grades 8–9), and one high school (grades 10–12), serving over 5,000 students.

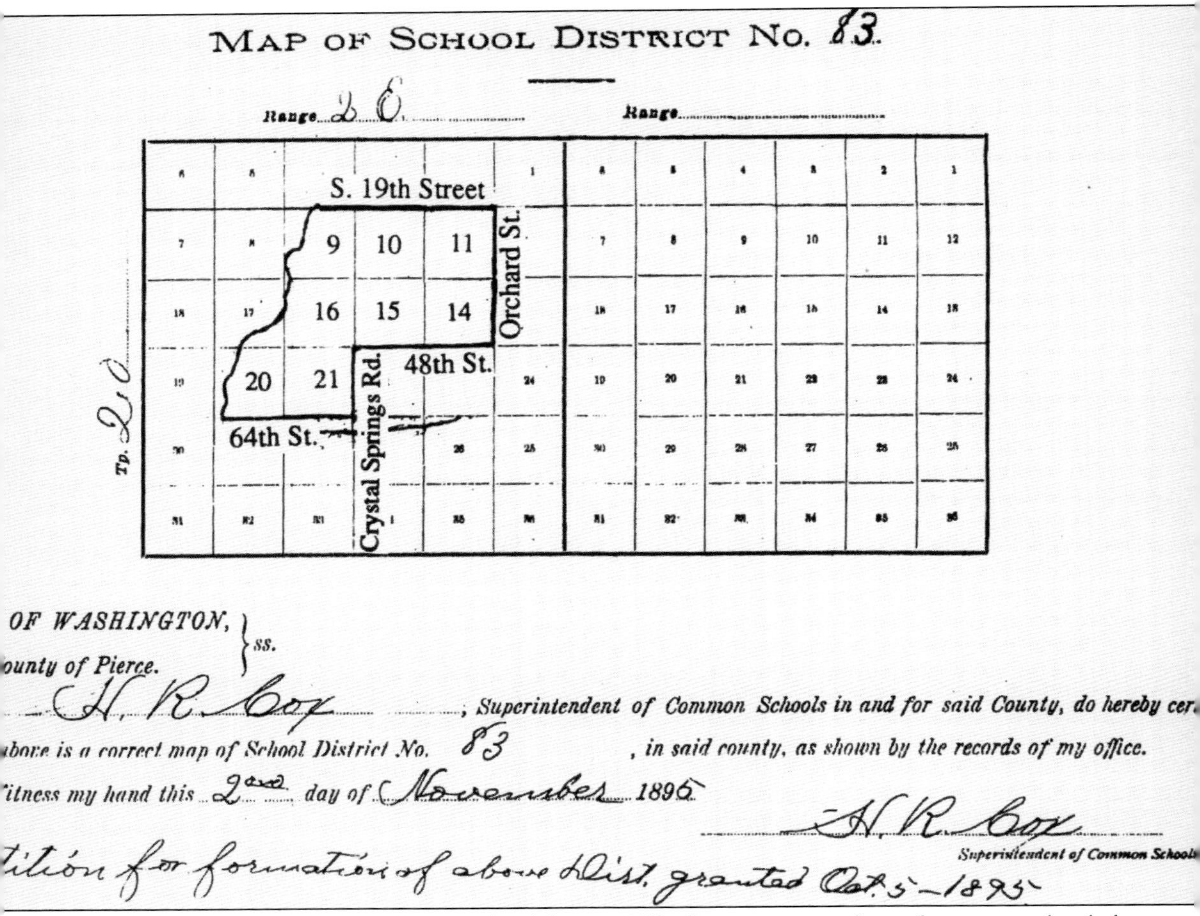

OF WASHINGTON, }
ounty of Pierce. } SS.

H. R. Cox, Superintendent of Common Schools in and for said County, do hereby cer.
bove is a correct map of School District No. 83, in said county, as shown by the records of my office.
'itness my hand this 2nd day of November 1895

H. R. Cox
Superintendent of Common Schools

tition for formation of above Dist. granted Oct. 5 - 1895

Based on a petition to form a new school district, H.R. Cox, superintendent of common schools for Pierce County, granted this request on November 2, 1895. The new district was called University Place, after the proposed university. The district encompassed about 10 square miles, with a northern border at Nineteenth Street, a southern border following Chambers Creek, a western border along the shores of Puget Sound, and a somewhat erratic eastern border with Fircrest and Tacoma. These are roughly the boundaries of the city of University Place today.

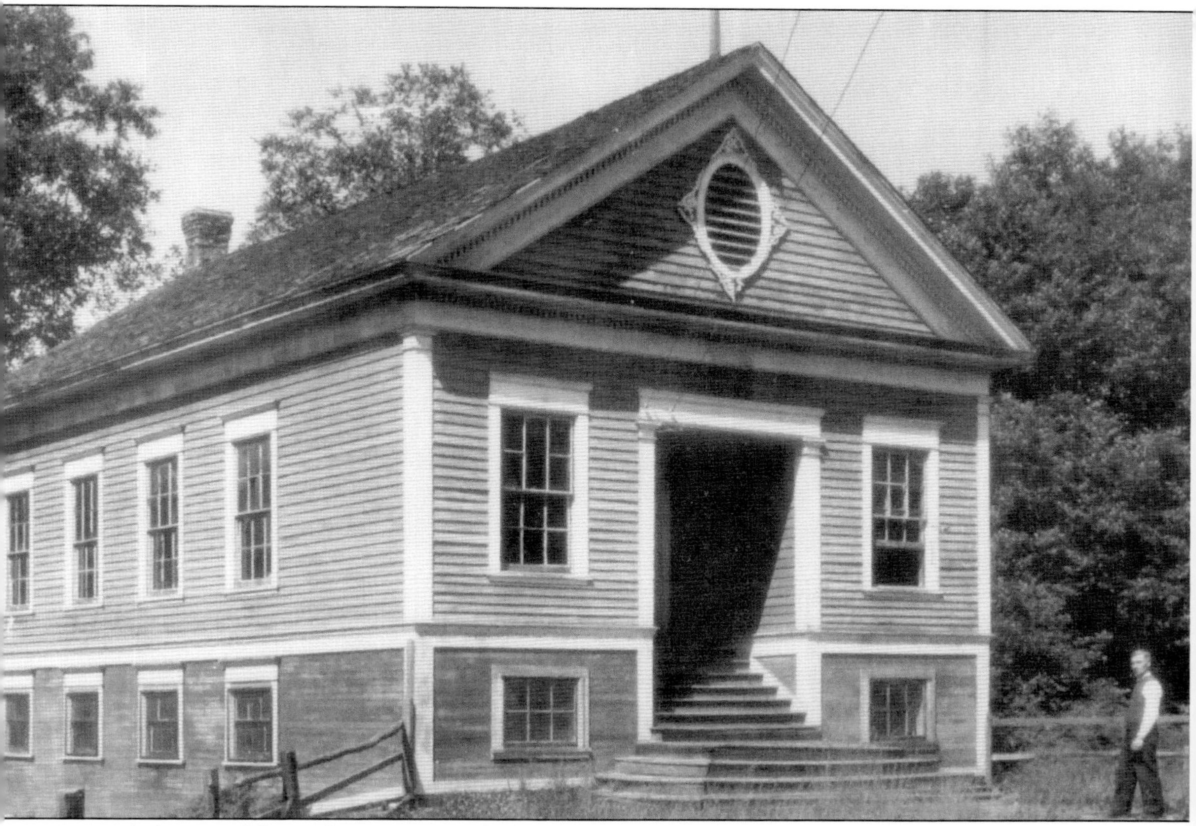

In 1896, this wood-framed structure was built on the corner of Twenty-seventh Street and Elwood Drive on a half-acre piece of property donated by the Elder family. It was called Lemon's Beach School, after pioneers John and Mary Lemon. It served as the district's school until a new four-room brick building was completed in 1916. After that, the building was used as a gymnasium and community center for many activities, including church services. This photograph was taken in 1926. The building was demolished in 1977. Julius Tollefson, the district's custodian and maintenance person, can be seen in the photograph.

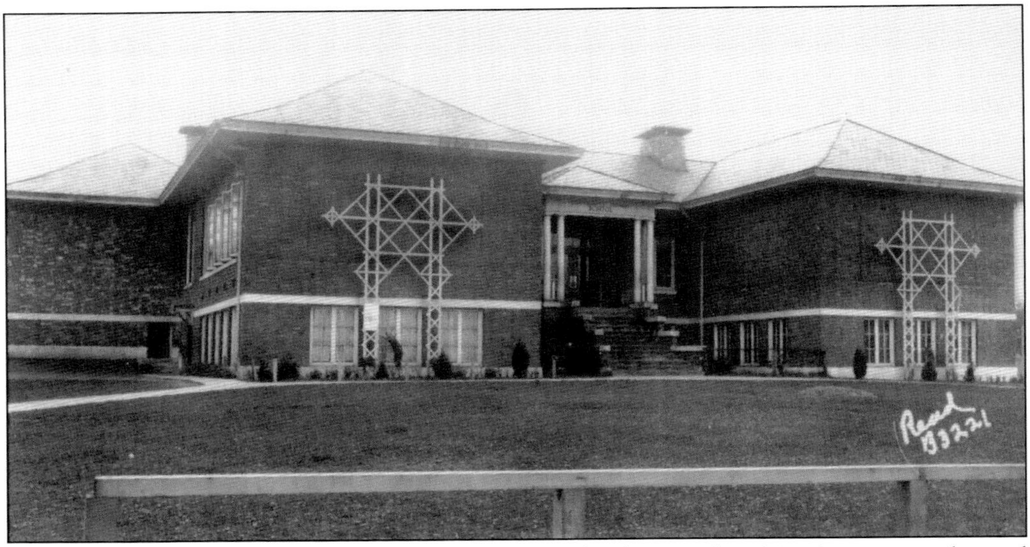

When the school district outgrew the Lemon's Beach School, voters, by a 34 to 2 margin, authorized a bond issue of $15,000 to buy land and construct a new school on the corner of Twenty-seventh Street and Grandview Drive. It was finished and opened to students in February 1916. The current UP Primary School is located on this property.

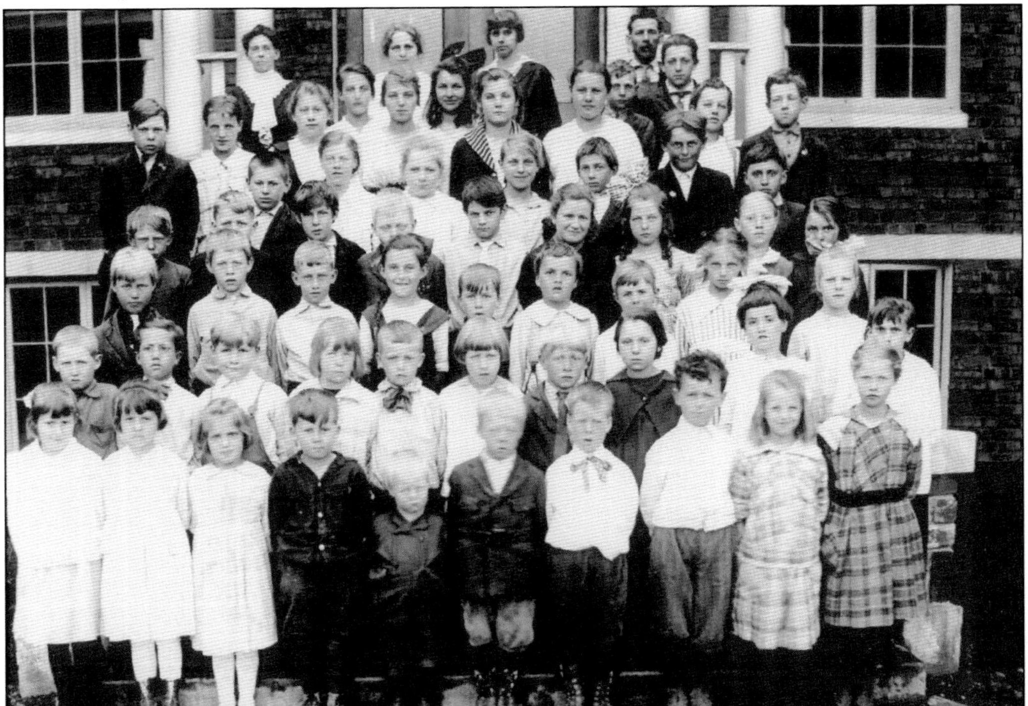

In September 1916, the new four-classroom University Place School began its first year of operation. It welcomed 65 children in grades one through eight and three teachers. The teachers were paid $60 per month and the custodian, Richard Colegate, $65 per month. The author's mother, Martha Tweiten Handeland, is in the first row, at far right. Colegate is in the back row, at far right.

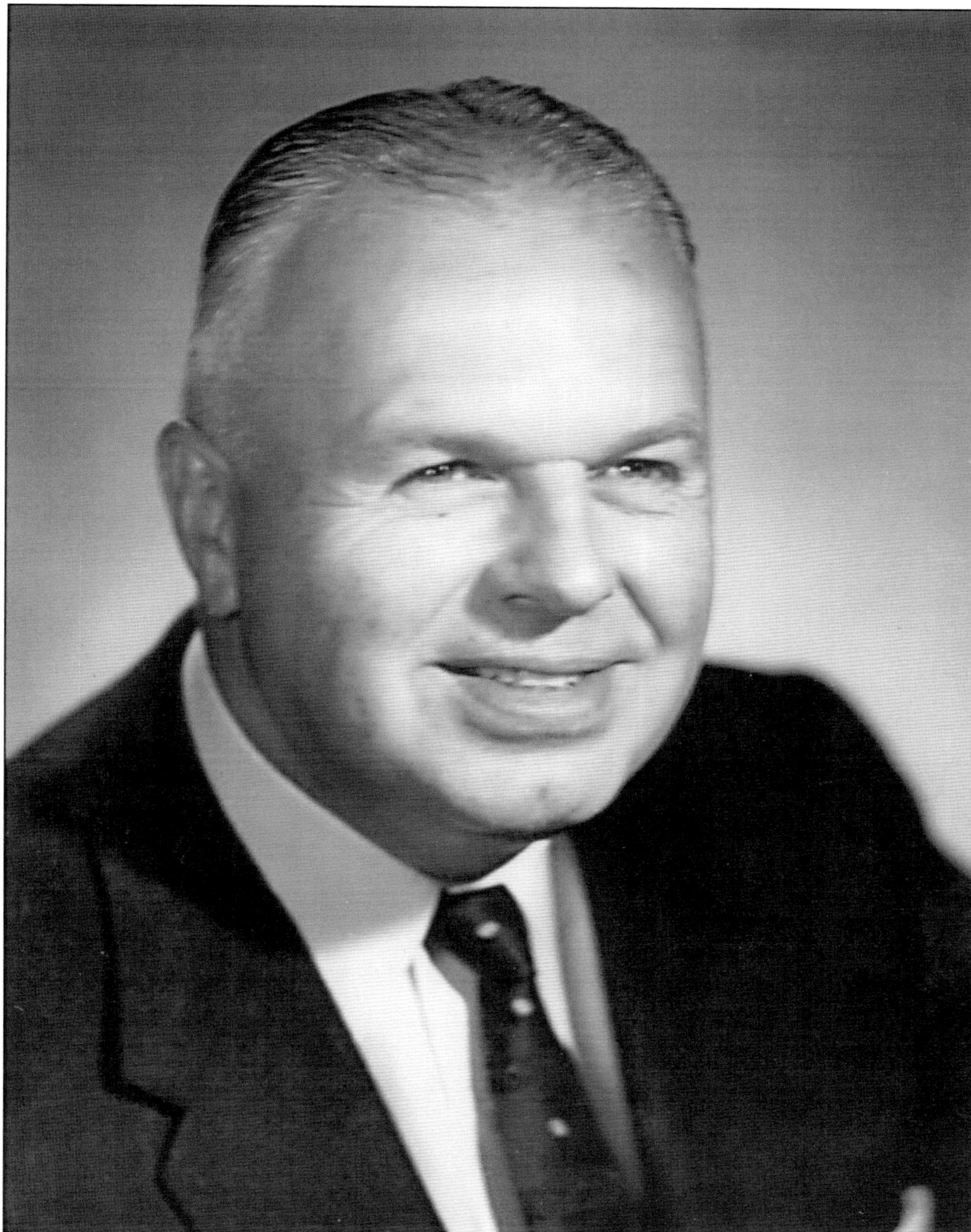
George R. Curtis was hired away from the Yelm School District to be the new principal of University Place School in 1927. He led the district for the next 50 years, guiding it from a single first-to-eighth grade school, to a district with three primary schools, a junior high, and a high school before he retired. The junior high and high school proudly bear his name. Because the school district and community were so intertwined, Curtis was often referred to as "Mr. University Place." He continued to attend school events and graduations until his death in July 2002 at the age of 97.

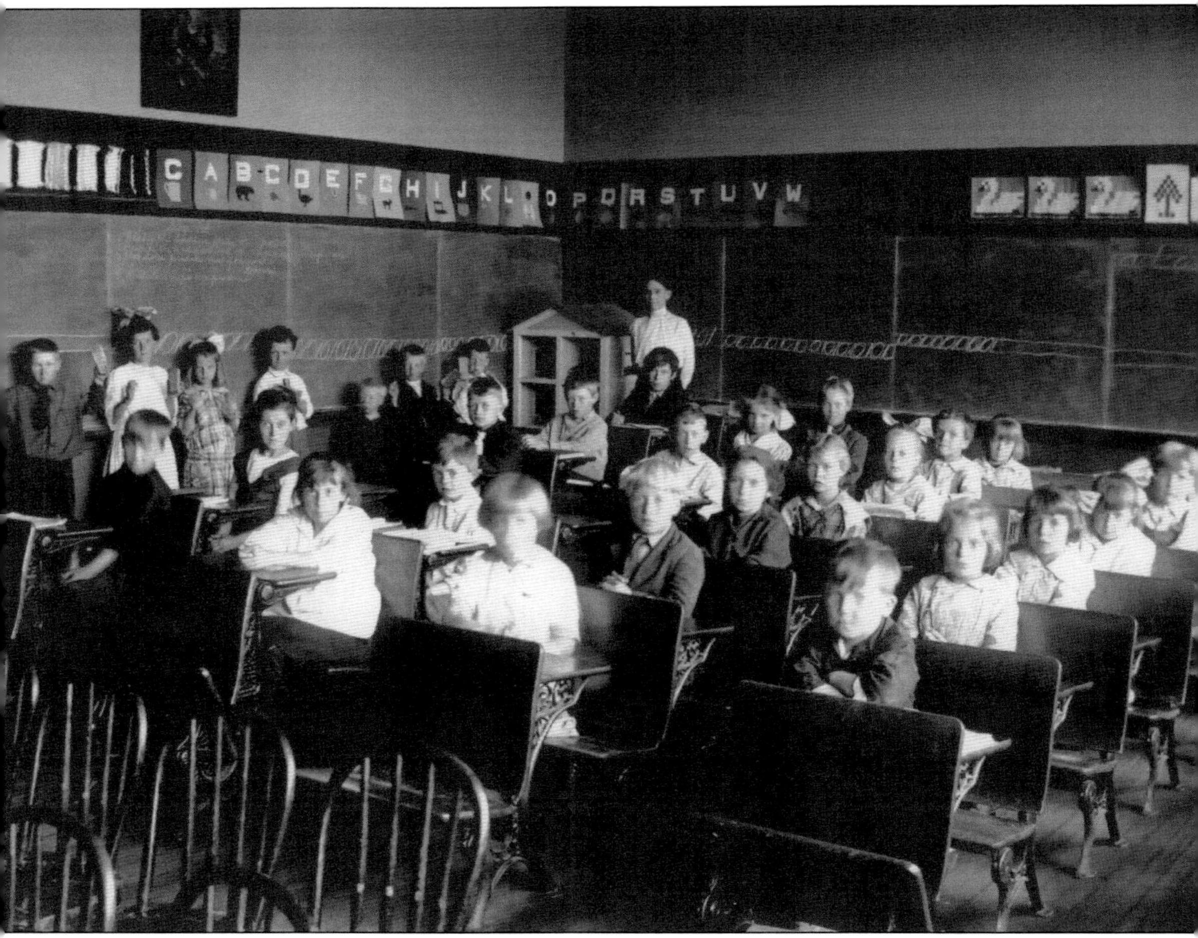

In 1919, the author's mom was in the fourth grade at UP School. This is a somewhat rare classroom interior view. By 1923, the school was overcrowded, so an additional two classrooms and gymnasium were approved by voters. Due to tight economic conditions, this would be the last expansion until 1939.

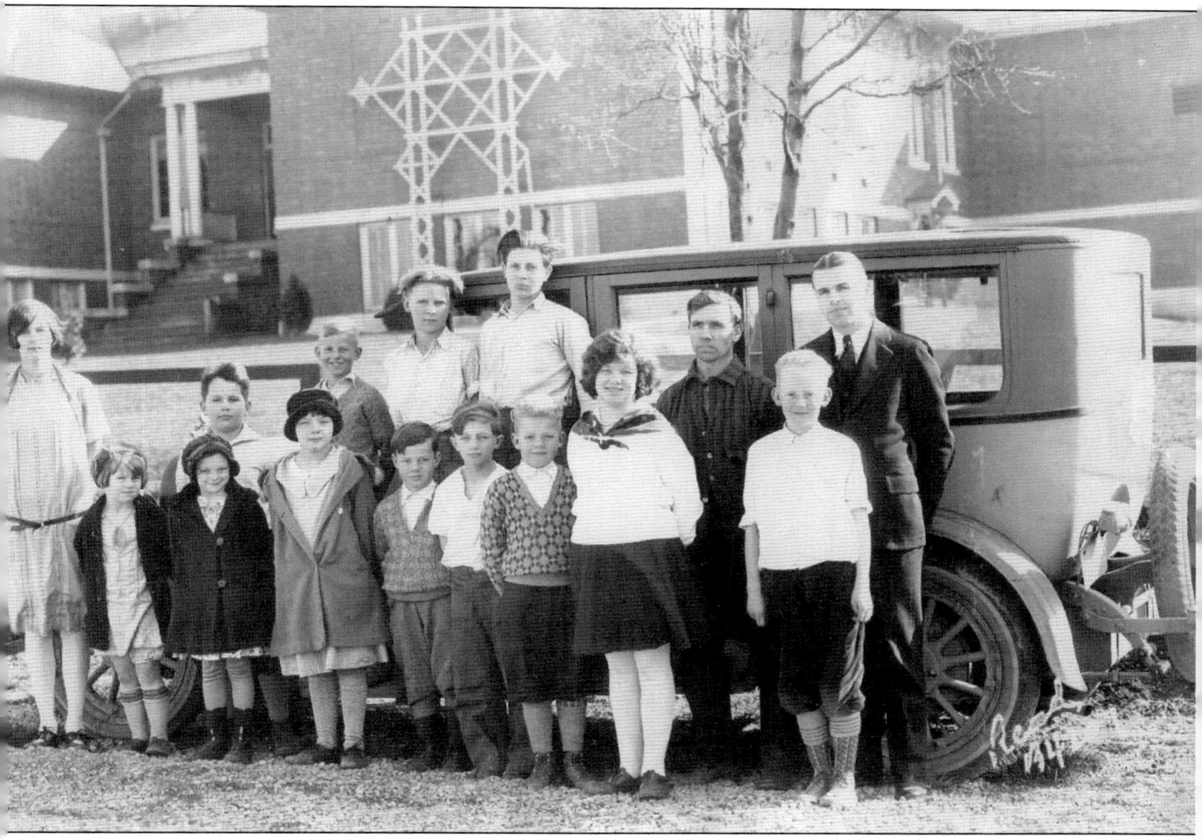

In the late 1920s, the school district began providing "bus" transportation for students living more than two miles from the school. As the district did not own a bus, it contracted the job to whomever offered the lowest rates. Julius Tollefson, the district's custodian and maintenance person, won the job. He picked up these students in his 1926 Chandler. It could hold up to nine passengers. In this 1928 photograph are, from left to right, (first row) Margaret Drexler, two unidentified, Bonnie Cole, Herbert Andersen, Maurice Kelso, Arthur Graham, Edna Anderson, and Thomas Graham; (second row) Paul Jarvis, Keith Graham, Frank Robins, Donald Slater, Julius Tollefson, and George Curtis. (Courtesy of John Tollefson.)

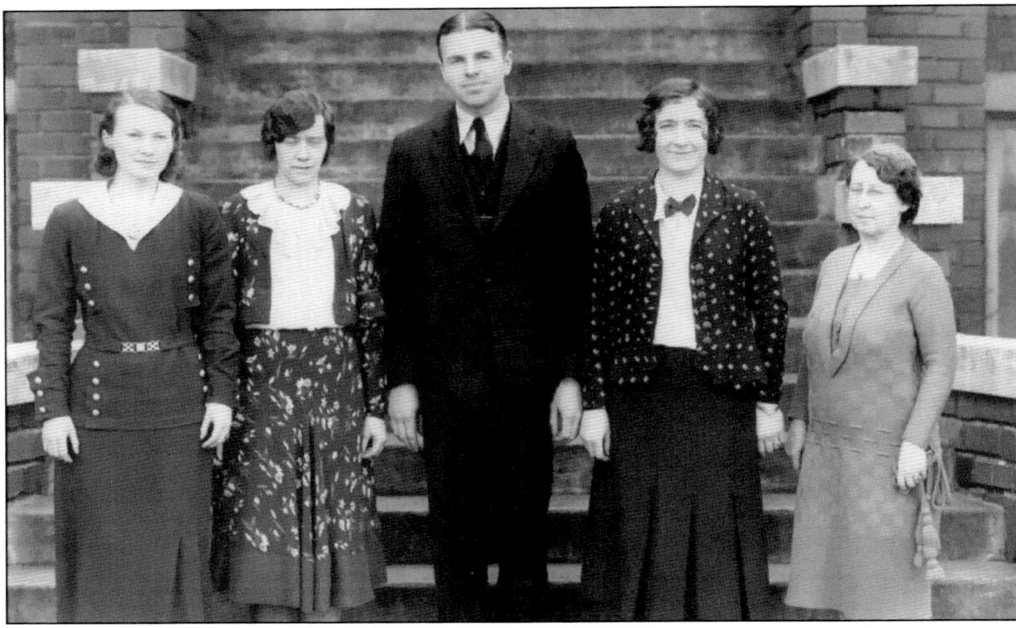

George Curtis poses with the UP School staff in 1932. The teachers are, from left to right, Miss Robinson, Miss Larson, Miss Hammerlund, and Miss Haltus. No married women were allowed to teach in UP schools at this time, and if a female teacher got married, she would lose her job. This ban was lifted in 1941. Enrollment had leveled off in the late 1920s, and the instructional staff, including George, remained at five until 1940. During the Depression, salaries were reduced each year from 1929 until 1936, when teachers received a slight raise after voters approved a new levy, 203 to 17. In 1934, teachers earned $80 per month for nine months. The custodian, Julius Tollefson, was contracted for $110 per month for 12 months.

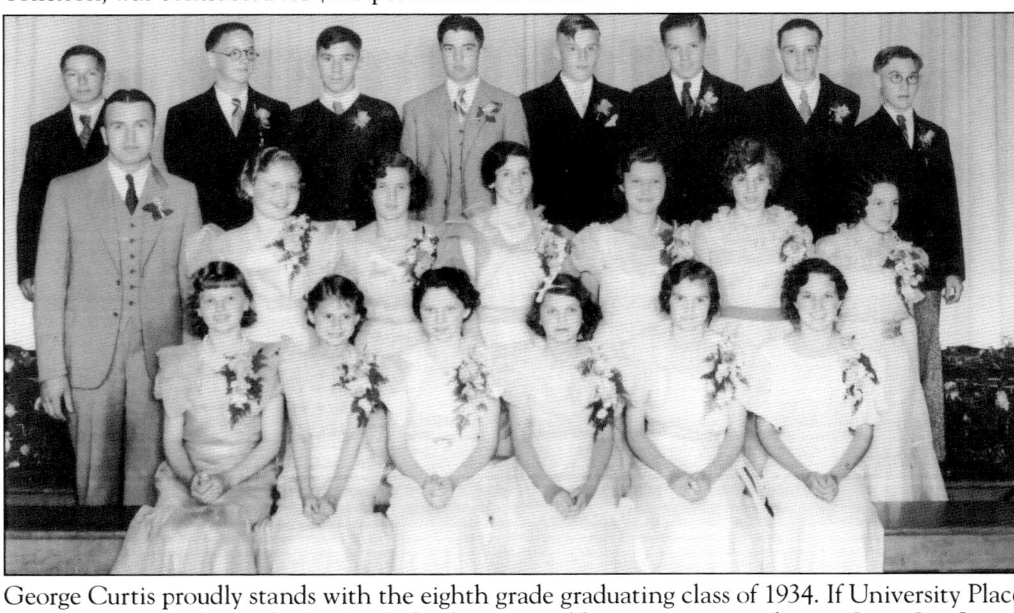

George Curtis proudly stands with the eighth grade graduating class of 1934. If University Place students continued on to high school, the district would pay to transport them to Jason Lee Junior High and then Stadium High School in Tacoma.

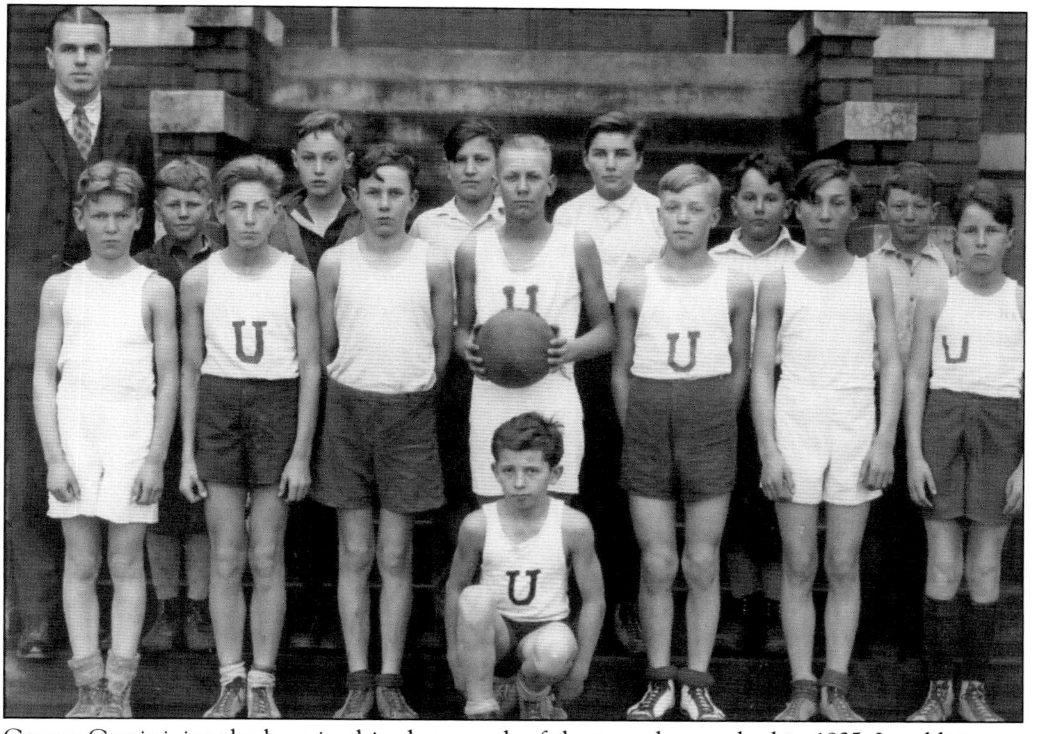

George Curtis joins the boys in this photograph of the team he coached in 1935. In addition to running a school, George became a part of these kids' and the community's life, at all hours of the day. He fished with them, coached them, and organized many activities. He even drove the school bus when needed.

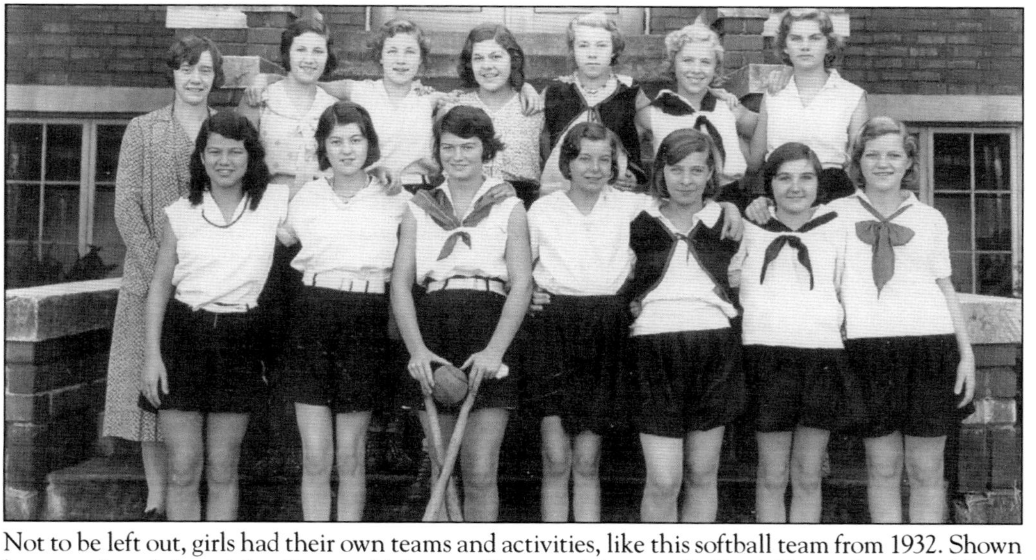

Not to be left out, girls had their own teams and activities, like this softball team from 1932. Shown here are, from left to right, (first row) Margaret Sarrazin, Margarie Rolland, Yvette Sarrazin, Clarice Cyr, Aleta Larson, Laura Robinson, and Helen Gullackson; (second row) Miss Hammerlund, Otis Rae Barnhart, Millie Barnhart, Gladys Brooks, Thelma Larsen, Emma Tollefson, and Mary Maltby. (Courtesy of John Tollefson.)

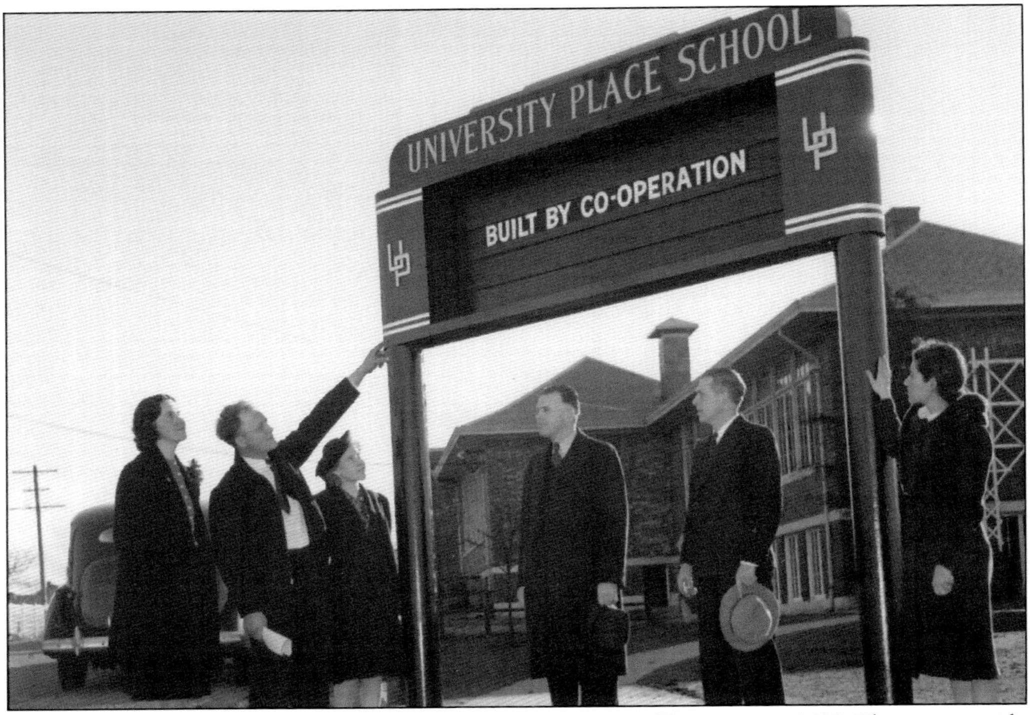

The first addition to UP School since 1923–1924 was approved by voters in 1939. The new outside bulletin board with neon lighting was erected by the University Place Improvement Club. In the photograph are, from left to right, Ruth Bolstad, "Bud" Bolstad, Anne Leland, George Curtis, Lester Magoon (designer of the board), and Pauline Bryant. (Courtesy of the Tacoma Public Library, Northwest Room, Richards Studio Collection.)

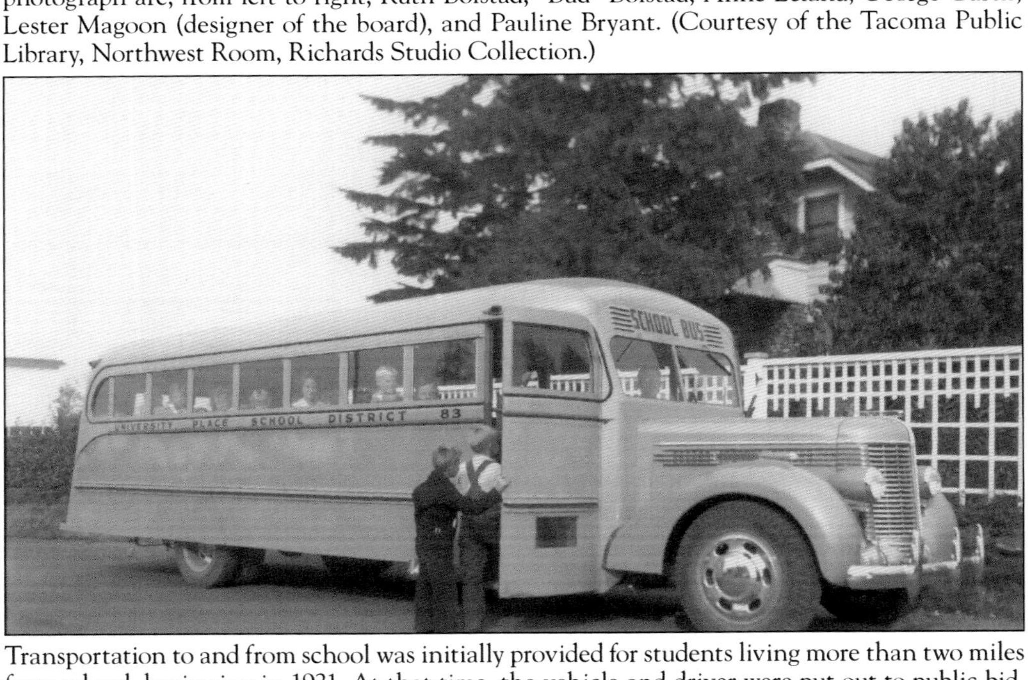

Transportation to and from school was initially provided for students living more than two miles from school, beginning in 1921. At that time, the vehicle and driver were put out to public bid. University Place School District bought this, the first district-owned bus, in 1939.

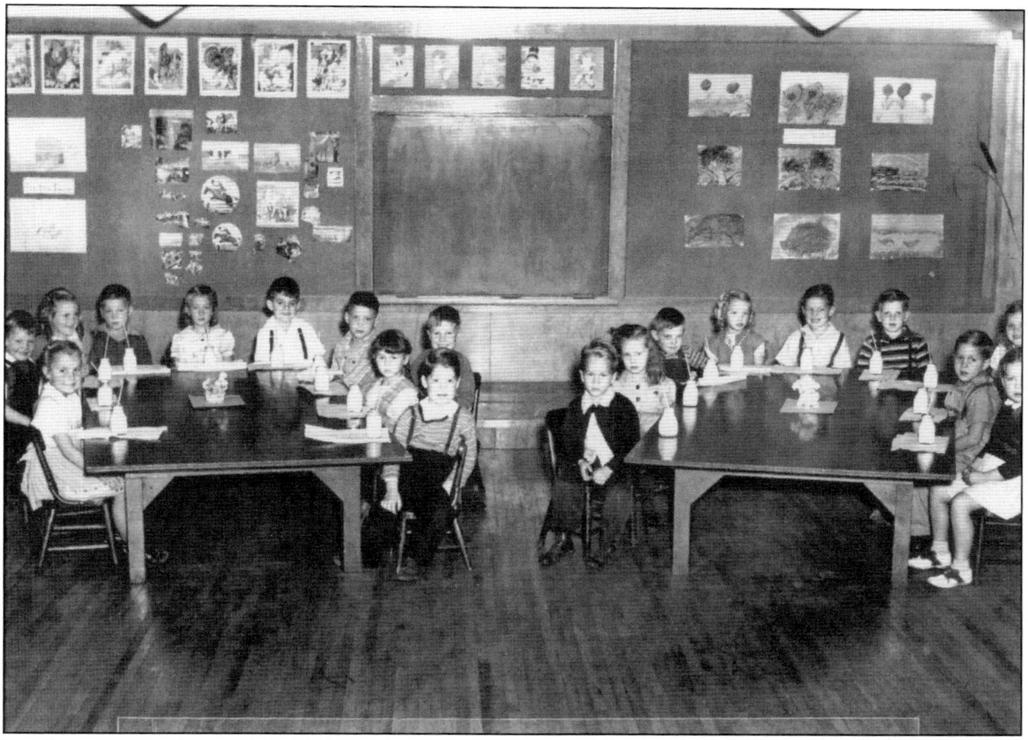

Kindergarten in University Place was added to the school curriculum in 1938. Although interrupted during World War II, it was resumed afterward. This photograph is of the kindergarten class of 1946–1947.

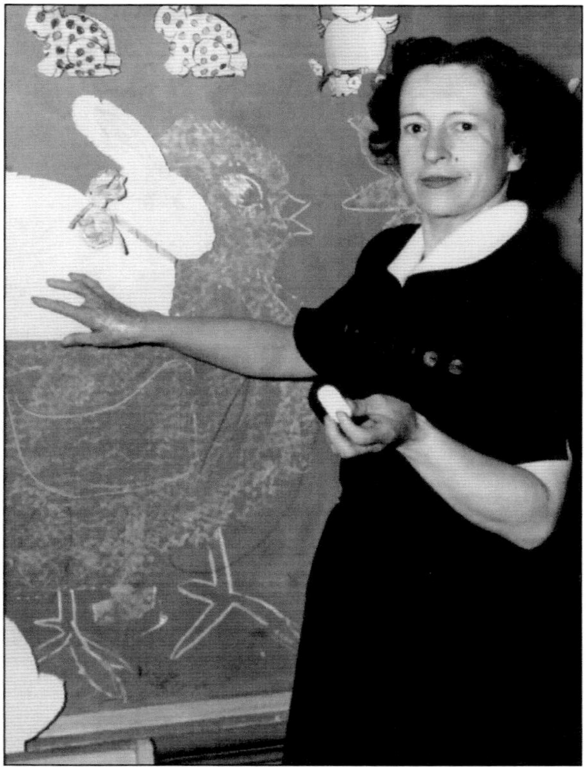

Vi White was the kindergarten teacher in UP for many years. She was one of the earliest persons to begin preserving and recording the history of University Place, for which the author owes a huge debt of gratitude.

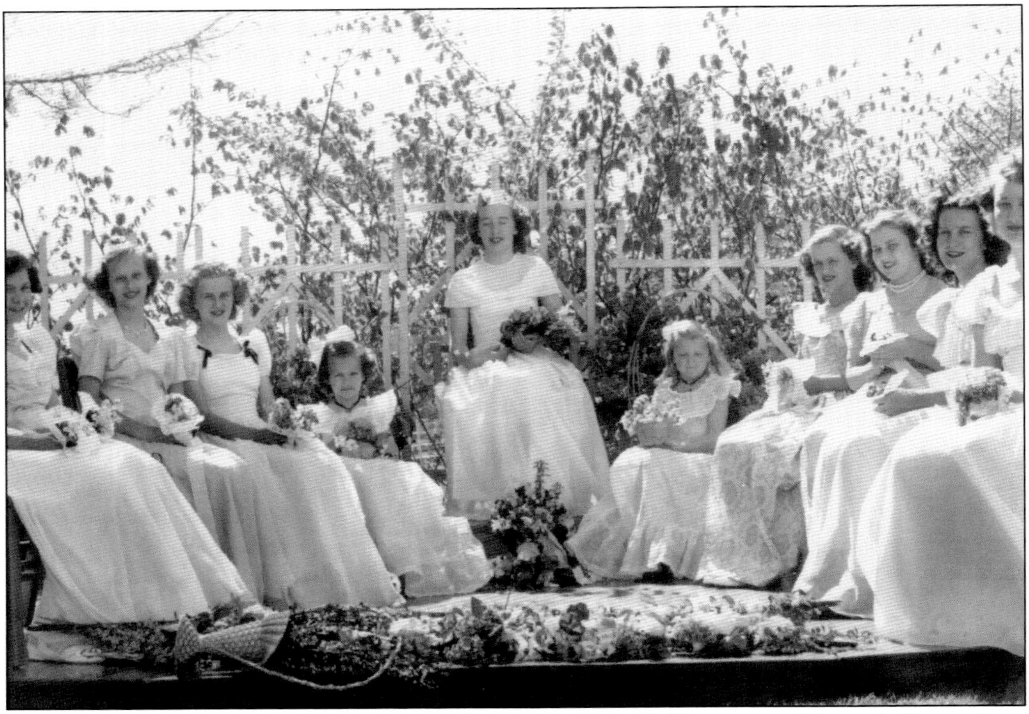

In celebration of May Day, the University Place community held an annual festival. Shown here are the 1946 May Queen, Carol Nelson (center), and her court.

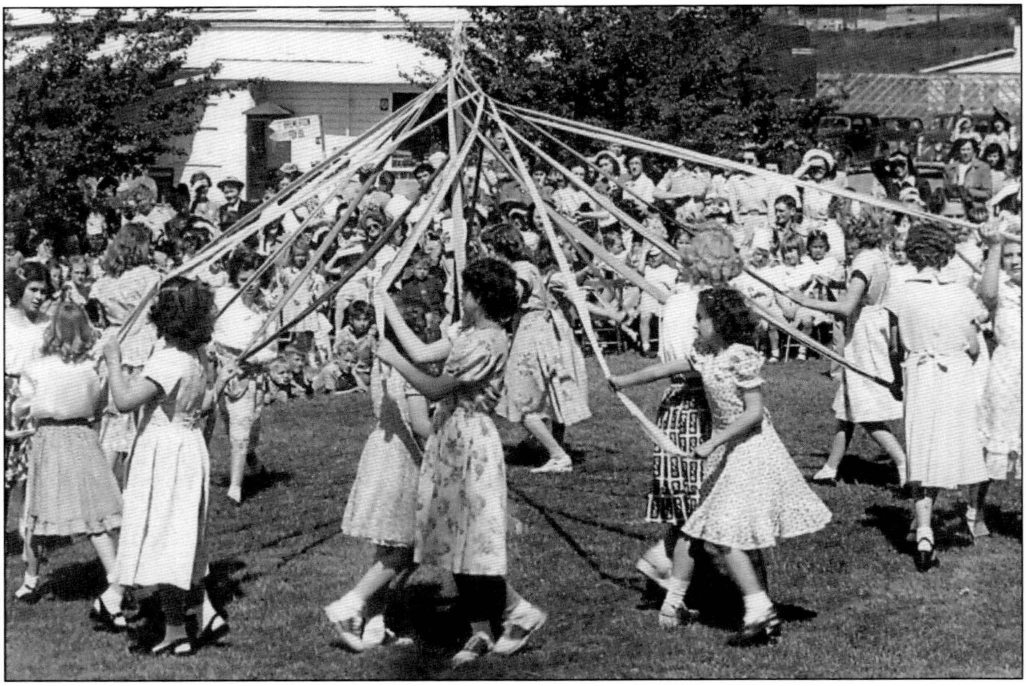

The dance around the Maypole was part of the annual May Day tradition. Sixth grade girls are the dancers in this photograph, taken in 1946.

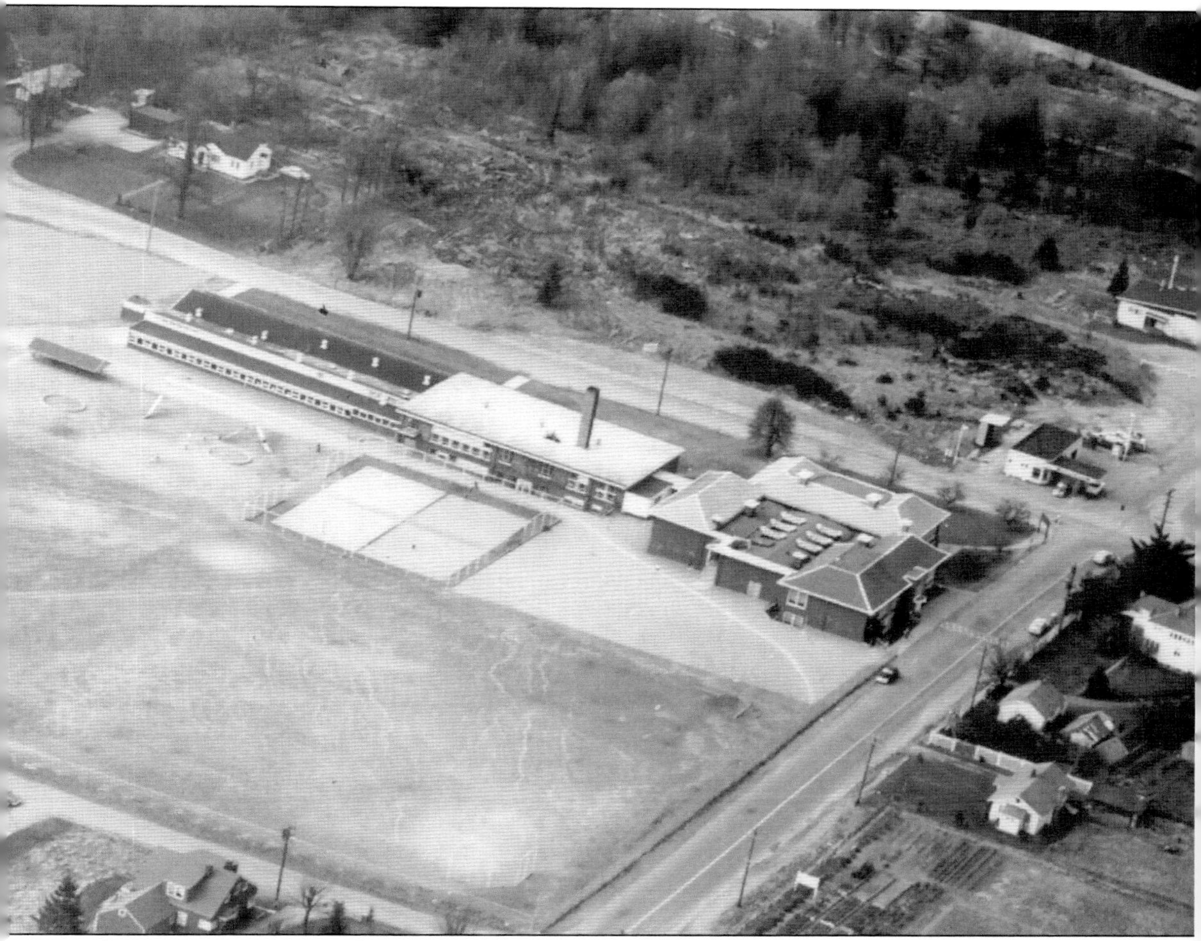

In the 1950s, expansion of University Place took off. As suburban living became the trend following World War II, University Place, with lots of available land, began growing rapidly. Several more additions were made at the UP School site, as can be seen in this aerial photograph, but overcrowding was still a problem. By 1952, there were over 750 students and 28 teachers, and a search for new building sites was begun. A 23.5-acre plot was purchased in November 1952 on the corner of Fortieth Street and Grandview Drive as well as another 15 acres adjoining it along Fortieth Street shortly after. These would become the locations for Curtis Junior and Senior High Schools. The district bought another 20 acres east of Fortieth Street that would become the location for a new primary school, Narrows View. The population of UP would reach 5,000 in 1952 and double to 10,000 by 1962. It was very difficult to keep up with this rapid growth. Overcrowded classrooms were the norm, but the district and community never lost sight of their commitment to providing the best possible education for their young people.

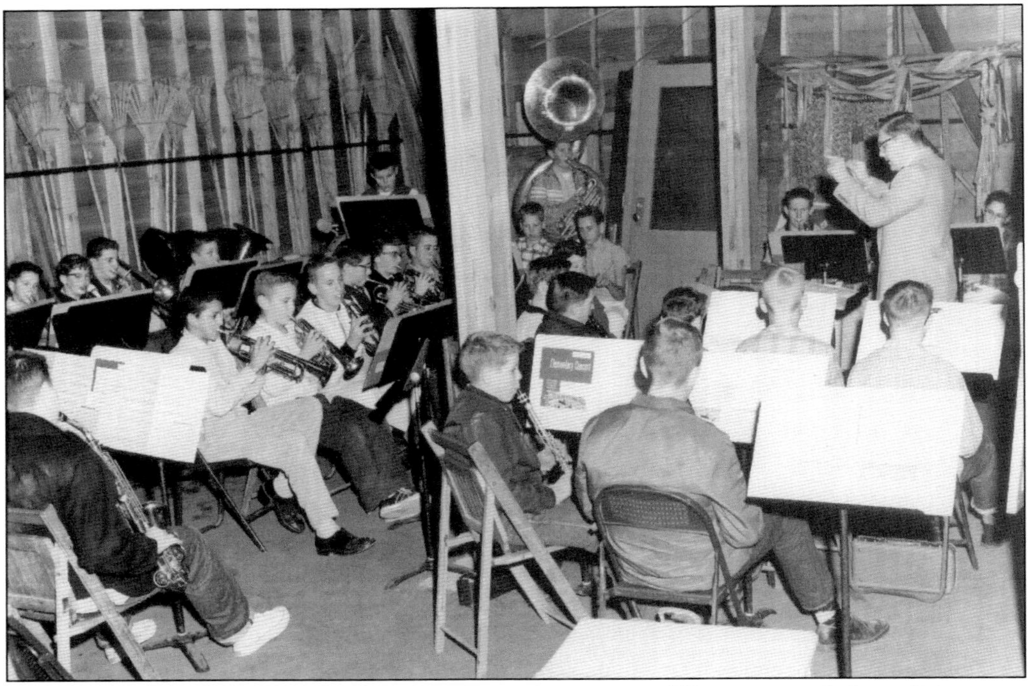

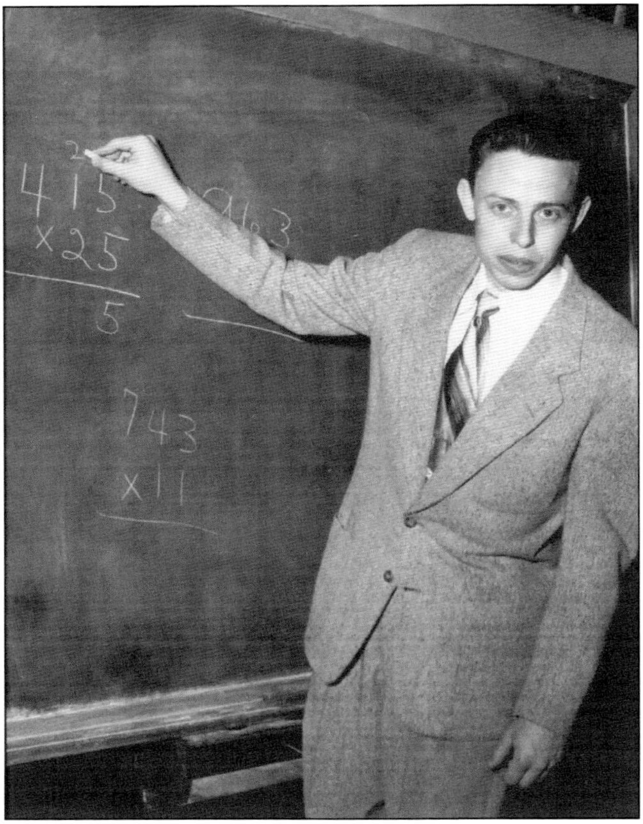

The overcrowded conditions are evident in the above photograph of the band class being held in a storage room—note the rakes along the wall. The band teacher is John Shartow.

George Luscombe taught at UP School for several years before becoming its principal. Much credit goes to Luscombe for recording the history of University Place schools for his master's thesis, which he completed at the University of Puget Sound in 1965.

In 1957, the great expansion began, as Curtis Junior High opened its doors on the property located at Fortieth Street and Grandview Drive. The gymnasium, main building, cafeteria/auditorium, and 200 building, all surrounded by undeveloped land, can be seen in this aerial photograph.

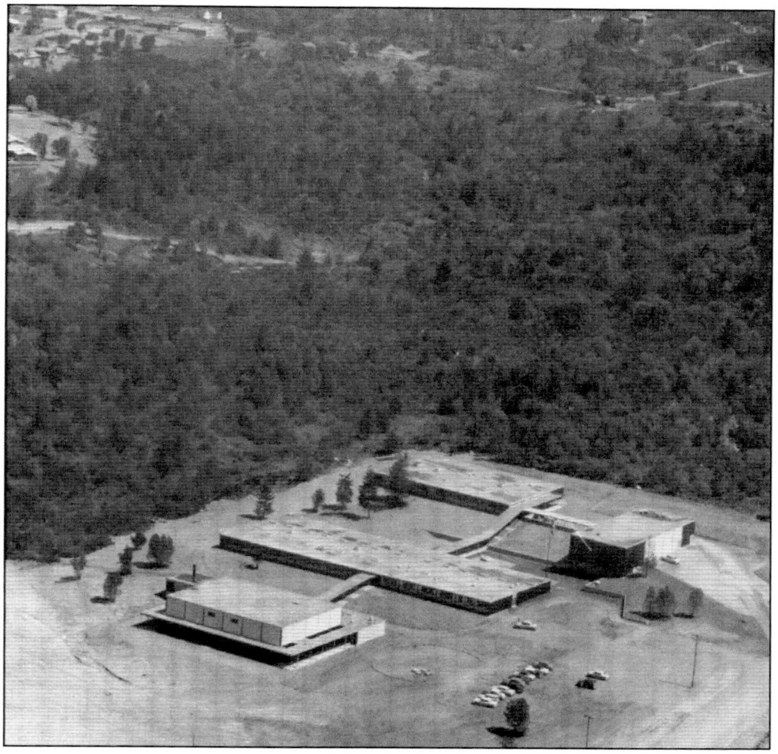

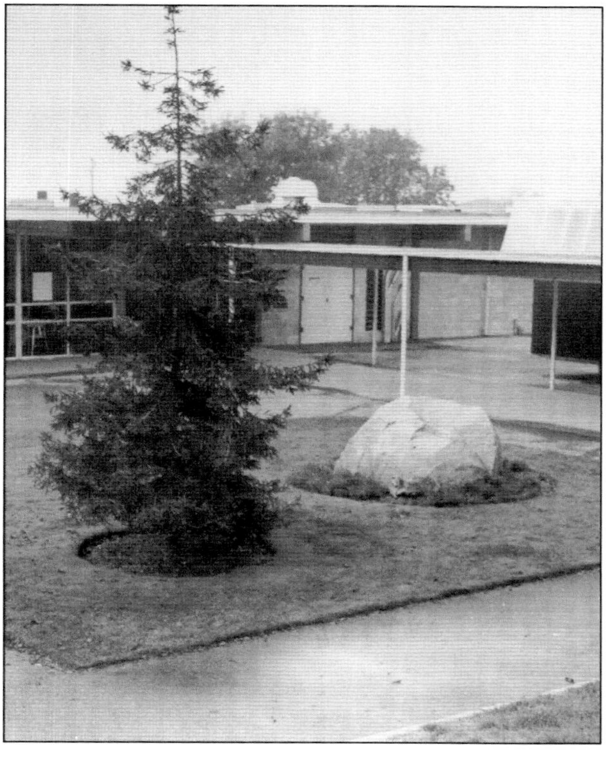

As the first class advanced through the grades, Curtis Junior High soon became Curtis Junior/Senior High School, and more buildings were added. The campus, designed by well-known architect Robert Price, was created using a California concept of spread-out buildings, so obtaining an all-encompassing photograph of the school was not possible. This photograph shows the courtyard by the main building. The infamous "Curtis rock" was moved to the high school campus when the junior high buildings were demolished in 2010.

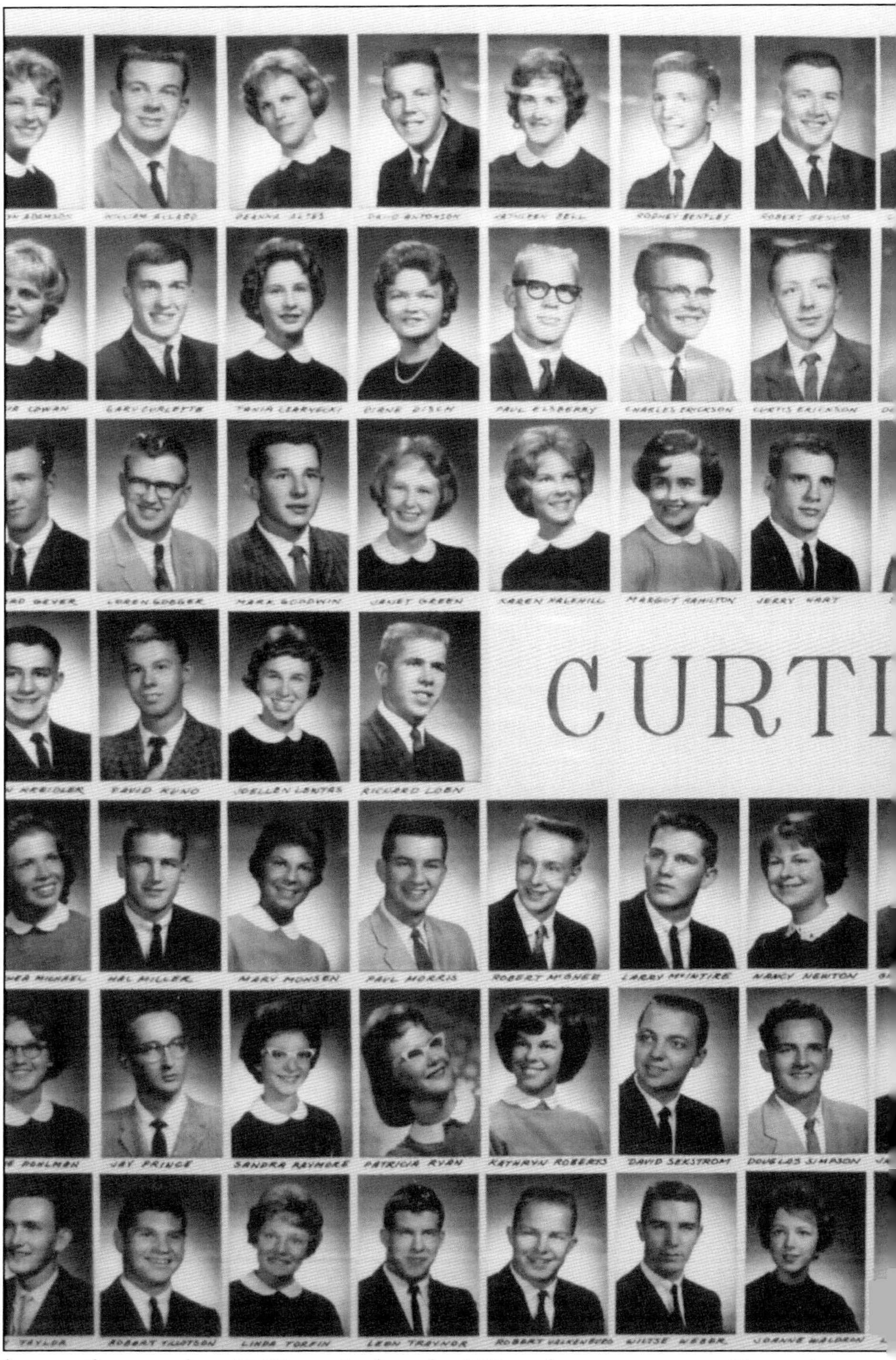

Finally, the dream of a complete K–12 curriculum for UP students came true. From the time that seven kids started school in a rented two-room house in 1894, until 99 seniors entered the gym to the strains of "When the Saints Come Marching In" in June 1962, the

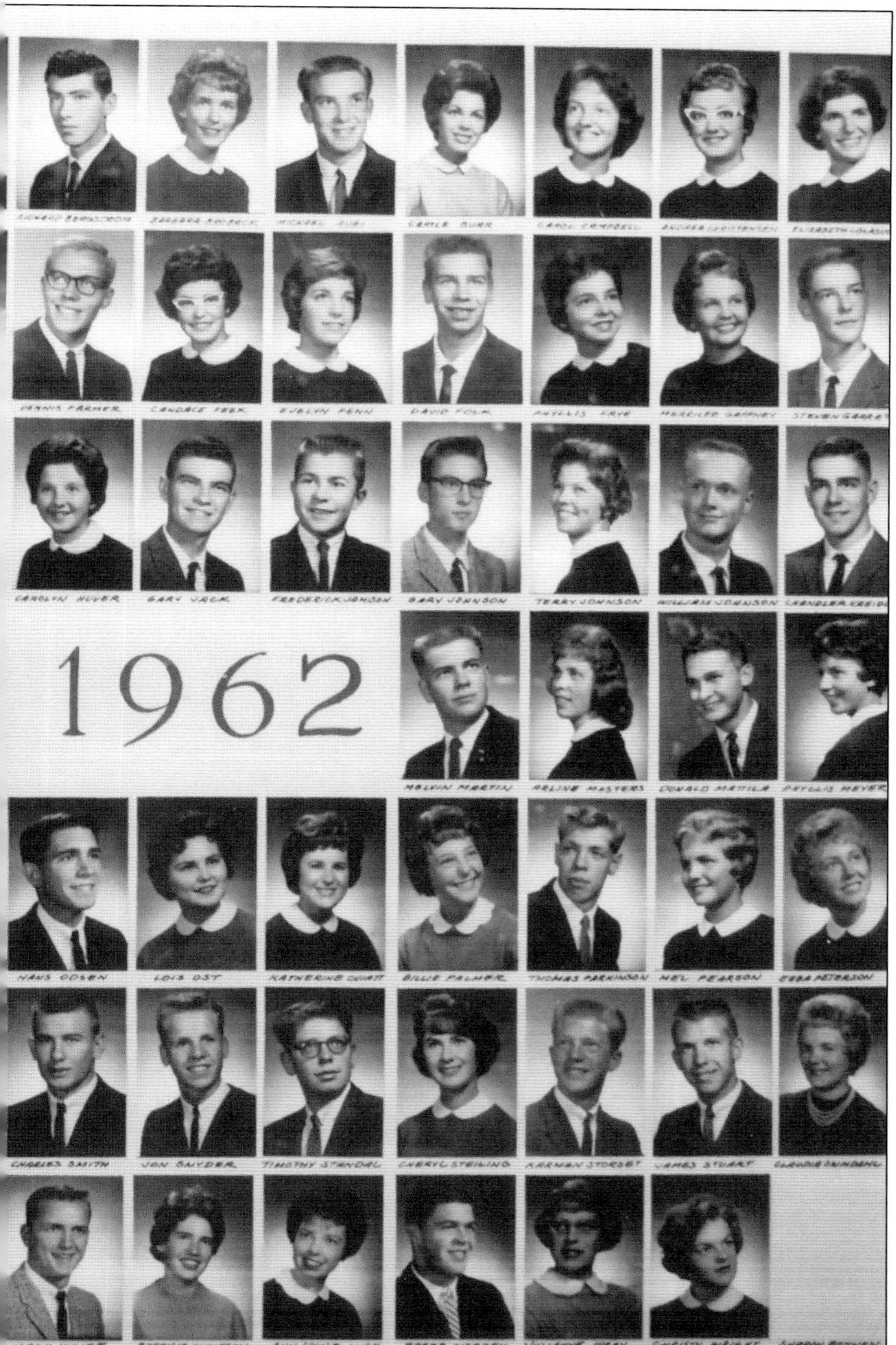

community embraced their schools completely. The class of 1962 was led by class president Paul Ellsbury and student body president George Mitchell. Curtis High School graduated its 50th class in June 2011.

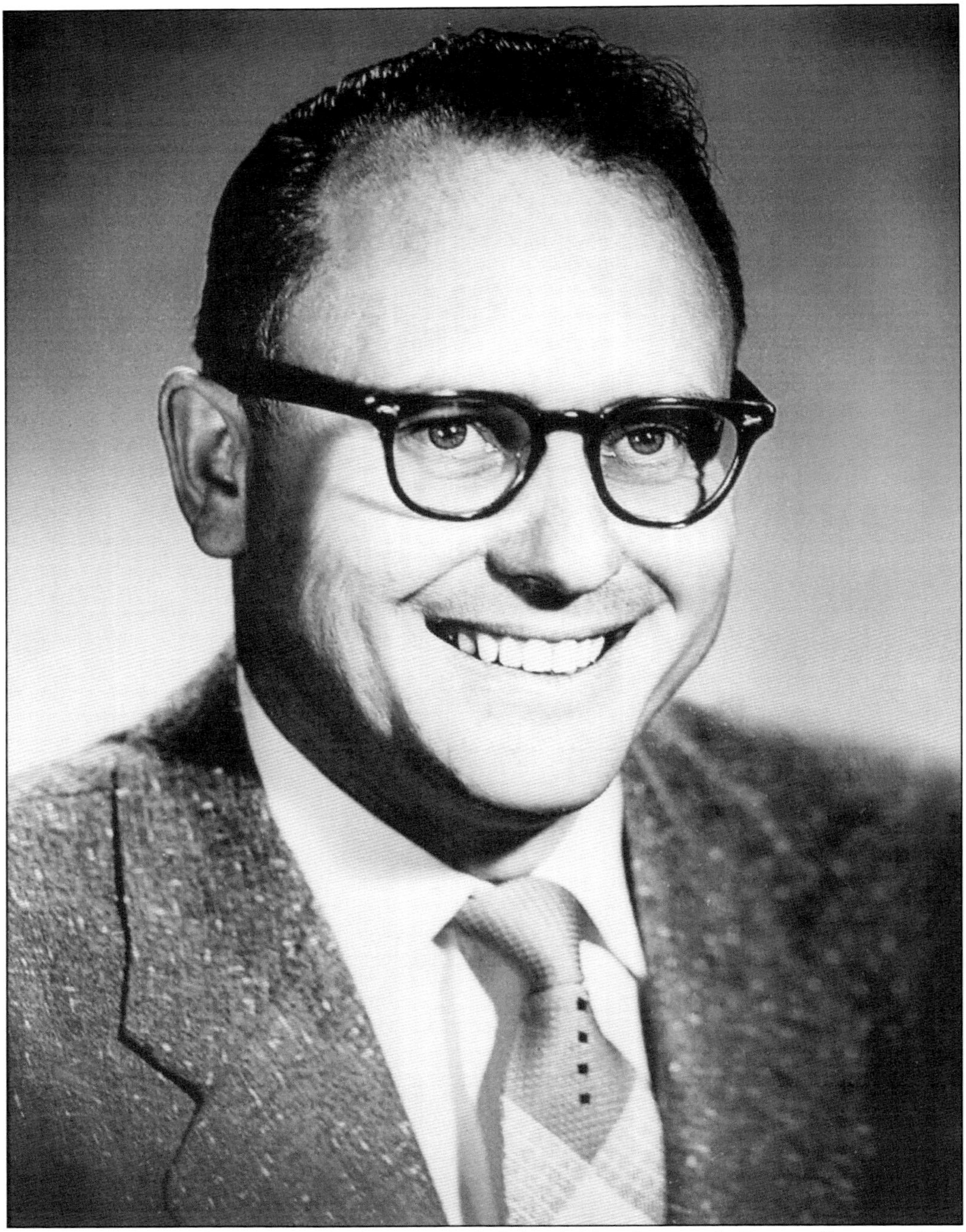

Ray Beard was the first principal of Curtis High School. He, along with George Curtis and the school board, continued the quest to provide an outstanding education for the children of UP—now all the way through high school. Beard led the transition of the high school to its new campus "up the hill" on Fortieth Street in the fall of 1969. He retired after the 1976–1977 school year.

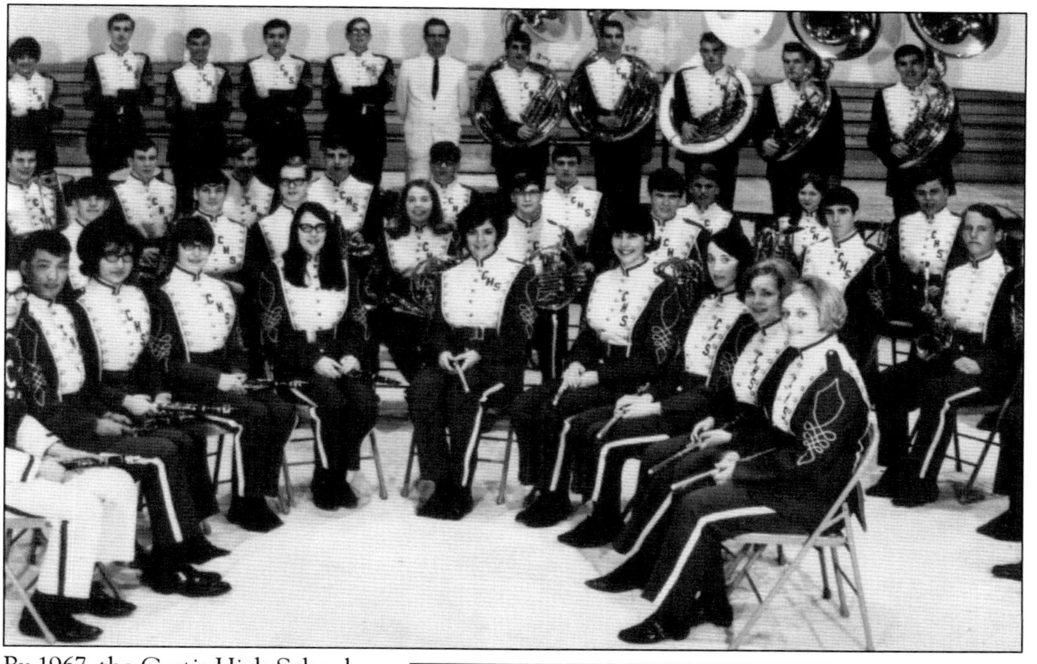

By 1967, the Curtis High School performing arts program was flourishing. The band program (above) was led by Gary Alshire, and the choir program was directed by Bob Northrop.

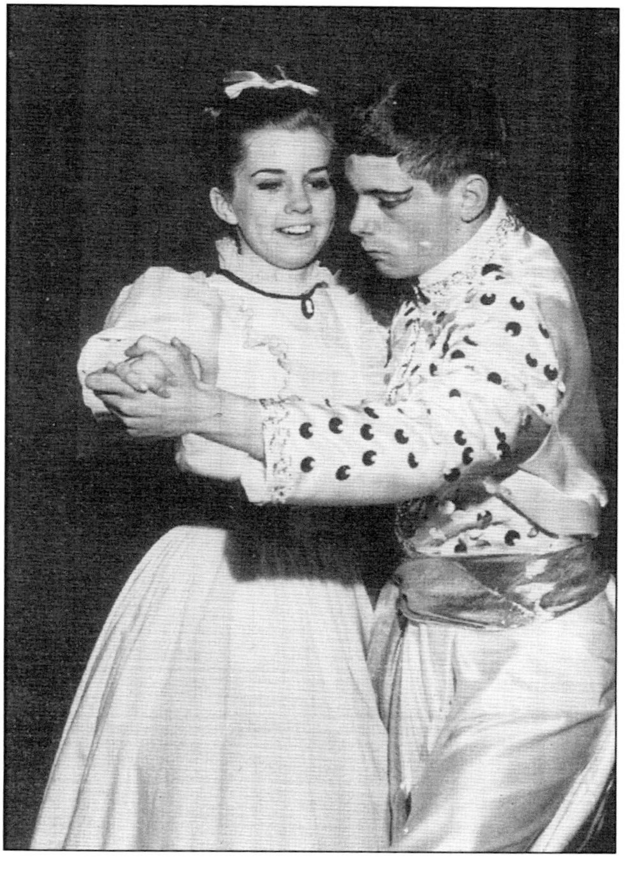

Another annual Curtis tradition and community highlight was born in the mid-1960s. The entire performing arts program of band, orchestra, choir, and drama combined to put on spectacular Broadway musicals. This photograph shows Steve Holmes, who starred as the King, and Sue Pagel as Anna in *The King And I*, the first musical to be staged at the new high school auditorium in 1969. Don Wolvers directed the production.

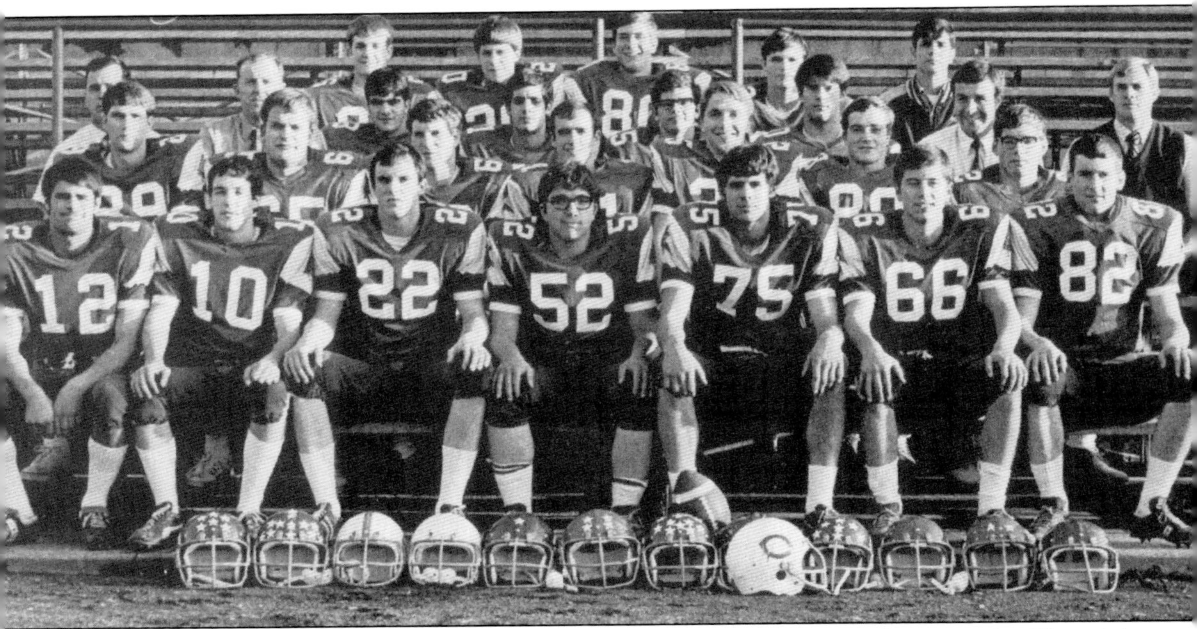

It did not take long for the Curtis athletic program to become a powerhouse in the Class AA Seamount League. In the early 1970s, the Viking football teams won 38 straight games and were named state poll champions three years in a row. The place to be on any fall Friday night was at the football game. Curtis also won Class AAA state championships in 1989 and 1990 and again in 1995 and 1996. This is the football team that started it all in the fall of 1970.

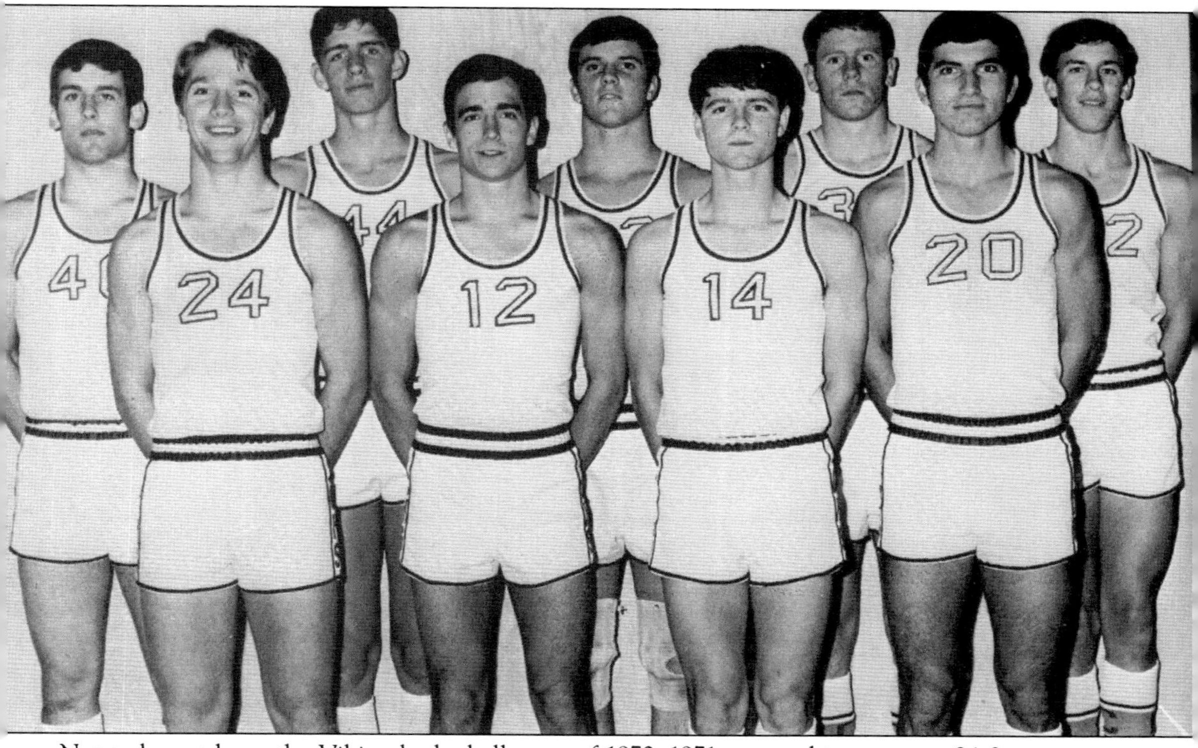

Not to be outdone, the Viking basketball team of 1970–1971 powered its way to a 24-0 season and the state championship. The team won every game by at least nine points and was inducted into the Tacoma–Pierce County Sports Hall of Fame in 2010. Shown here are, from left to right, (first row) Tim O'Connell, Mark Wells, Tom Shoemaker, and Tom Hargadon; (second row) Paul Zurfluh, Mike Berger, Tim Beard, Brian Roark, and Jim Ball. Not pictured are coaches Jerry Redburg, Mike Mullen, and Arne Handeland and manager Dave Berger.

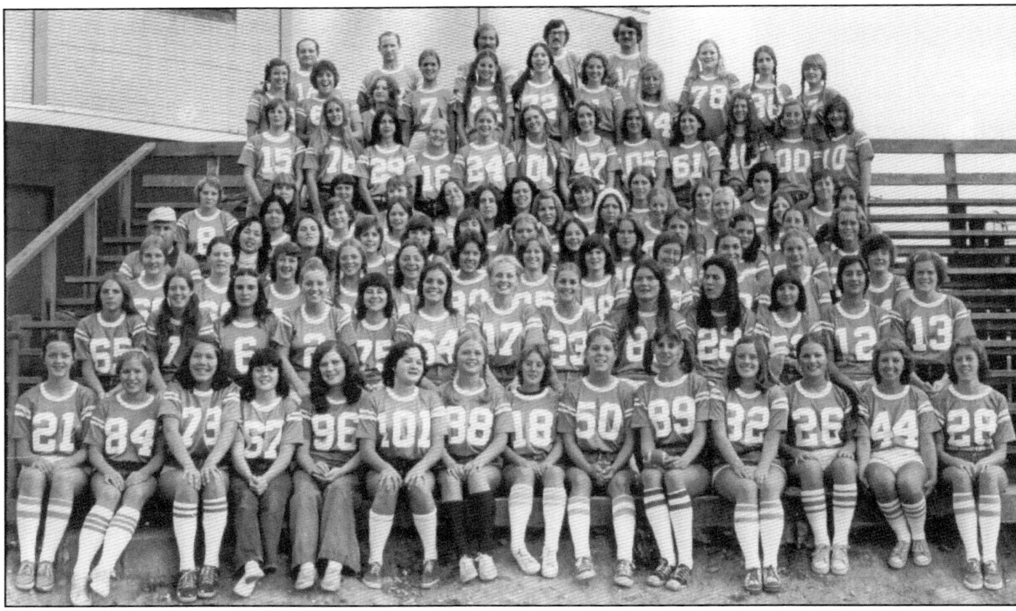

One tradition that was started by school counselor Bill Doucette in the late 1960s was the annual powder-puff football game between the juniors and seniors. For many girls, this game was a major highlight of their high school years. In pre–Title IX days, it was not unusual to have over 100 girls from each class participate in this event. This photograph was taken in the fall of 1973.

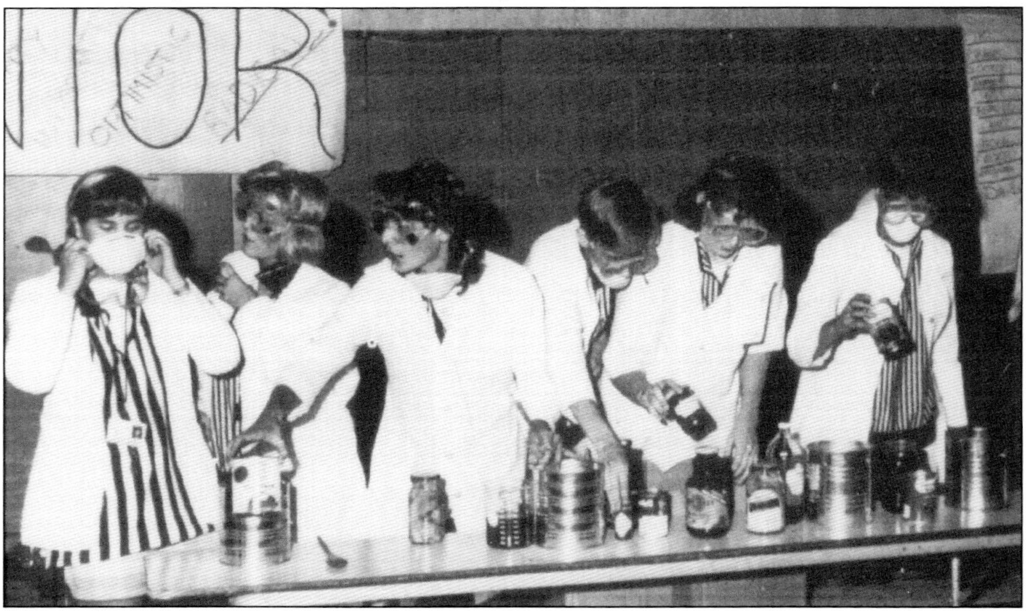

Homecoming Week at Curtis is another tradition started by Bill Doucette. The week consists of choosing a theme, decorating the entire school, dress-up days, class competitions during lunches, and finally a huge evening assembly, with the students and community packing the gym to watch class and faculty competitions and games, ranging from the octets to the ever-popular ugly drink. The evening culminates with the crowning of the homecoming royalty. This photograph shows the student body officers concocting the ugly drink at the 1984 assembly.

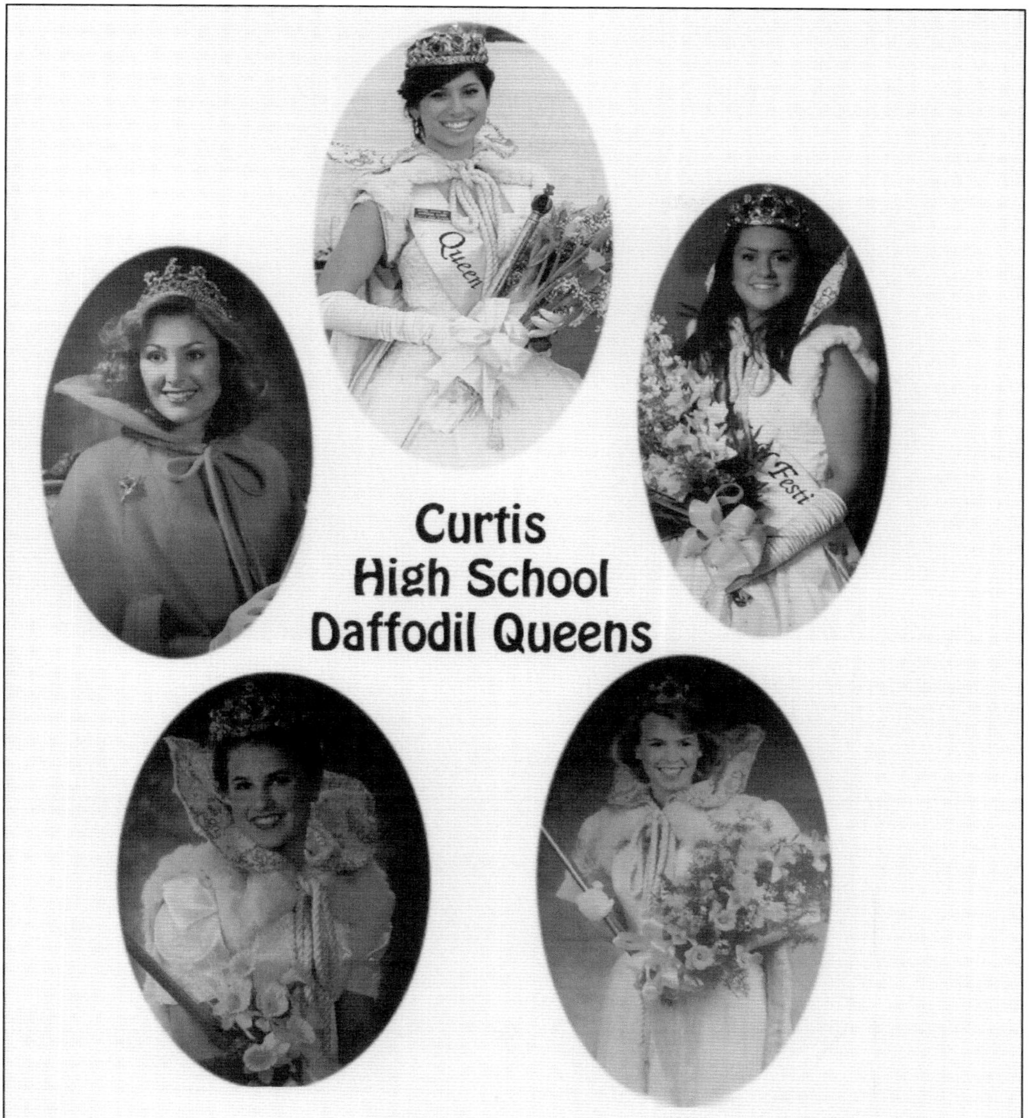

When Curtis became a full-fledged high school in 1962, it became eligible to participate with all other high schools in the Puyallup Valley Daffodil Festival. Every year, princesses from each school are chosen and compete to become the reigning queen. Five times, the Curtis princess has won the honor to be the queen and highlight the floral parade. The winners are, shown clockwise from the top, Claire Fleming (2011), Molly Ruiz (2006), Heidi Johnson (1988), Allison Porter (1998), and Paula Nelson (1979). (Photo collection arranged by Laurent Jarvis.)

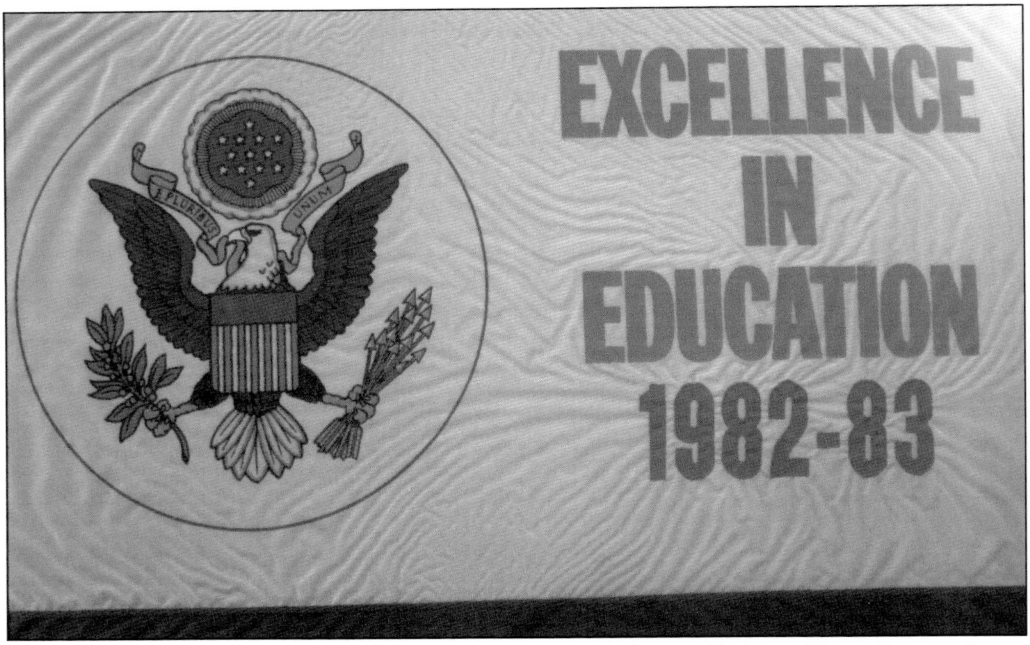

These two awards represent what University Place schools are all about. From George Curtis to all of the administrators, school boards, and staff through the years, nothing has been more important than providing the very best possible academic education for UP children. Year after year, University Place students score well above state and national averages. The quality of the schools attracts many parents to the area. In 1982–1983 and again in 1999–2000, Curtis High School was chosen as a National School of Excellence by the Department of Education. (Both, courtesy of Laurent Jarvis.)

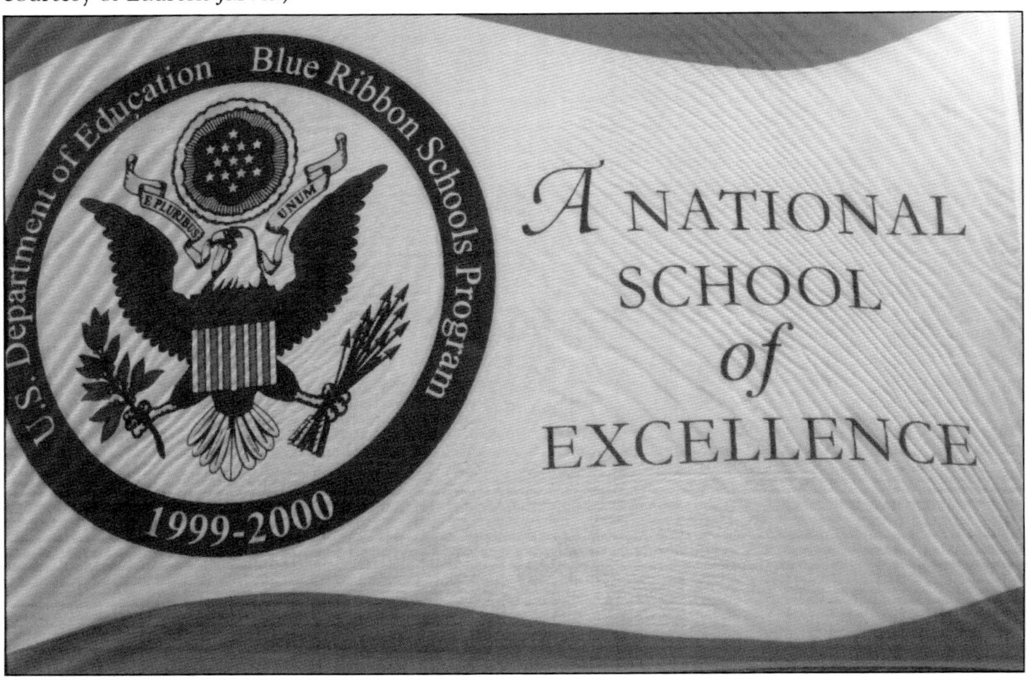

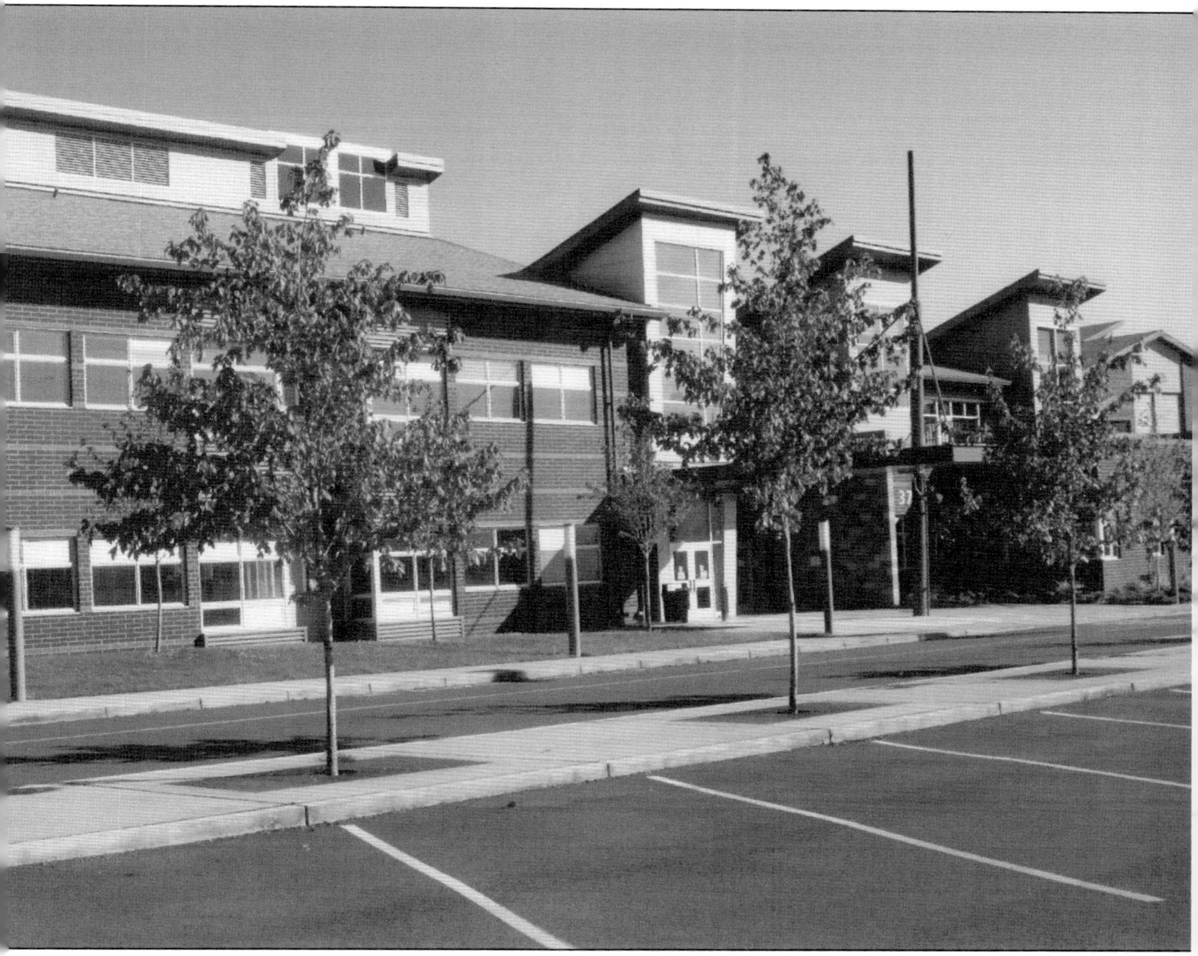

Due to the ever-continuing support of community voters throughout the years, the University Place School District (UPSD) has worked hard to keep up with the demands of University Place's growing population and with the deterioration of older facilities. In a massive bond issue passed in 2007, voters agreed to fund the total replacement of University Place Primary, Curtis Junior High, and the high school gym and a complete renovation of the pool. New athletic fields, replacement turf on the football field, covered stands on the visitors' side of Viking stadium, and four new tennis courts are now complete. The facilities provided by UPSD are truly cutting edge and ready for the 21st century. This photograph shows the new Curtis Junior High School, which opened its doors in the fall of 2010. (Courtesy of Laurent Jarvis.)

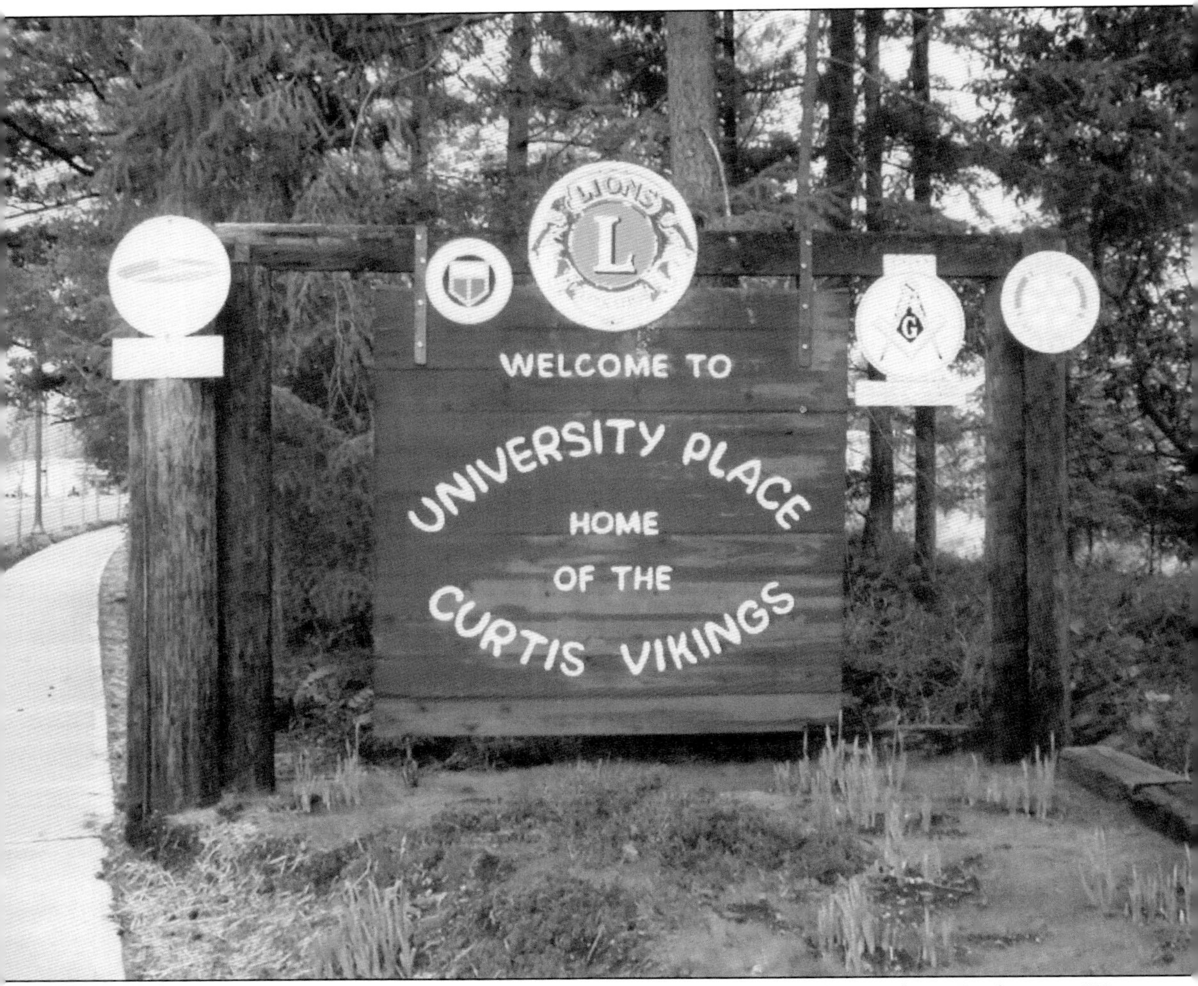

This sign greets everyone coming into University Place from Lakewood via Bridgeport Way: "University Place—Home of the Curtis Vikings." The central focus and public pride and joy of University Place has always been its schools. The sign also features several UP service organizations (Lions, Rotary, Masons, Kiwanis, and chamber of commerce), but they seem to pale in relation to the focus on the Curtis Vikings.

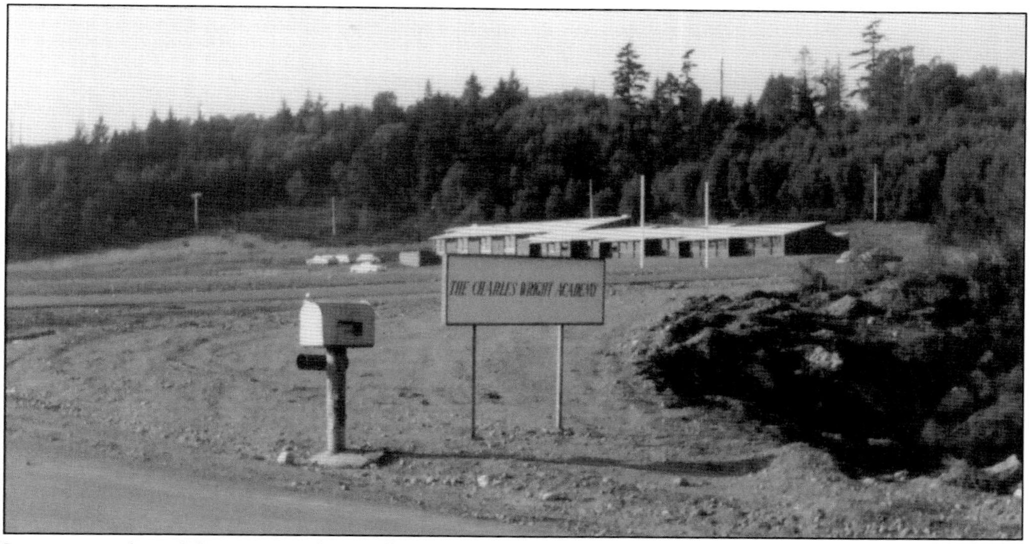

In writing about University Place schools, not mentioning Charles Wright Academy would be a major oversight. This Episcopal-based private school has been here for over 50 years, providing an outstanding educational experience for thousands of students. Founded as a complement to Annie Wright Seminary for girls in Tacoma, Charles Wright Academy was first opened to boys, kindergarten through fourth grade, and kindergarten girls in 1957 with the goal of adding one grade yearly until a complete K-12 program was realized. The academy graduated its first senior class in 1964. (Courtesy of Charles Wright Academy.)

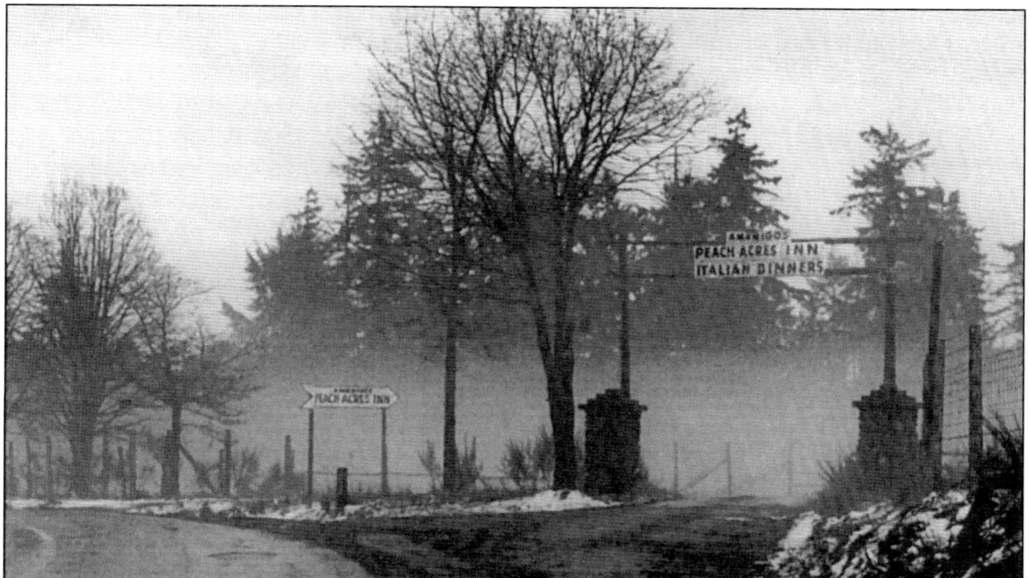

The founders of Charles Wright Academy began looking for a suitable location near Lakewood and discovered a 127-acre parcel in the south end of University Place, known as Peach Acres. The property was owned by Amerigo and Clorinda Centori, who operated an Italian restaurant called Amerigo's as well as tending the peach orchard. Unfortunately, two severe winters had killed the peach trees, and the Centoris decided to sell. This became the campus of Charles Wright Academy. (Courtesy of Charles Wright Academy.)

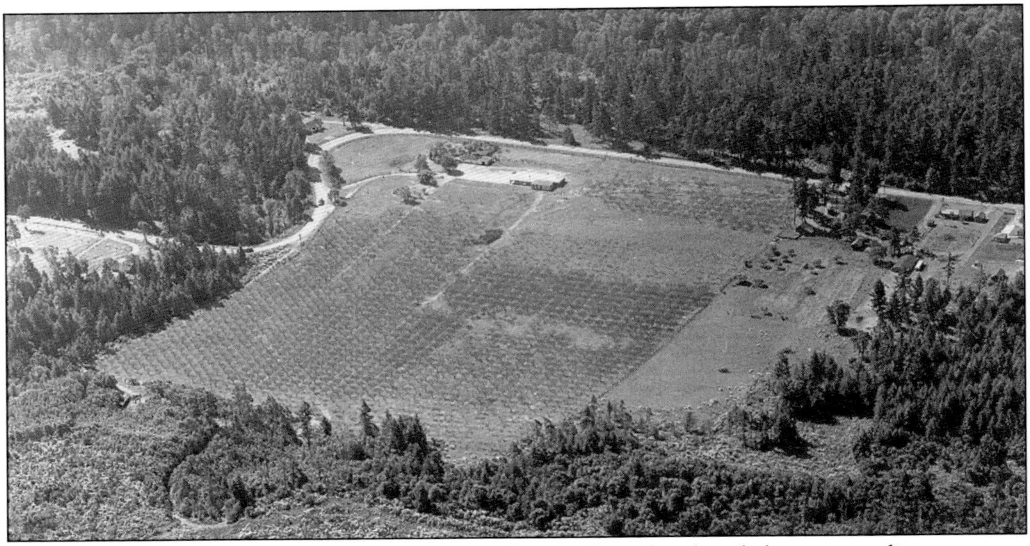

This aerial view of Peach Acres estate shows the peach orchard and the surrounding property of the Centori estate in 1956, before it became Charles Wright Academy. (Courtesy of Charles Wright Academy.)

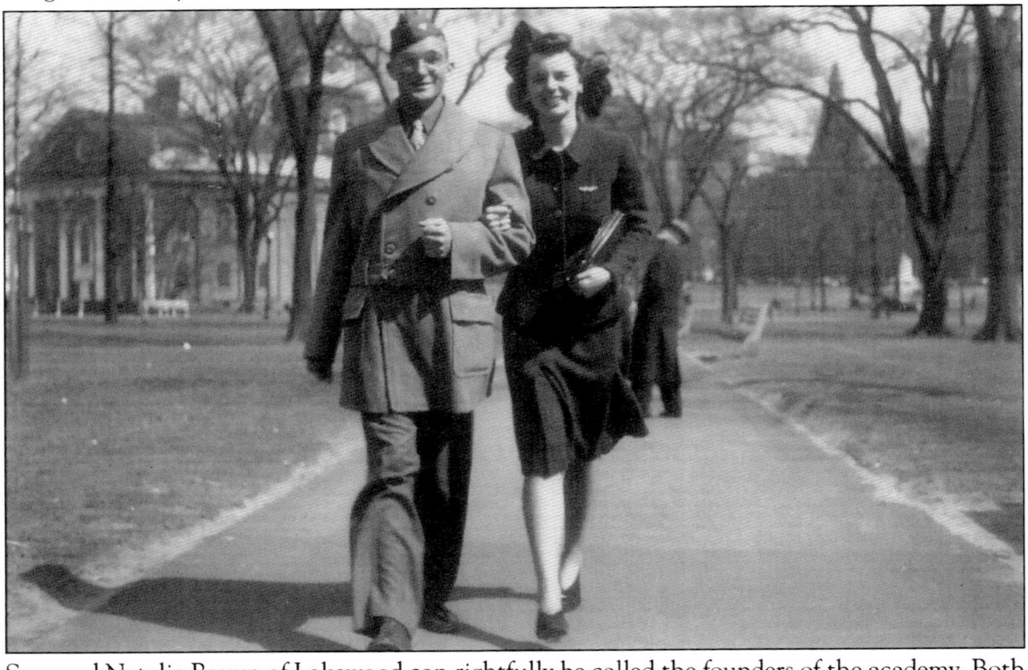

Sam and Natalie Brown of Lakewood can rightfully be called the founders of the academy. Both were educated in well-established East Coast private schools and came west to work for the Weyerhauser Company. They had three sons and three daughters. The Annie Wright Seminary in Tacoma provided an opportunity for their girls, but no non-Catholic private school program existed in the area. The Browns posted an announcement in the *Lakewood Log* calling for a meeting on November 14, 1956, for those interested in starting an independent day school for boys. To their amazement, over 50 people showed up, and Charles Wright Academy was born. (Courtesy of Charles Wright Academy.)

An old bell from a Northern Pacific Railroad locomotive was donated to Charles Wright Academy in recognition of the role that Charles Wright, as president of Northern Pacific, played in selecting Tacoma as the western terminus of the first transcontinental railroad to the Northwest. (Courtesy of Charles Wright Academy.)

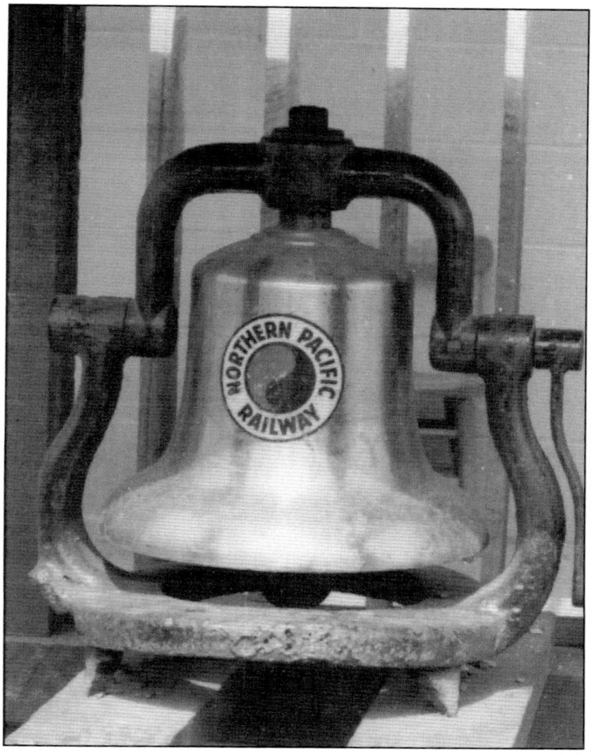

Below is one of the first Charles Wright Academy school buses. These boys are arriving for classes in September 1961. At one time, the academy's bus routes crossed 23 different public school districts. (Courtesy of Charles Wright Academy.)

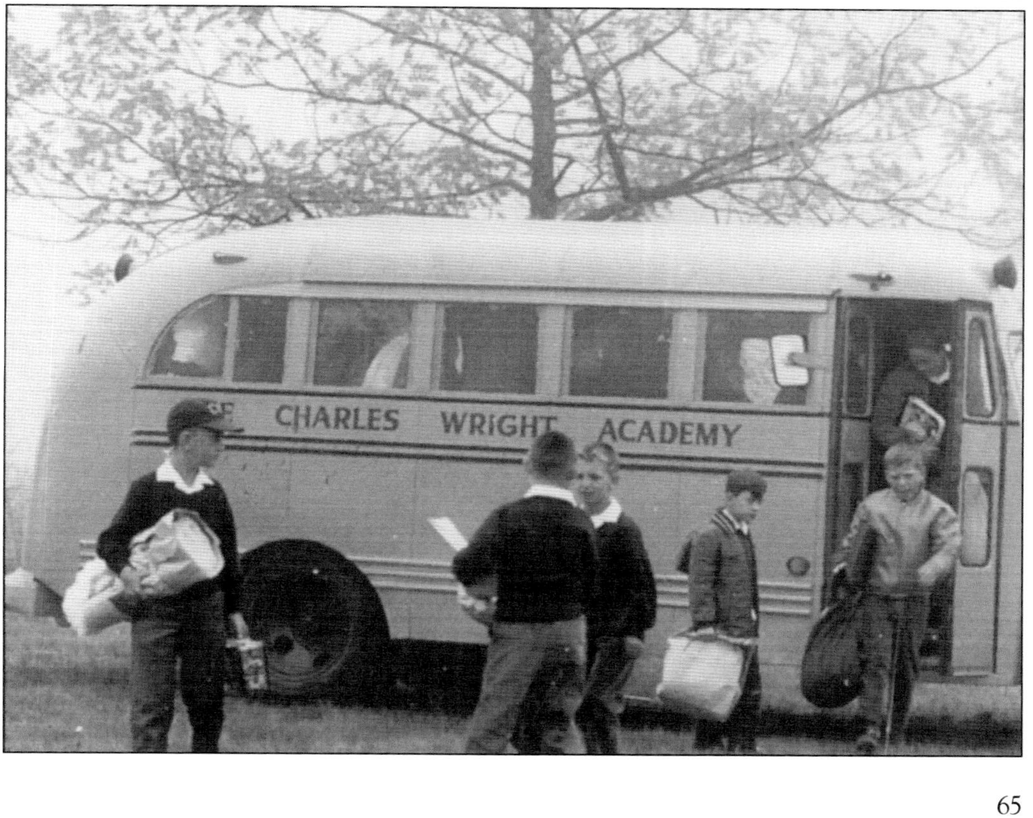

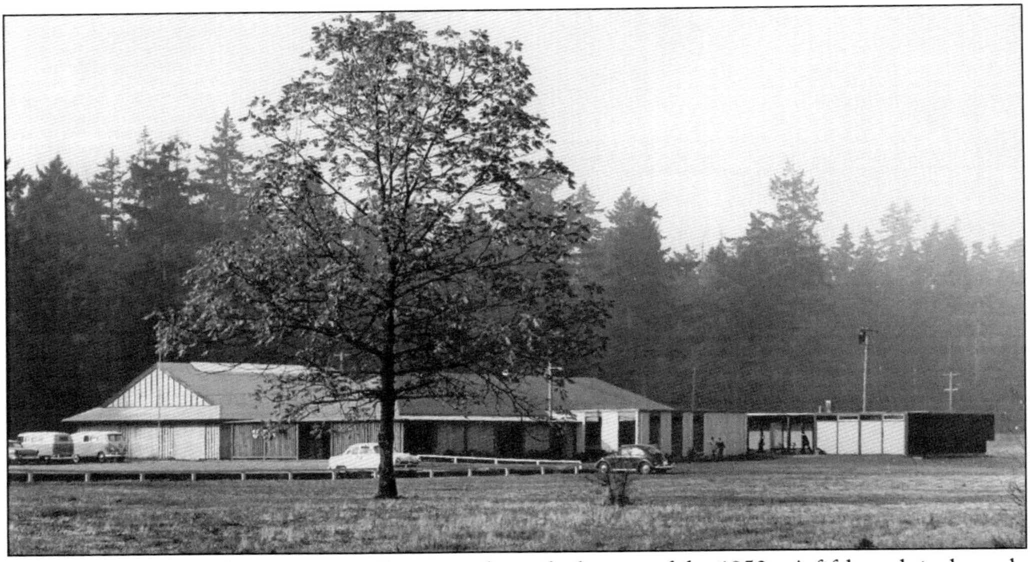

Charles Wright Academy continued to grow through the rest of the 1950s. A fifth and sixth grade were added for the 1958–1959 school year, and 83 students were enrolled. In addition, three new classrooms were added on, at a cost of $15,000. The Upper School opened in September 1960. (Courtesy of Charles Wright Academy.)

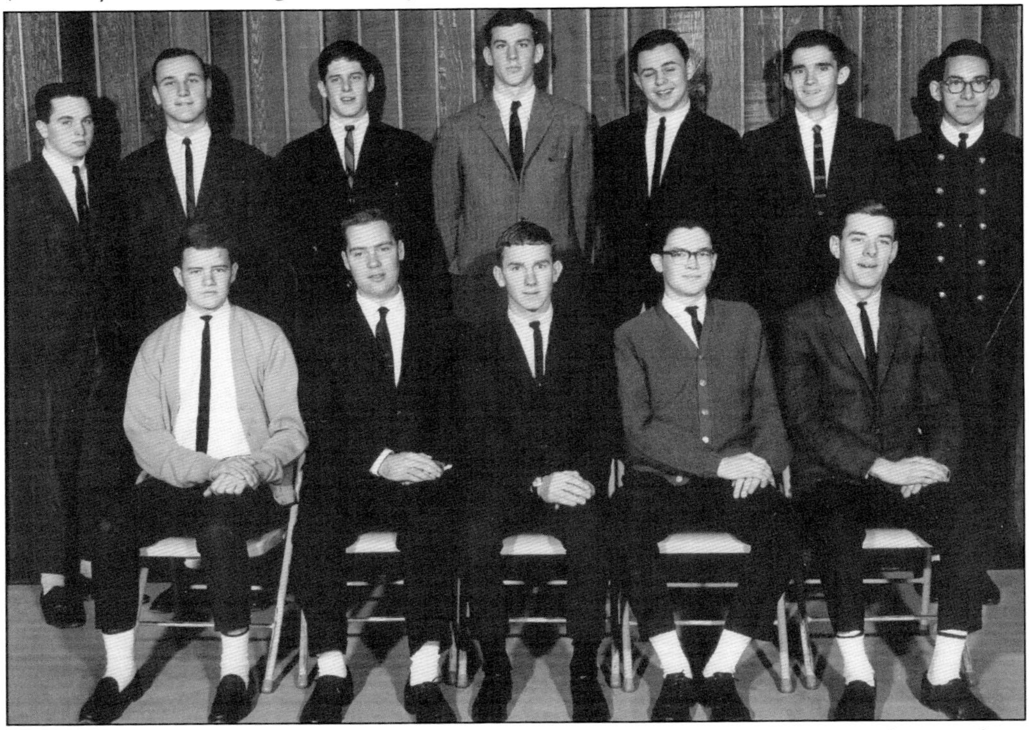

The 12 young men of the first graduating class got their diplomas on June 5, 1964. They are, from left to right, (first row) Mark Wyatt, David McKay, John Long, William Armstrong, and Philip Pasco; (second row) John Allen, Bruce McKendry, Michael Shanahan, Clarke Palmer, Howard Lincoln, Michael Roberts, and Peter Shapiro. (Courtesy of Charles Wright Academy.)

Four
Growing Pains and Gains

Until the 1950s, University Place's growth was very gradual. New residents that came were looking for more space to live and raise their children but not too far away from the work and other amenities that Tacoma offered. Many had farms, raising cows and chickens and growing crops mostly for their own consumption. Those with orchards of peaches, apples, or cherries sold their crops commercially, but sometimes they got hit hard by weather conditions. For a time in the 1930s, University Place became well known for its tomatoes and even had a tomato growers' association with its own packing shed. On Day Island, the Willits brothers were making their remarkable canoes. Relatively speaking, University Place was devoid of any major industries, with the exception of the lumber mill at the end of Nineteenth Street and the sand and gravel pit at the south end of UP near Chambers Creek. The sawmill burned to the ground in 1934, but the gravel pit operated until the late 1990s, when it became the property of Pierce County. Much of it has now been converted to recreational property, including the world-class Chamber Bay Golf Course, which will be the site of the US Open Golf Championship in 2015.

As University Place grew, the need for community services became more and more evident. When the Tacoma-Steilacoom streetcar line shut down for good in the late 1920s, more roads were necessary before bus and car transportation would be feasible. Other public services were becoming necessary, including extension of electric and telephone service, a consistent water supply, mandatory refuse service, and a local firefighting presence. University Place was growing up.

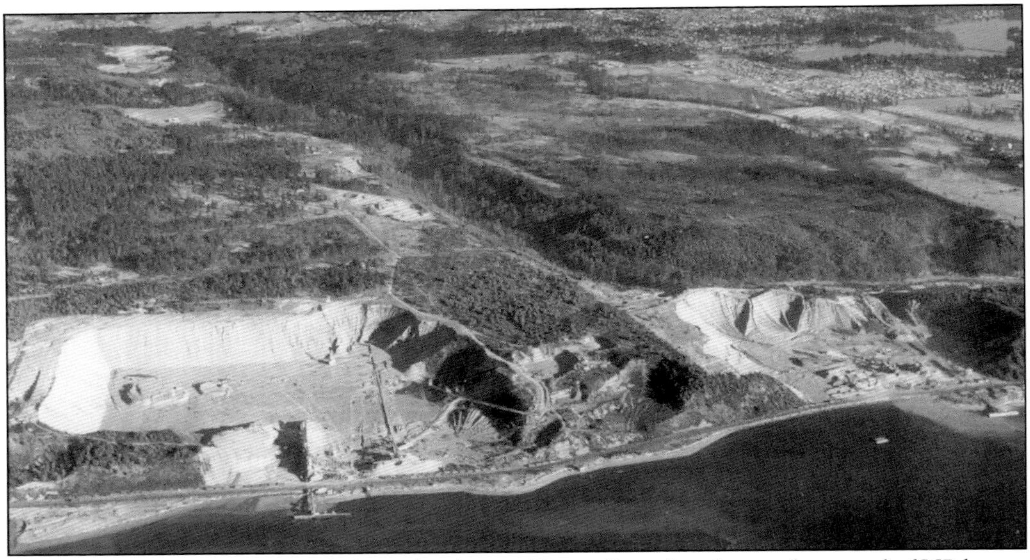

The mining of sand and gravel along the shore of Puget Sound at the southern end of UP began in the 1890s, when the federal government began construction of Forts Warden, Flagler, and Casey at strategic locations on the Sound. Pacific Bridge Company got the contract and began mining the site. When the forts were completed in 1905, the mine was sold to Martin Sand & Gravel, and then to Pioneer Sand & Gravel in 1910. Glacier Sand & Gravel began operation of a new mine that same year, at the south end of the site. This photograph shows the two mining operations in the early 1960s.

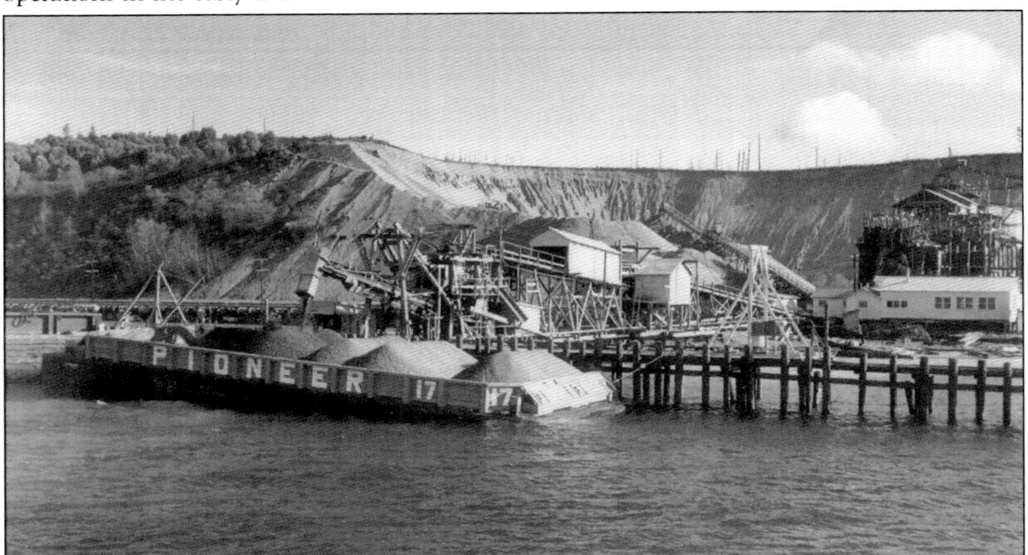

The sand and gravel companies were the biggest companies, and largest employers, for many years in UP. Located in the largely unoccupied southern portion of University Place, the pits did not seem to bother anyone and were a welcome tax asset to the community, especially the school district. As the community expanded and the addition of coal-exporting docks and an asphalt plant were proposed, opposition to the mines began to grow, especially among environmentally conscious residents like George and Adriana Hess.

The sand and gravel from these sites were incredibly "pure," as can be seen in this photograph of gravel being loaded onto a Pioneer barge. Very little processing was required before shipping the product to market. It was known as "Steilacoom Grade" and was used in construction projects around the world.

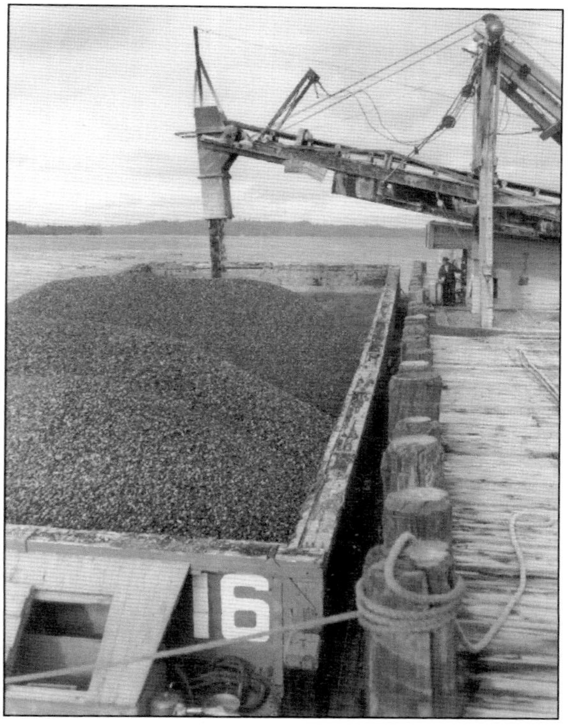

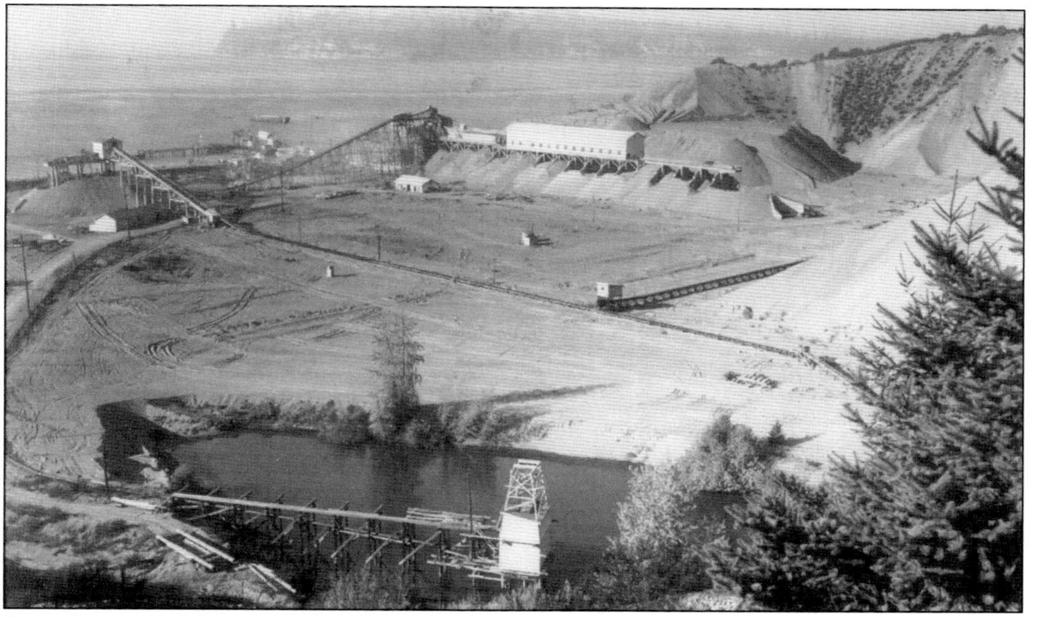

Several aspects of the Pioneer Sand & Gravel operation, shown in this photograph, are recognizable to those that currently use the trail and Central Meadow at Chambers Bay. Remnants of the sorting bins, seen in the center of the photograph, are next to the trail and the 18th-hole fairway of the golf course. The pillars standing at the end of Central Meadow are visible in the upper left of the photograph. The gravel operations ended in the late 1990s, and the property was sold to Pierce County. The county has converted it into a phenomenal recreation area.

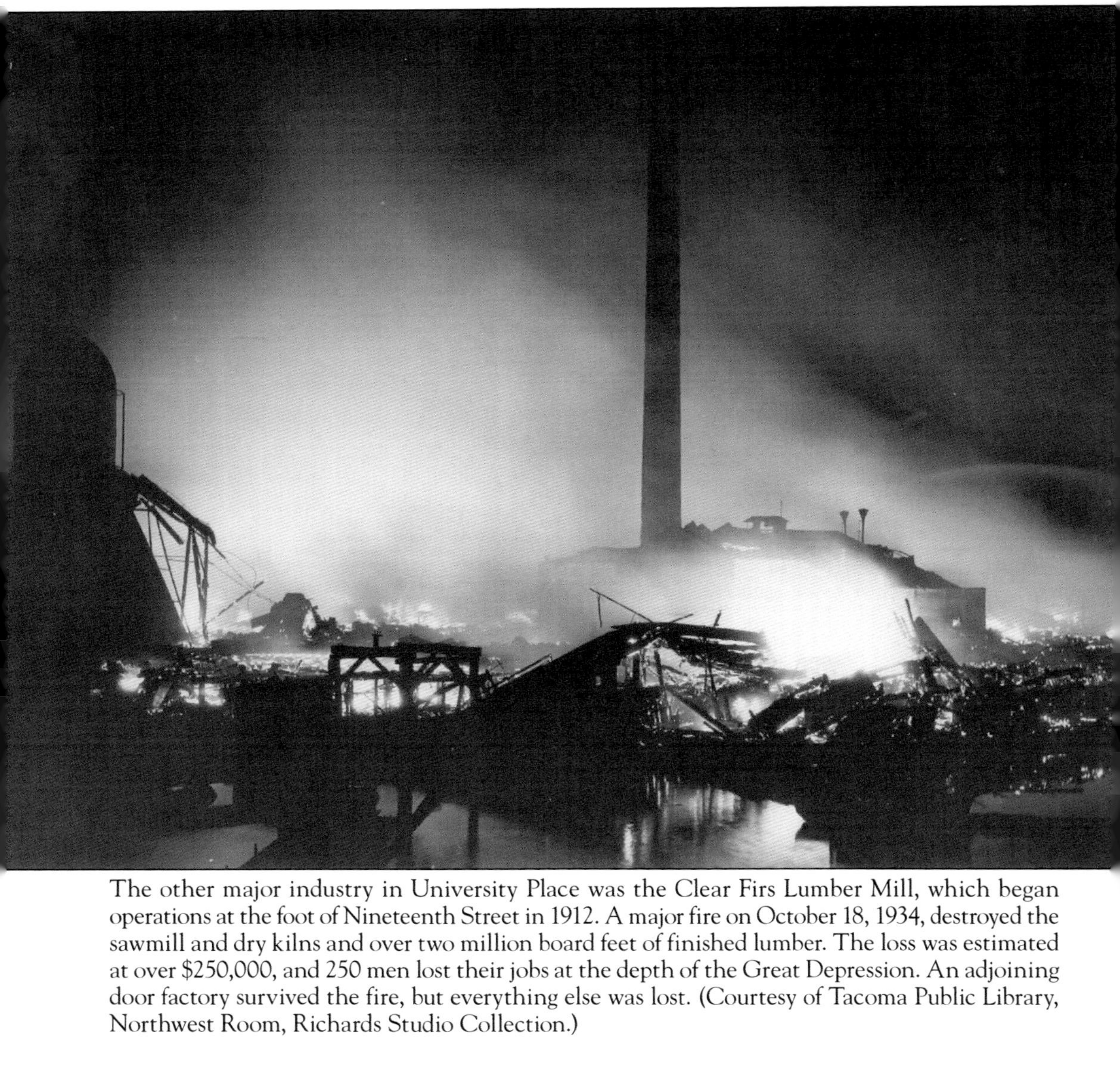

The other major industry in University Place was the Clear Firs Lumber Mill, which began operations at the foot of Nineteenth Street in 1912. A major fire on October 18, 1934, destroyed the sawmill and dry kilns and over two million board feet of finished lumber. The loss was estimated at over $250,000, and 250 men lost their jobs at the depth of the Great Depression. An adjoining door factory survived the fire, but everything else was lost. (Courtesy of Tacoma Public Library, Northwest Room, Richards Studio Collection.)

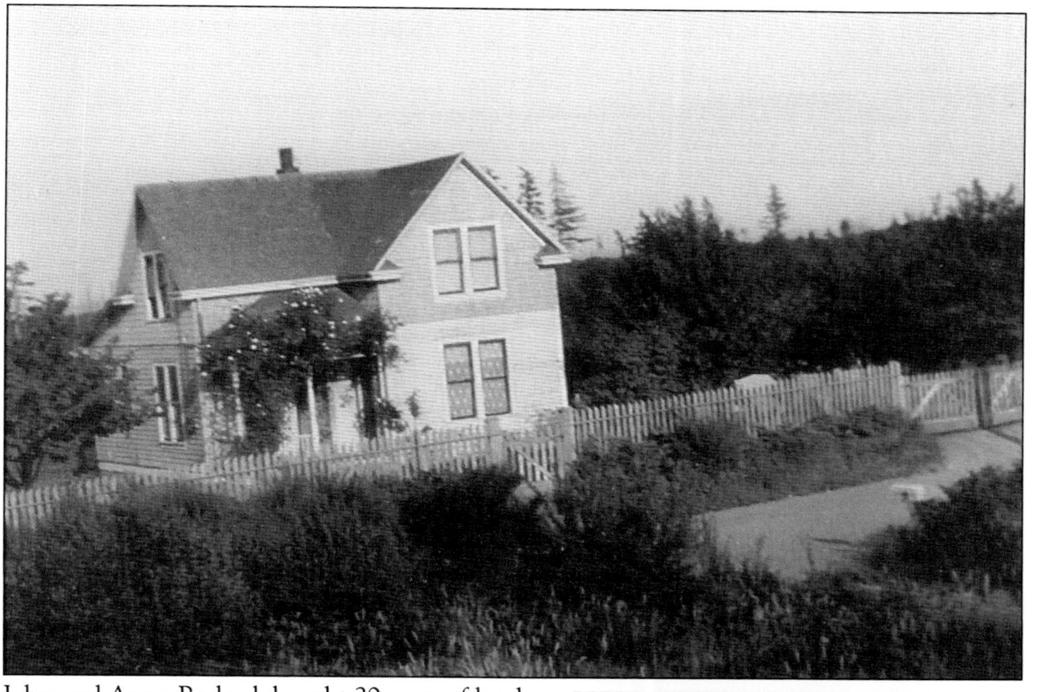

John and Anna Broback bought 20 acres of land on the west side of Bridgeport Way near Thirty-seventh Street in 1931 and moved to the country with their seven children. John continued to work in the shipyards of Tacoma, and he was also a cabinetmaker. The rest of the family farmed the land, at various times growing oats and tomatoes and raising cows, goats, rabbits, and chickens. The Brobacks also had an orchard. Bridgeport Way of the 1930s can be seen in front of the white picket fence. (Courtesy of Art Broback.)

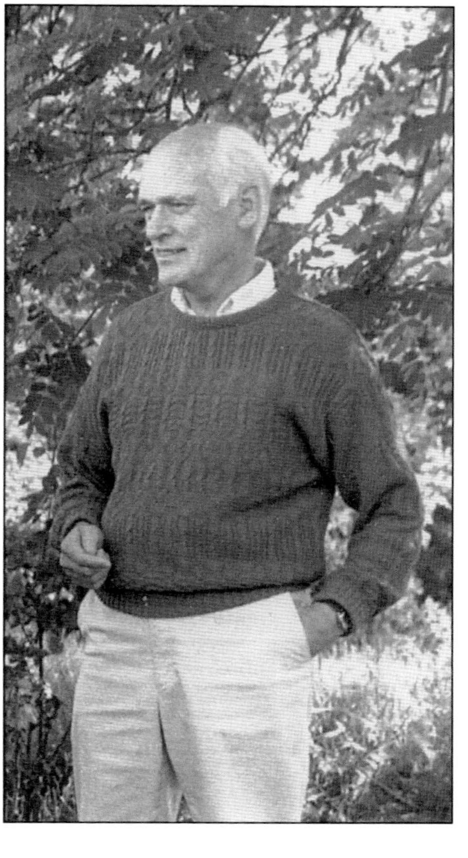

The Brobacks became a well-known family in University Place. Art Broback (right), the youngest son of John and Anna, became a major developer. He built many homes in University Place as well as Windmill Village, which is the current home of city hall. The Homestead Park, next to city hall, is part of the 20 acres that Bert, Art's brother, bought next to his parents' property. (Courtesy of Art Broback.)

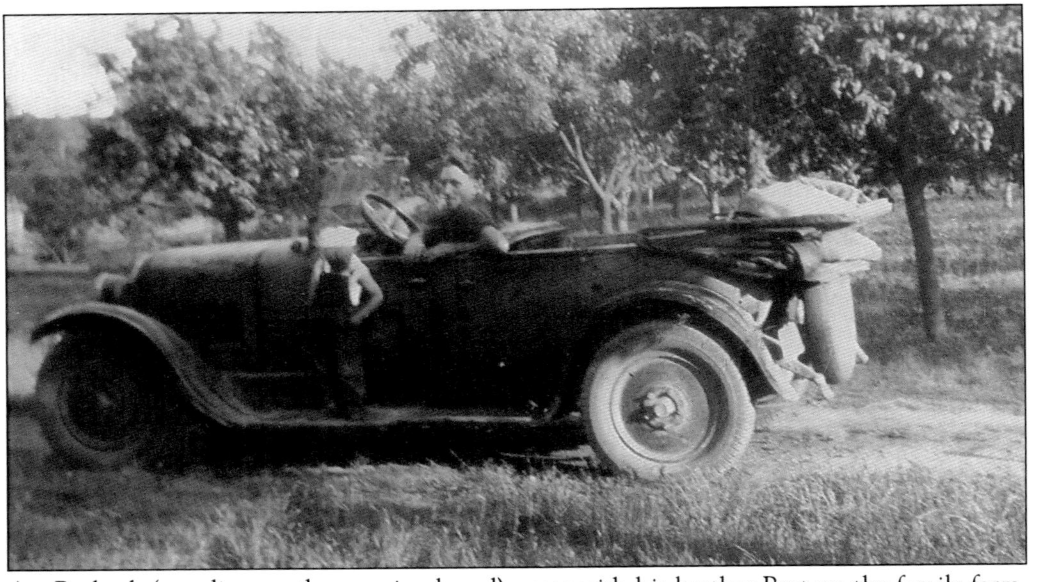

Art Broback (standing on the running board) poses with his brother Bert on the family farm. Their orchard is in the background. (Courtesy of Art Broback.)

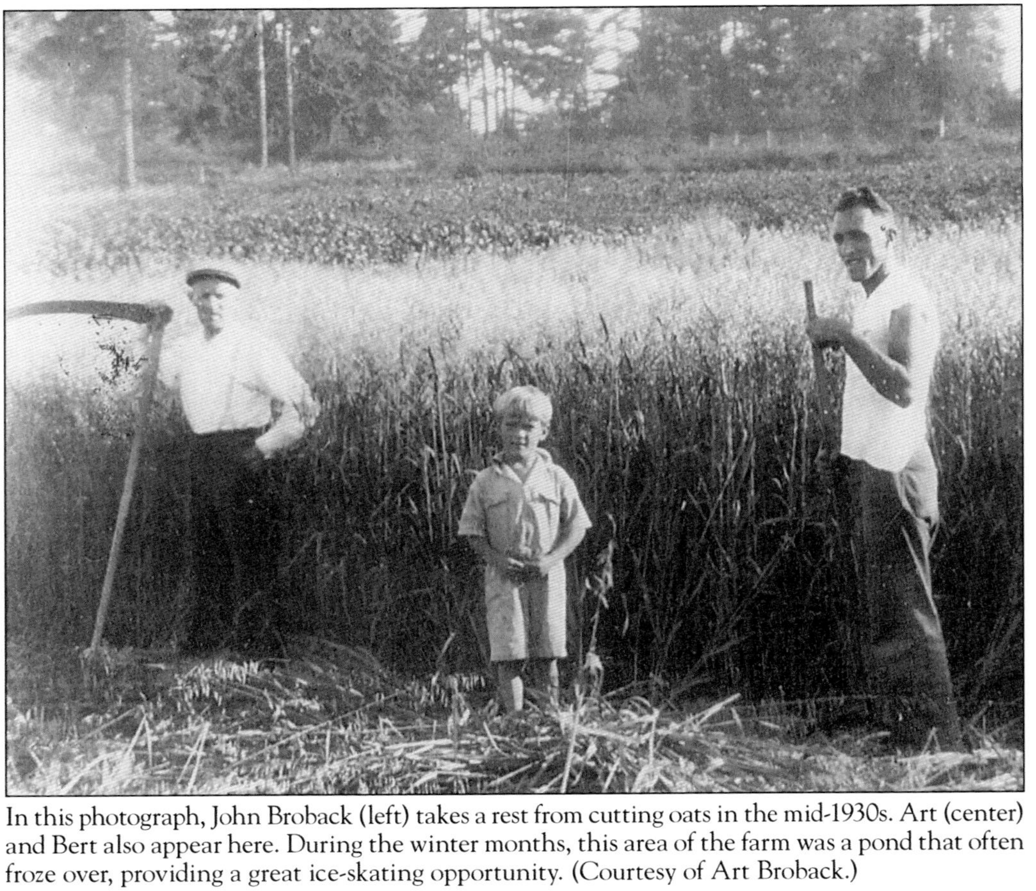

In this photograph, John Broback (left) takes a rest from cutting oats in the mid-1930s. Art (center) and Bert also appear here. During the winter months, this area of the farm was a pond that often froze over, providing a great ice-skating opportunity. (Courtesy of Art Broback.)

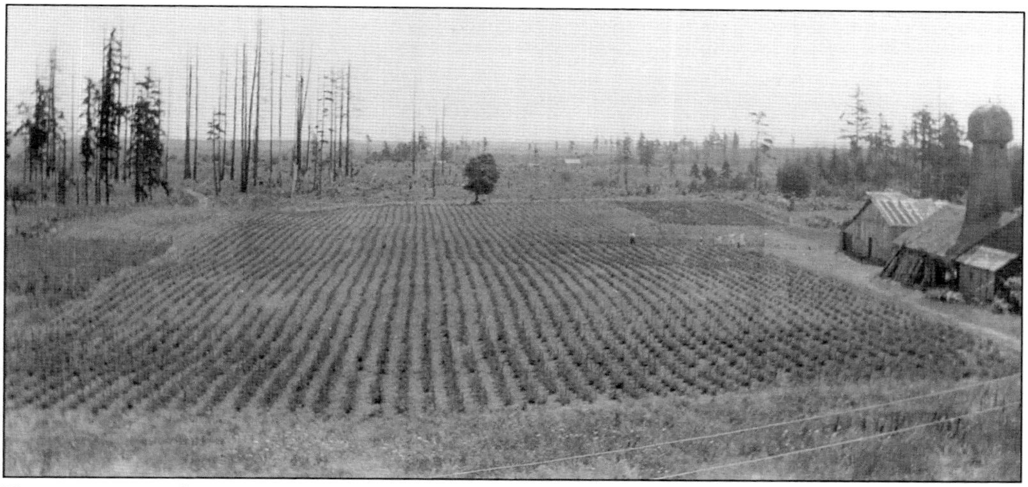

Tomato-growing became a major venture in University Place during the Great Depression. Shown here is the tomato field on the Broback farm. The original barn and water tower can be seen on the right-hand side of the photograph. (Courtesy of Art Broback.)

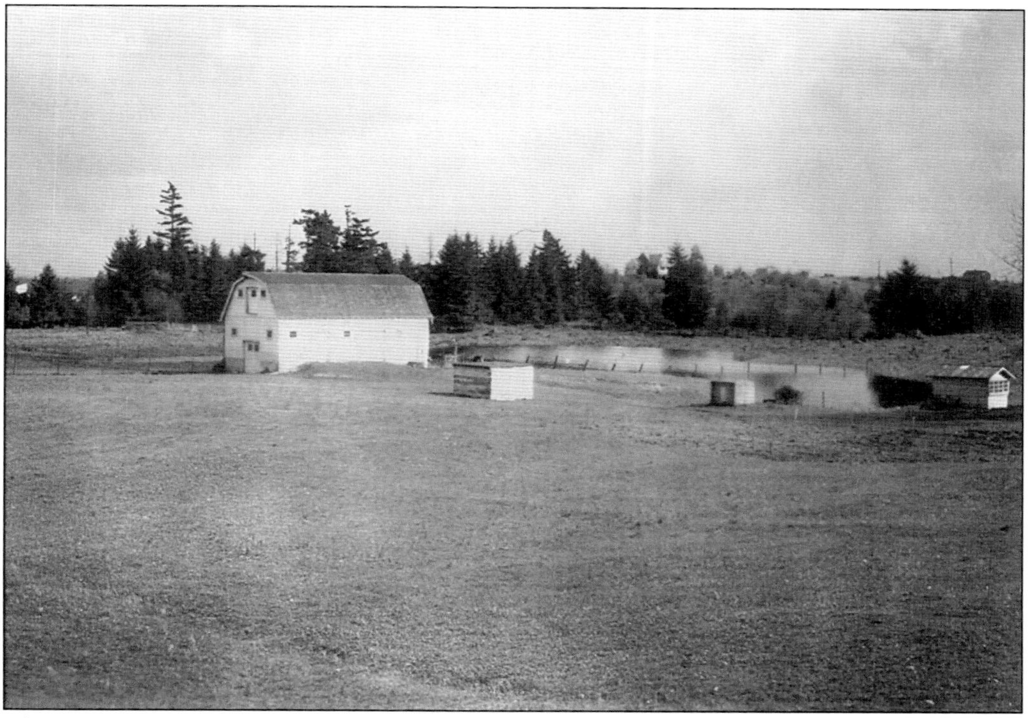

The new barn was built in 1936 or 1937. The pump house for the well can also be seen in the photograph, as can the pond mentioned on page 72. (Courtesy of Art Broback.)

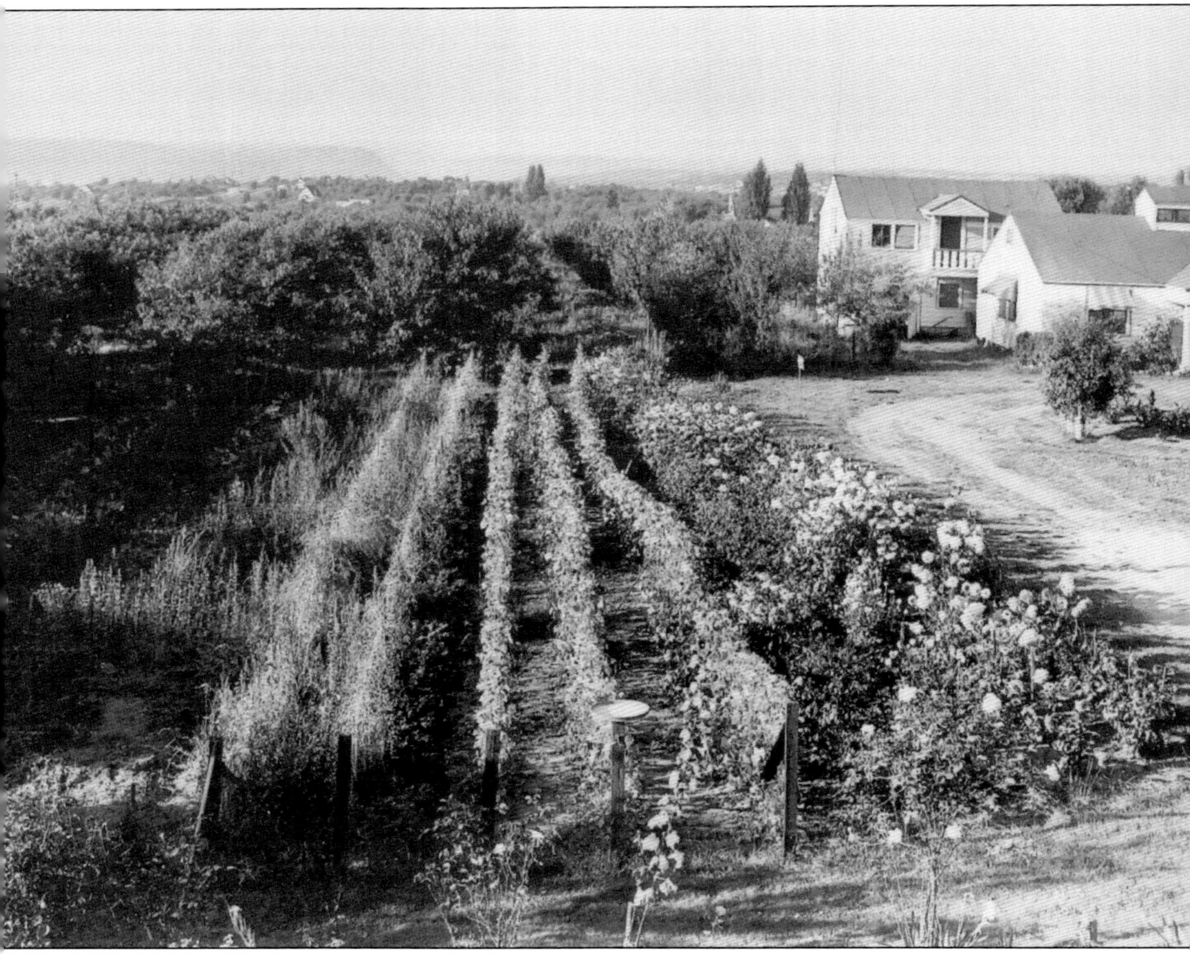

The Ford Fruit Farm was started by Delta Ford when he bought 10 acres of land in 1929 along Madrona Way (now Forty-fourth Street). He later added another seven-and-a-half acres stretching to Sunset Drive. At the time, there was no water or electricity this far from the center of UP along Twenty-seventh Street. The Fords raised chickens, grew tomatoes, sold dahlia bulbs, and started a peach orchard. They sold the farm to John and Viva Maitland in 1947, who renamed it Narrows View Farms. The Maitlands added a packing shed and cannery, both of which can be seen in this photograph. They also added a five-acre strawberry patch alongside the peach orchard. The strawberry patch was sold on a handshake with George Curtis and became the site of Narrows View Primary School (now Narrows View Intermediate School) that opened in 1958.

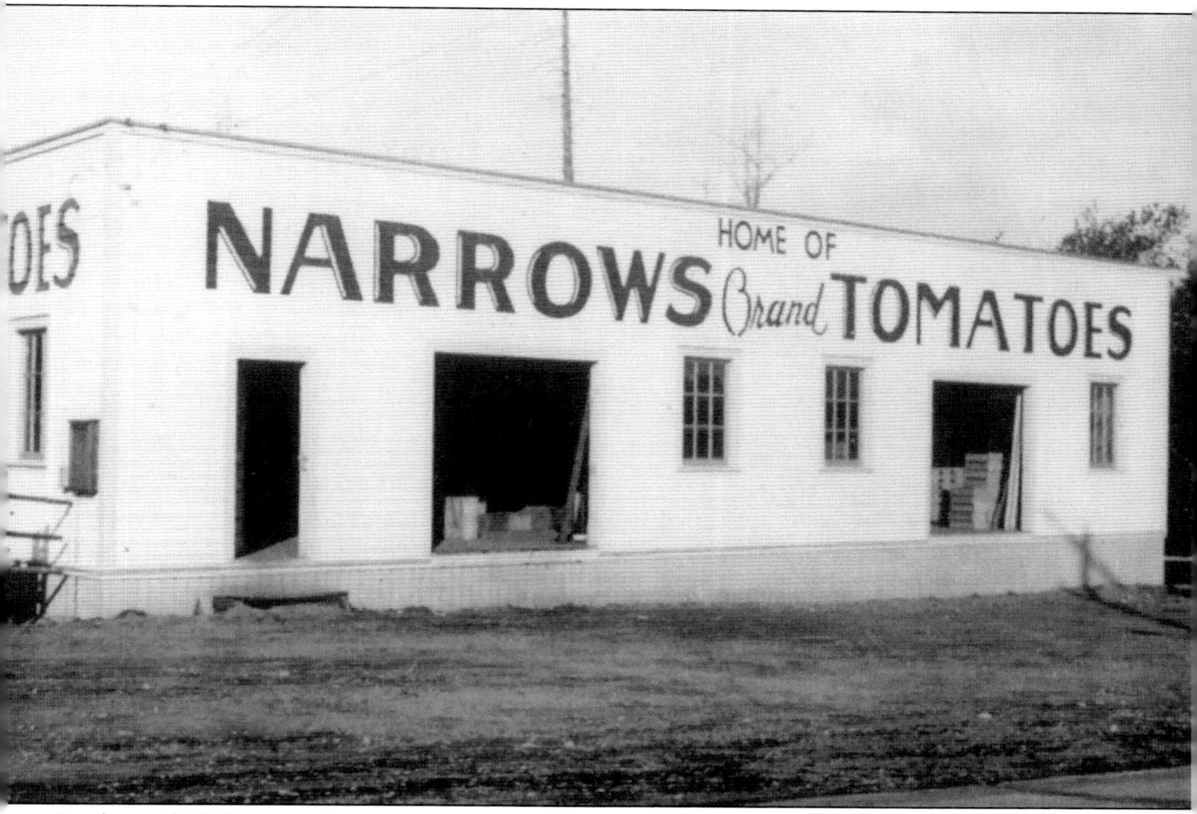

In the mid-1930s, several tomato growers in University Place, including Gunder Leland and Delta Ford, partnered with Joe Thomas to form the University Place Growers Association. This tomato-packing shed was built on the Thomas' property, near Twenty-seventh Street and Grandview Drive. Growers from all around the area brought their tomatoes here to be packed and shipped. When the University Place Volunteer Fire Department started in 1941, the tomato shed was converted into UP's first fire station. It was later used by many area churches as a place to worship while their sanctuaries were being built. UP Parks and Recreation has also used the building, and it now houses the UP Senior Center. (Courtesy of Inez Leland Glass.)

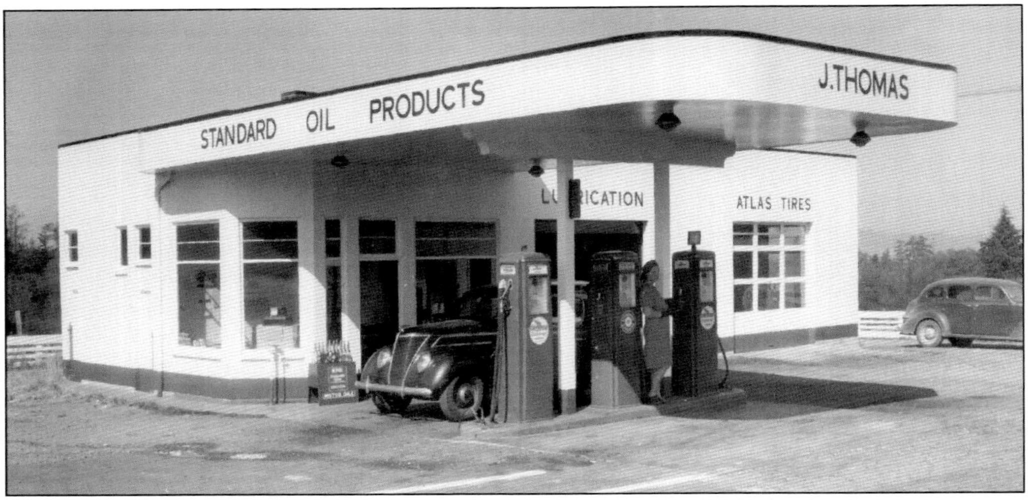

The Thomas brothers, sons of Frank and Agnes Thomas, who built the first grocery store in UP, started several businesses on their property north of Twenty-seventh Street and Grandview Drive. Joe Thomas, with his wife, Loretta, owned the Standard Oil (Chevron) service station seen in this 1945 photograph. (Courtesy of the Tacoma Public Library, Northwest Room, Richards Studio Collection.)

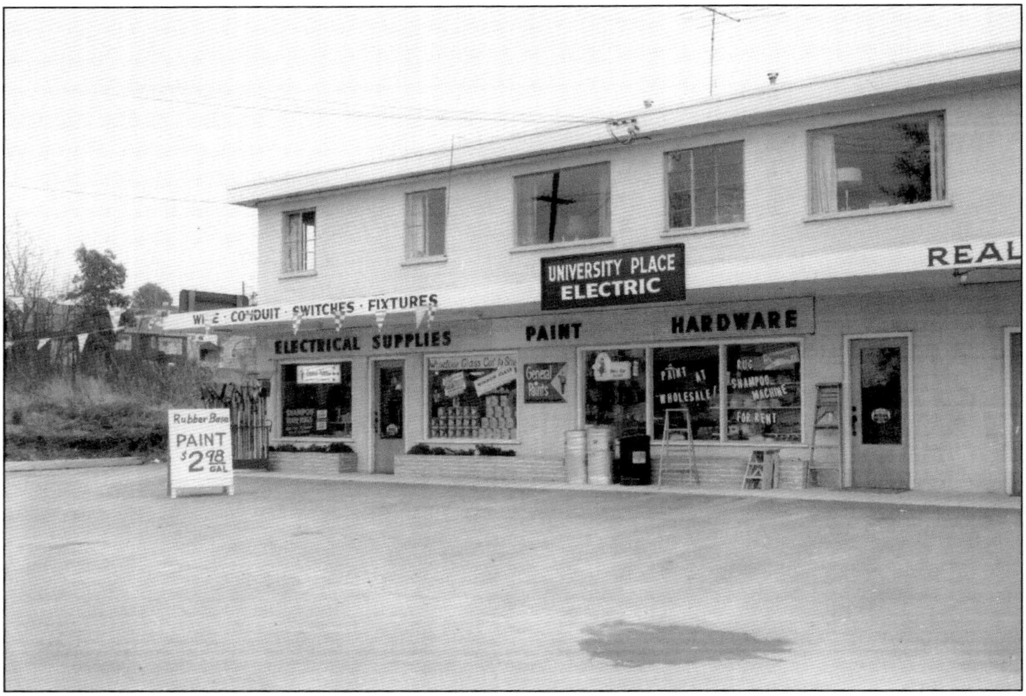

University Place Electric was located on the south side of Twenty-seventh Street, near Locust Avenue. It sold electrical supplies, paint, and hardware and offered contracting services. Note the price of paint at $2.98 per gallon. University Realty was its next-door neighbor. This photograph was taken in early 1958. (Courtesy of the Tacoma Public Library, Northwest Room, Richards Studio Collection.)

The need of the residents for a reliable water supply existed at the very beginning of University Place. Most settlers dug their own wells. In the early 1900s, water was brought by the streetcar to the Ferndale Station at the Drexler home on Thirty-fifth Street and Bridgeport and could be purchased for 25¢ a barrel. UP Water Company got its start in the 1920s. This water tower, located on Fortieth Street east of Bridgeport, supplied water beginning in the early 1960s, but it could not keep up with the rapid growth of the community that had started in the 1950s. Eventually, Tacoma City Water took over the system. (Courtesy of the Tacoma Public Library, Northwest Room, Richards Studio Collection.)

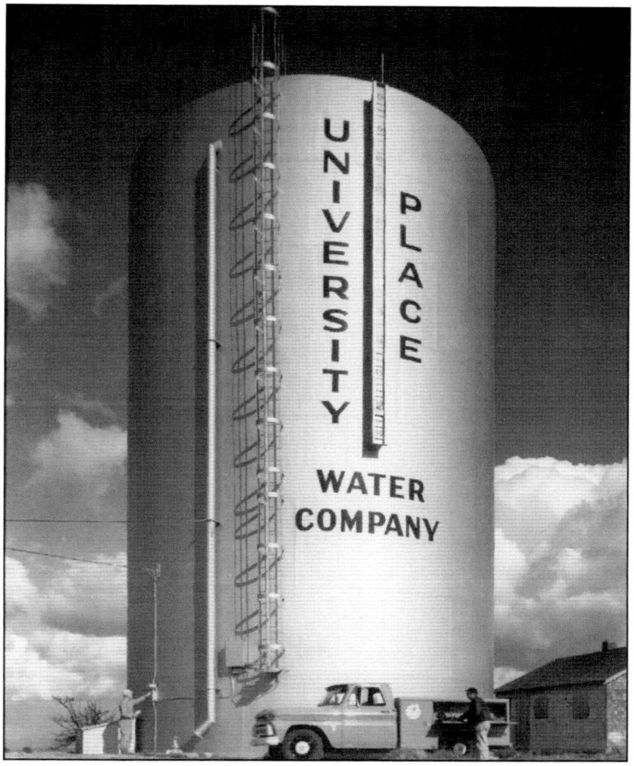

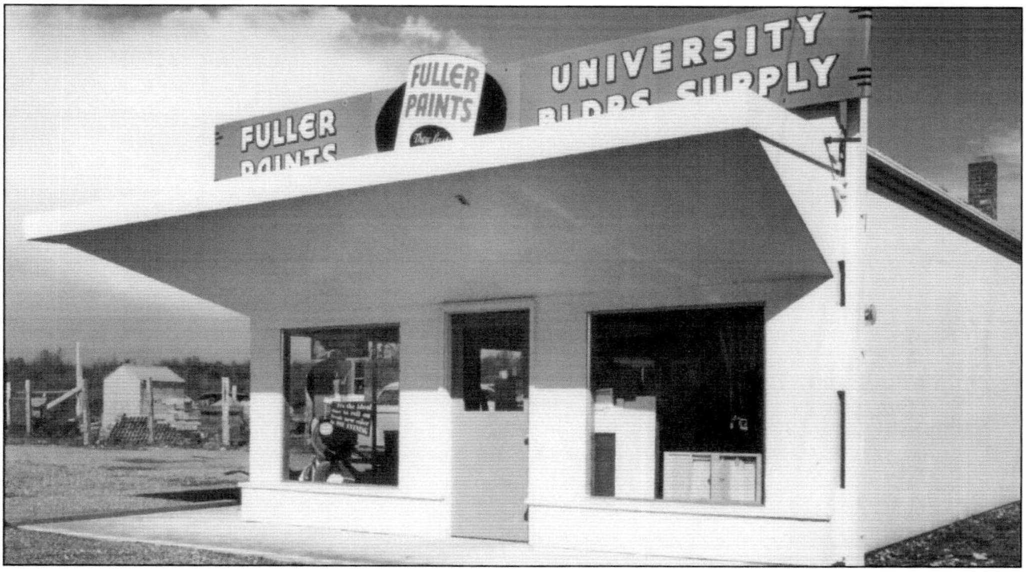

The University Builders Supply, on the southeast corner of Nineteenth Street and Bridgeport Way, came to UP around 1950, just as the community's rapid growth commenced. This small, one-story structure provided building materials for the newly emerging neighborhoods in the North End of Tacoma and University Place. The company continued to expand and became a UP fixture until it closed in the mid-1990s. The buildings were torn down to make way for a small strip mall. (Courtesy of the Tacoma Public Library, Northwest Room, Richards Studio Collection.)

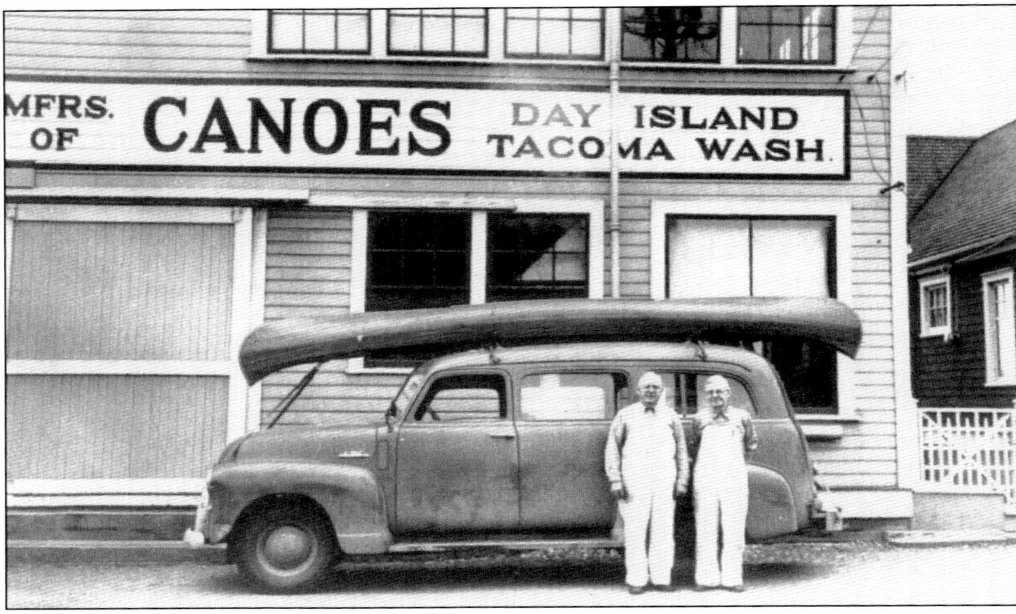

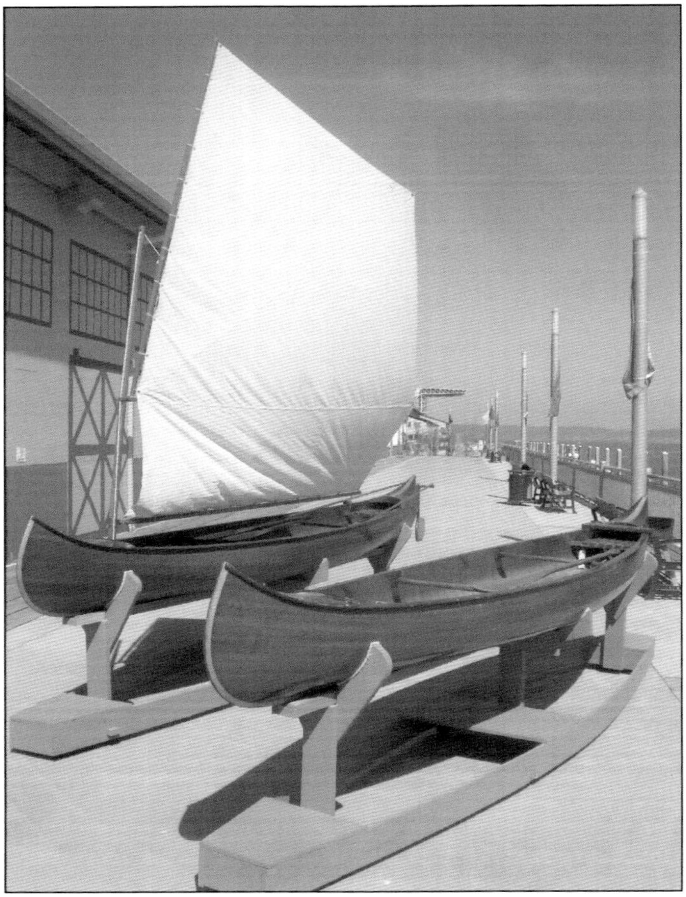

Earl and Floyd Willets (above) began manufacturing wooden canoes on Day Island following their service in World War I. Between the early 1920s and 1962, when Floyd died, the brothers built nearly 1,000 canoes. Their canoes were so sought after that customers had to wait as long as seven years for their order. Only the two brothers built the canoes, with Earl milling out the various pieces using templates to produce identical parts, and Floyd assembling them.

Shown here are two Willets canoes still around today. The one with the sail was built in the 1930s, and the "plain" one in the 1950s. They are extraordinary!

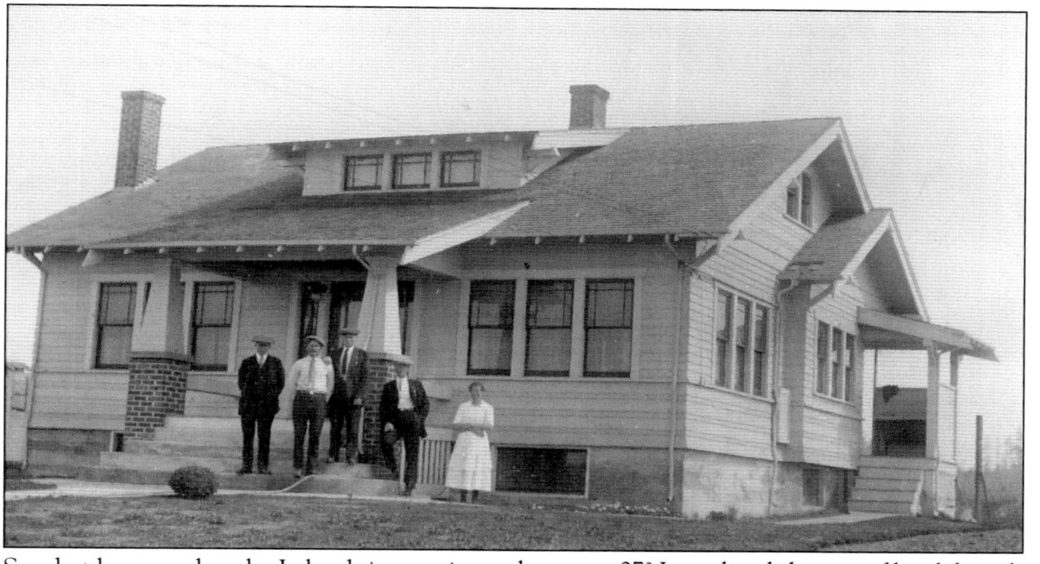

So what happened to the Leland sisters, pictured on page 27? Inger lived the rest of her life with her husband, Oscar Leland, in the house he built on Sunset Drive (pictured on page 28). Bertha lived with her husband, Tom Olson, in the house shown here in the above photograph, built in the 1920s, until she passed away in 1946. It was located at Twenty-seventh Street and Mountain View Avenue. In the photograph, Tom is standing in the center and Bertha is on the far right. In the 1950s, the house was moved to a lot between Twenty-ninth and Thirty-first Streets on Locust Avenue. It is now oriented in a north-south direction, with the porch facing Locust Avenue. The house in the photograph below, located near Thirty-third Street on Mountain View Avenue, was built in the mid-1940s by the author's father, Torvald Handeland. Pauline's husband, Ommund Tweiten, had already passed away, and she lived here with her son Carl until her death in 1969. She can be seen sitting on the front porch.

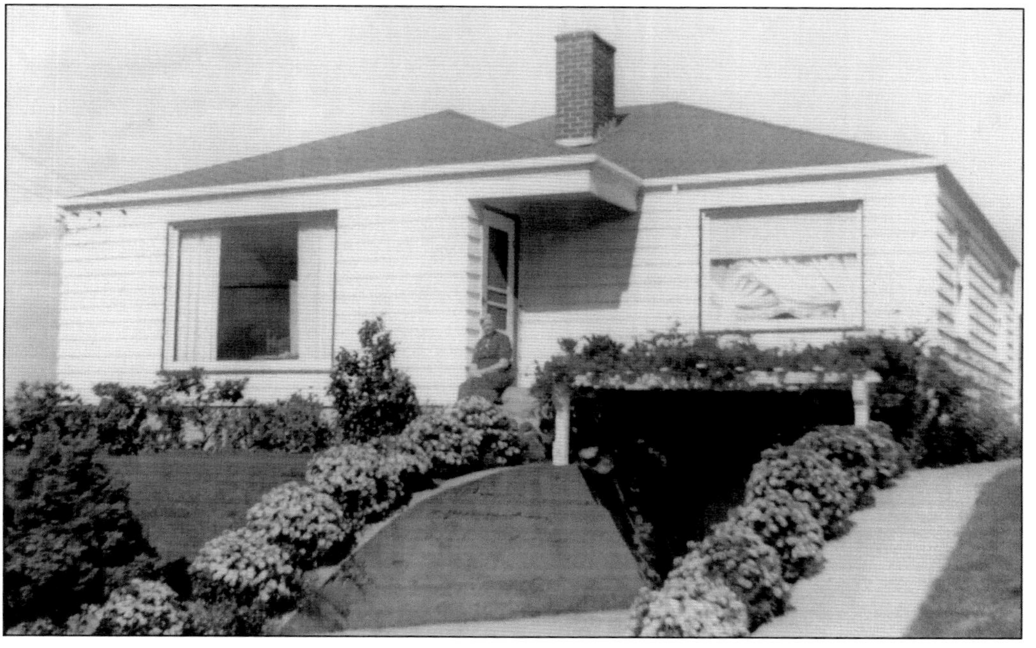

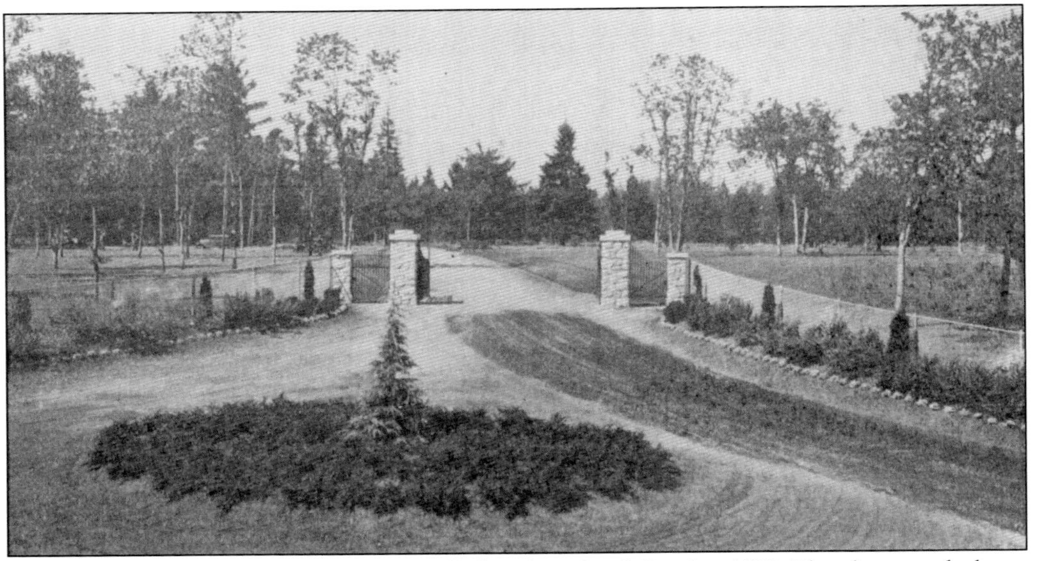

The New Tacoma Cemetery got its start off Chambers Creek Road in 1932. The photograph shows the entrance in that year. The cemetery comprises about 125 acres of land, which it continues to develop. Henry "Jack" Harding, who started working at the cemetery over 50 years ago, is now its president. (Courtesy of Jack Harding.)

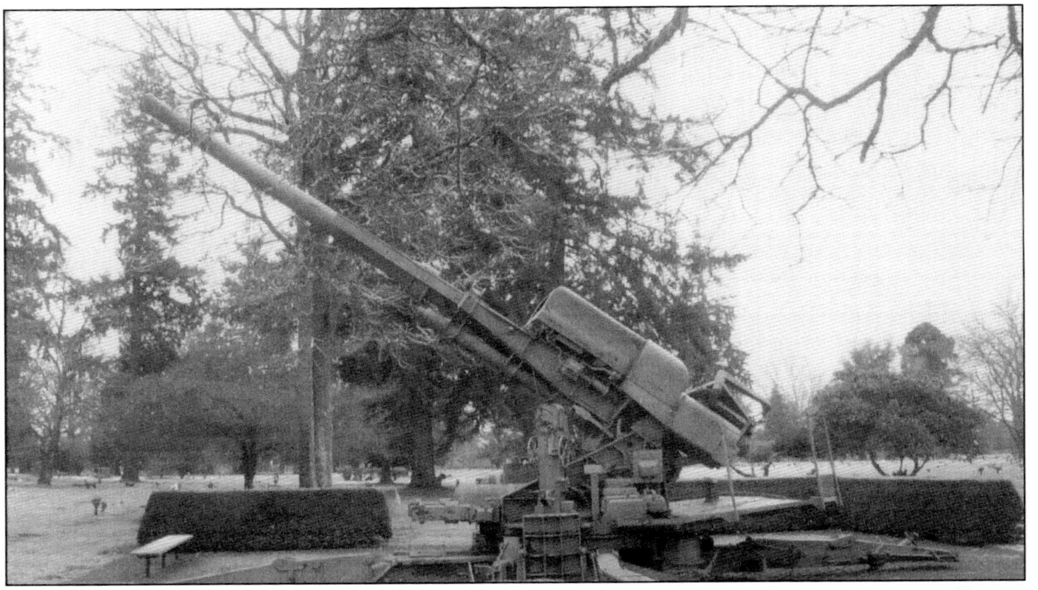

The New Tacoma Cemetery has one of the largest veterans sections in the Tacoma area. Shown here is a Sky Gun, in service during World War II. It was placed at the cemetery by the Wild West Post No. 91, Veterans of Foreign Wars, in June 1961. (Courtesy of Jack Harding.)

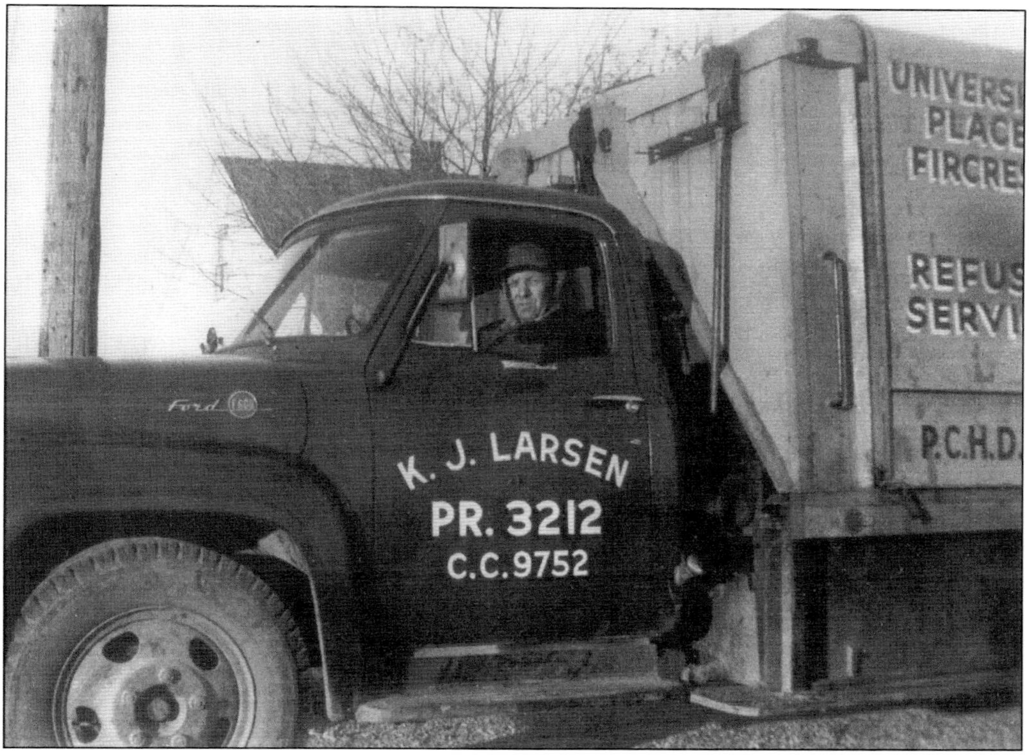

The University Place Refuse Service was started by Kordiel Larsen in 1941. The original truck was a flatbed 1929 Model AA Ford that had formerly been used to transport workers from UP to the shipyards in Tacoma. Larsen had 111 customers and charged 50¢ a month, and he would collect by going door to door. The refuse was taken to the city dump in Fife. The photographs show Kordiel with two of his early trucks. The UP Refuse Company is still owned and operated by the Larsen family. (Both, courtesy of the Larsen family.)

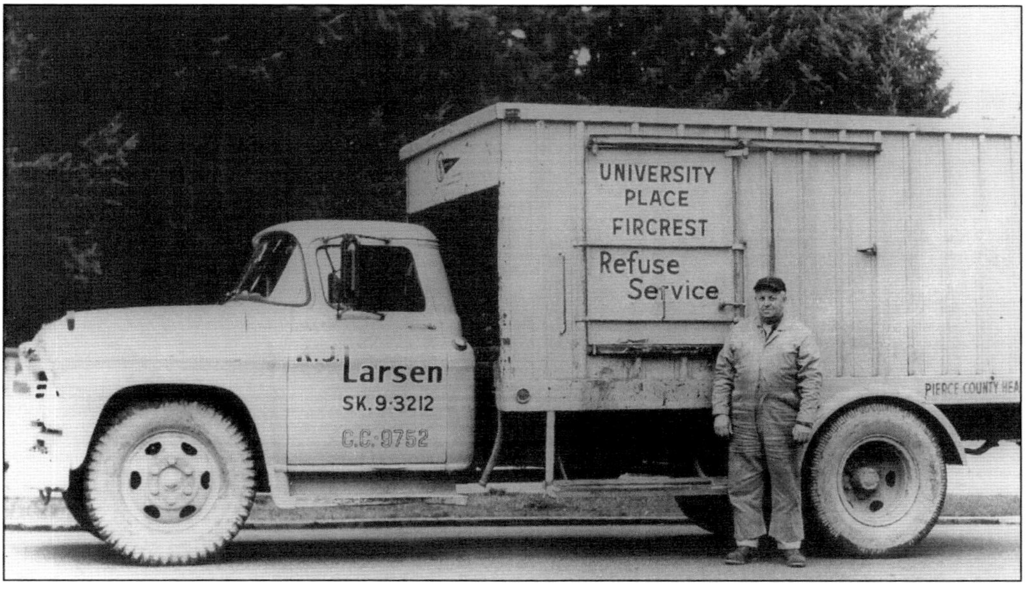

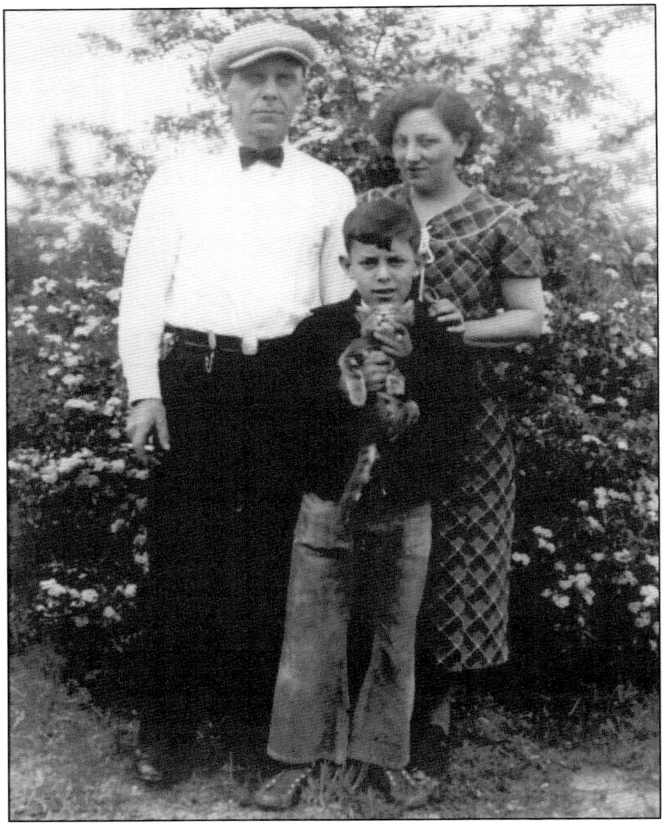

Edd and Eva Bush came to UP in the mid-1920s and built a home at 2726 Mountain View, where they raised their family. Edd worked at the Clear Firs Lumber Mill until it burned in 1934. The photograph at left shows Edd and Eva with their son Edward. Edward's son, Bill, worked as a UP fireman for many years and was chief of the department in the early 2000s. The photograph below, of the Bush home, shows Eva with her two children, Anne and Edward, probably in 1929.

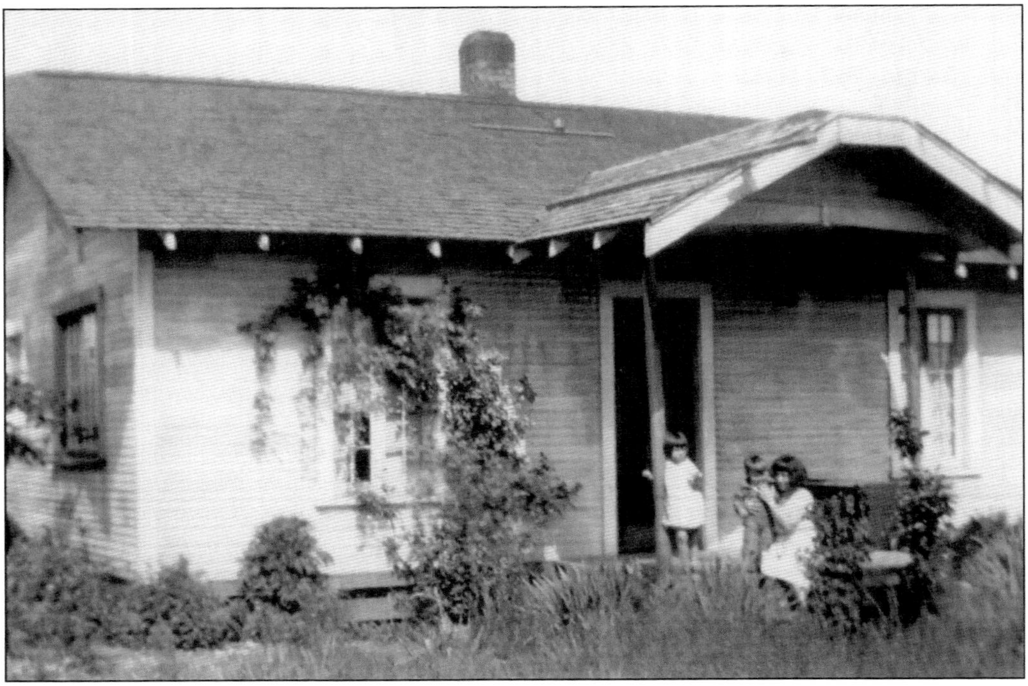

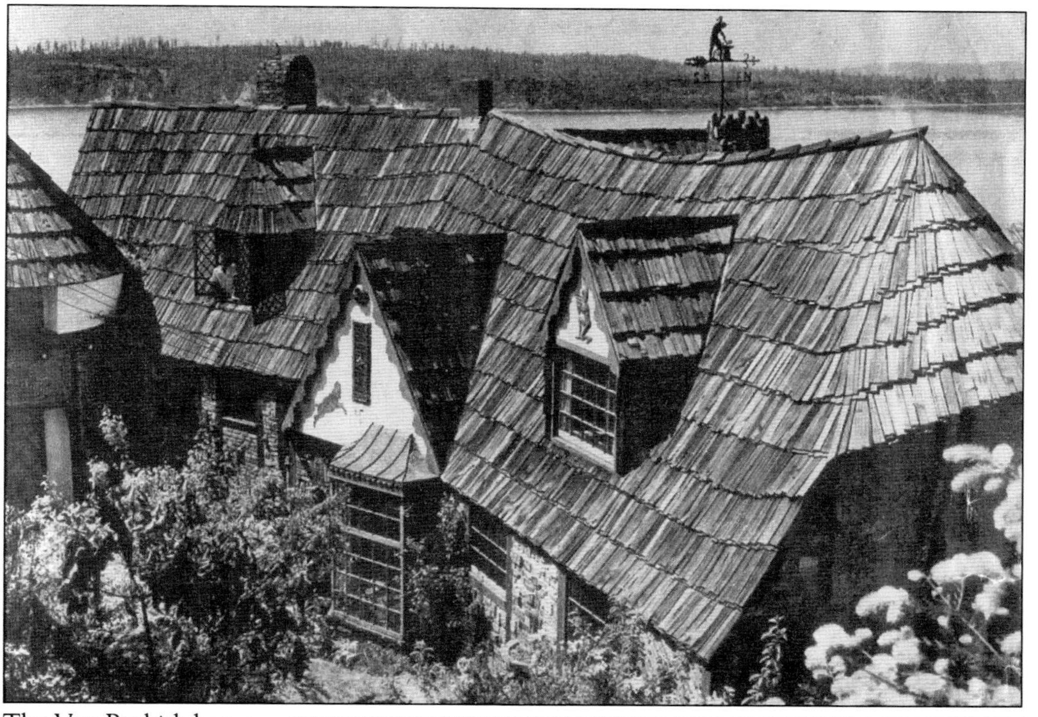

The Van Buskirk home was built on the hill overlooking Sunset Beach in 1947 and is probably the most well-known home in UP. The house is often referred to by University Place residents as "the castle." Bob and Gladys Van Buskirk built the home using an English Tudor design with many unique features. The Van Buskirks lived there until they developed and moved into the Prestige Center, off Twenty-seventh Street and Mountain View Avenue in 1963. The photograph at right shows Gladys at the hand-carved front entrance, on which was the family crest, made by her husband, Bob.

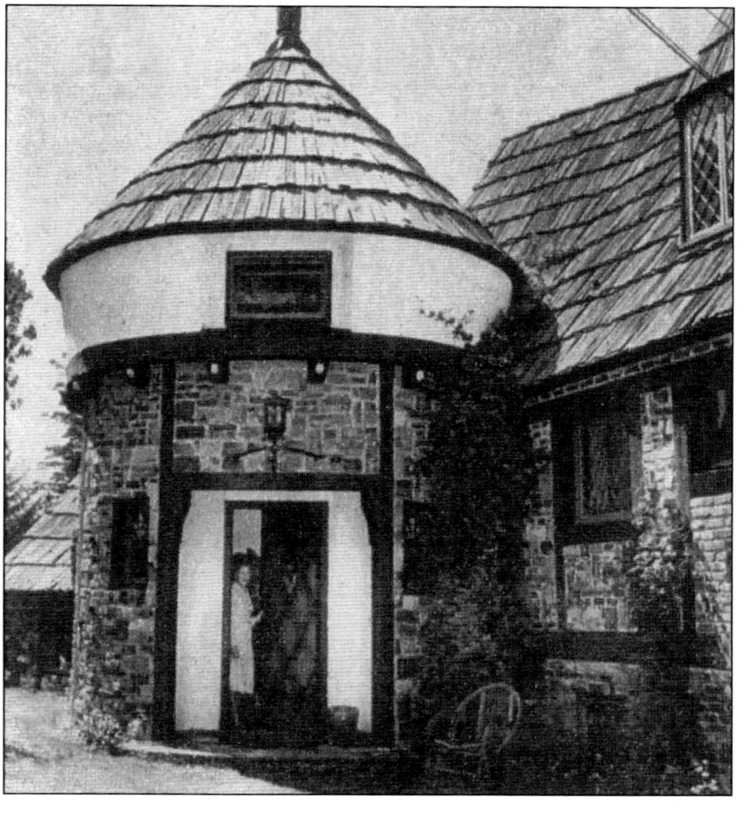

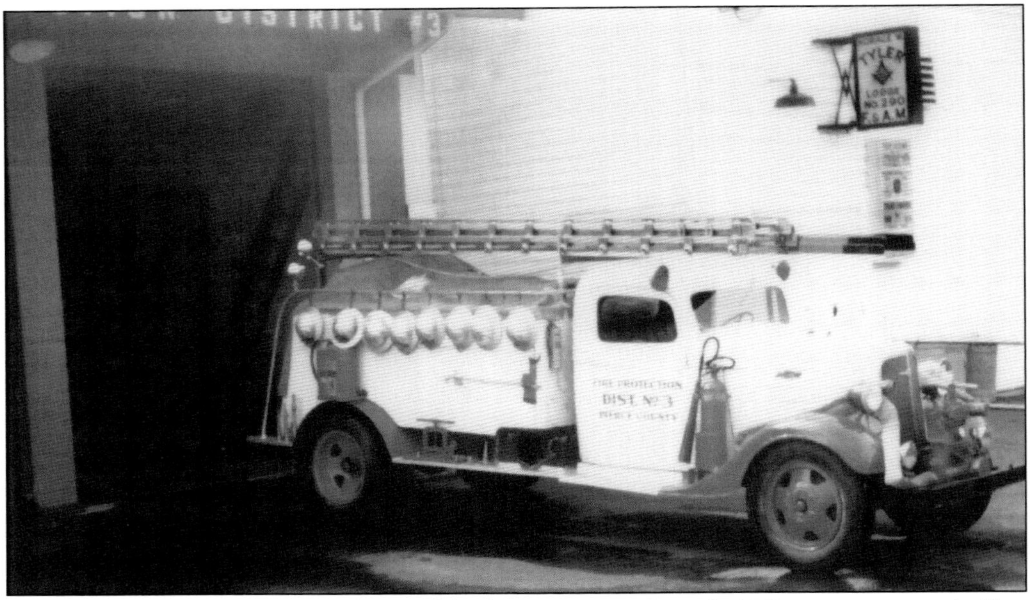

As the community grew, so did the need for fire protection. In early 1941, a meeting was held at UP School to discuss the formation of a volunteer fire department, and by March, the UP Fire Department was born. Its first fire truck was a used 1936 Chevy truck (above) purchased from South Tacoma Chevrolet for $229.50. It cost another $250 to transform it into a full-fledged fire truck. Below is the list, dated March 28, 1941, of the charter members of the UP Volunteer Fire Department.

CHARTER MEMBERS

UNIVERSITY PLACE FIRE DEPARTMENT

MARCH 28, 1941

LESLIE B. McGAW
BUD BOLSTAD
LESLIE MAGOON
AL THOMAS
JOE THOMAS
JACK REESE
CLARENCE STOUT
LOREN CAMPBELL
JOHN STILL
HERMAN SWENSON
SAM LISTER
HERB OAKLEY
MARK BRYANT
RALPH HUGHES
RAY CAMPBELL
CARL KRAUSE

ELMER NELSON
FORREST CAYTON
FRANK PROULX
CHARLES PROULX
KEN PANCHOT
ALONZO NIGH
ED TURNER
FRED EHMKE
RUSSELL JORGENSON
CARL E. ANDERSON
FLOYD STOUT
LOREN B. LARSON
HAROLD LARSON
VERNON PAIGE
EARL WILLETS

Leslie B. McGaw was chosen as the first fire chief of the new Pierce County Fire District No. 3 in March 1941. This photograph of Chief McGaw was taken in 1952. The UP Fire Department remained a mostly volunteer organization through the 1950s. The first full-time, paid firefighter was Lin Wicks. He was hired in 1950. By 1960, there were 30 volunteers, including one woman, and three full-time firemen in addition to Chief McGaw. He retired in 1965. (Courtesy of the Tacoma Public Library, Northwest Room, Richards Studio Collection.)

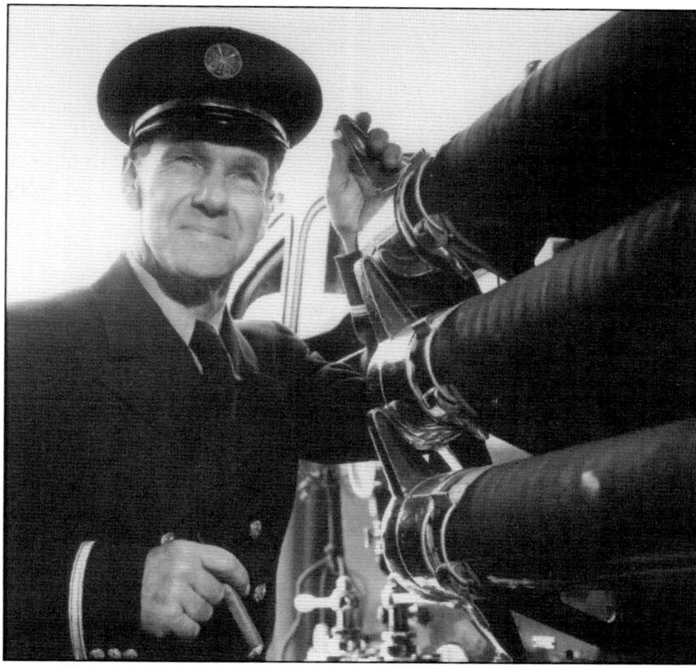

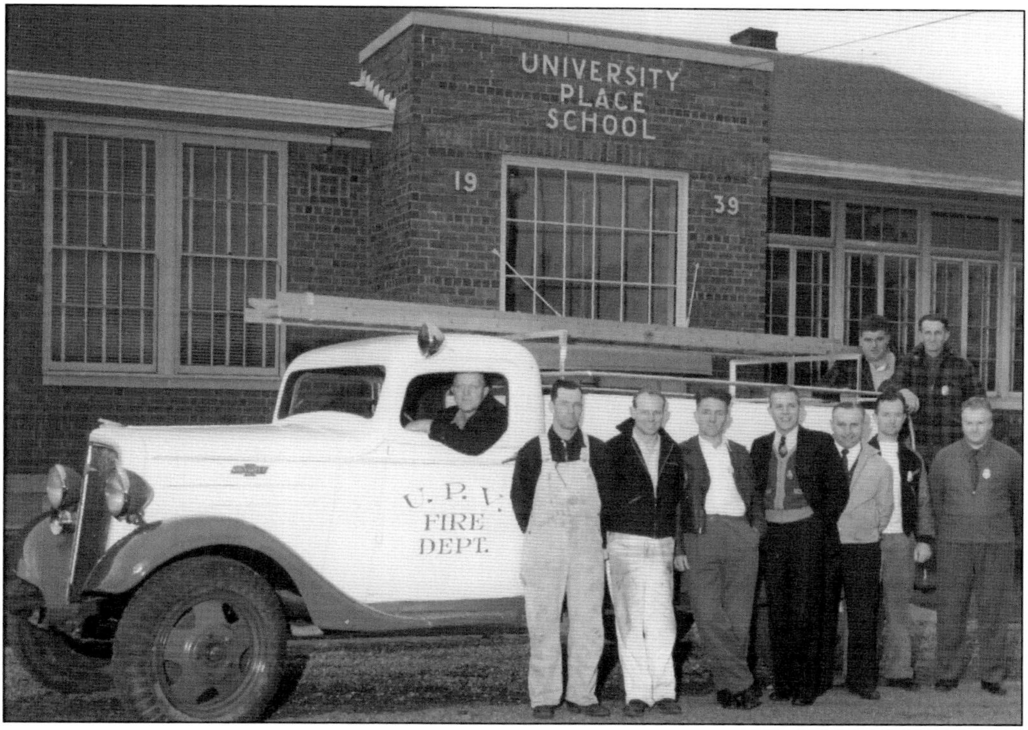

Some of the early volunteers pose with the new truck in front of UP School, probably in 1941. Shown here are, from left to right, Capt. Bud Bostad (seated in the truck), Chief Les McGaw, Joe Thomas, C.L. Stout, Les Magoon, Al Thomas, Lorne Camphill, and Sam Lister. Floyd Stout and John Still are in the back of the truck.

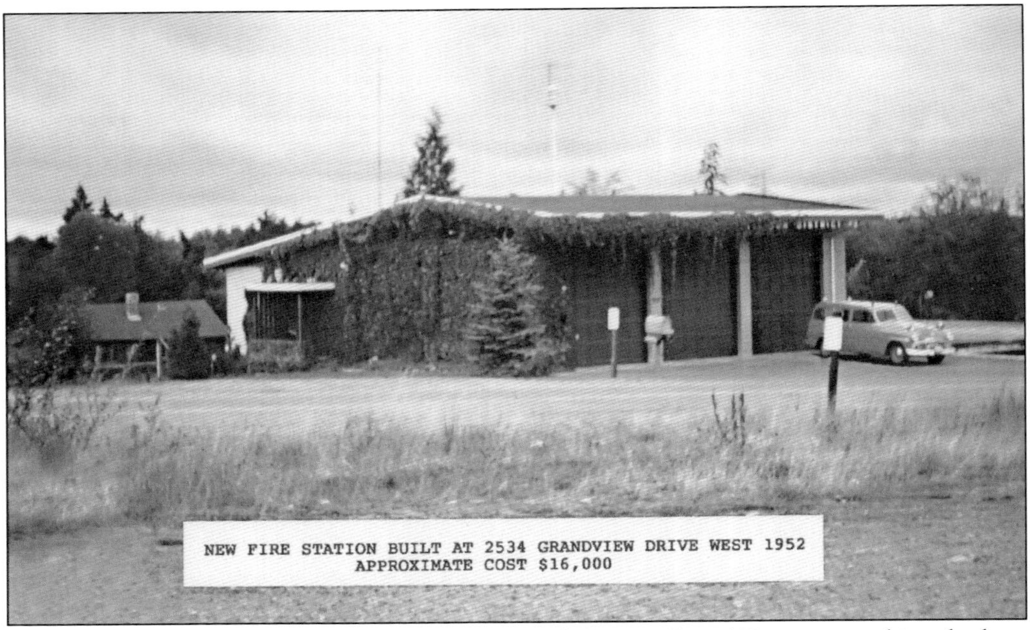

The first UP fire station was located in the converted Narrows Brand Tomatoes packing shed, on Twenty-fifth Street and Grandview Drive. In 1952, a new, three-bay station was built next door on Grandview Drive, and in 1957, an identical station was constructed at 7909 Fortieth Street West. Both stations were used until two more bays were added to the Fortieth Street station in the early 1960s. The old station was then turned over to UP Parks and Recreation. Today, it is the Senior Center.

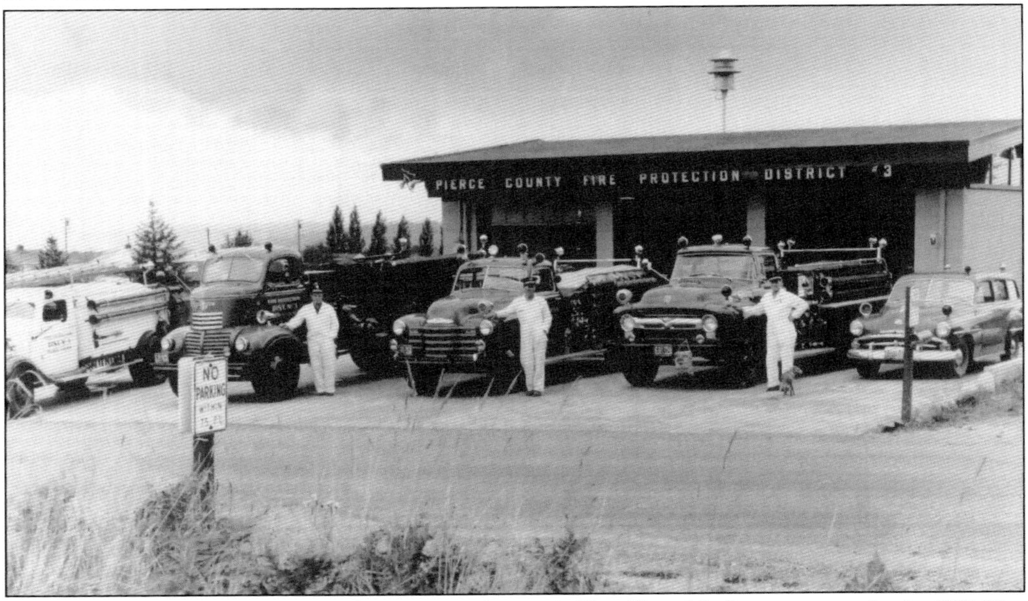

From left to right, Wayne Gotchy, Lin Wicks, and Chief Les McGaw pose with the UP Fire Department fleet in the late 1950s. The original 1936 Chevy truck can be seen on the far left. The other vehicles are, from left to right, a 1942 GMC, a 1948 Chevy, a 1956 Ford, and a 1952 Plymouth (the chief's car).

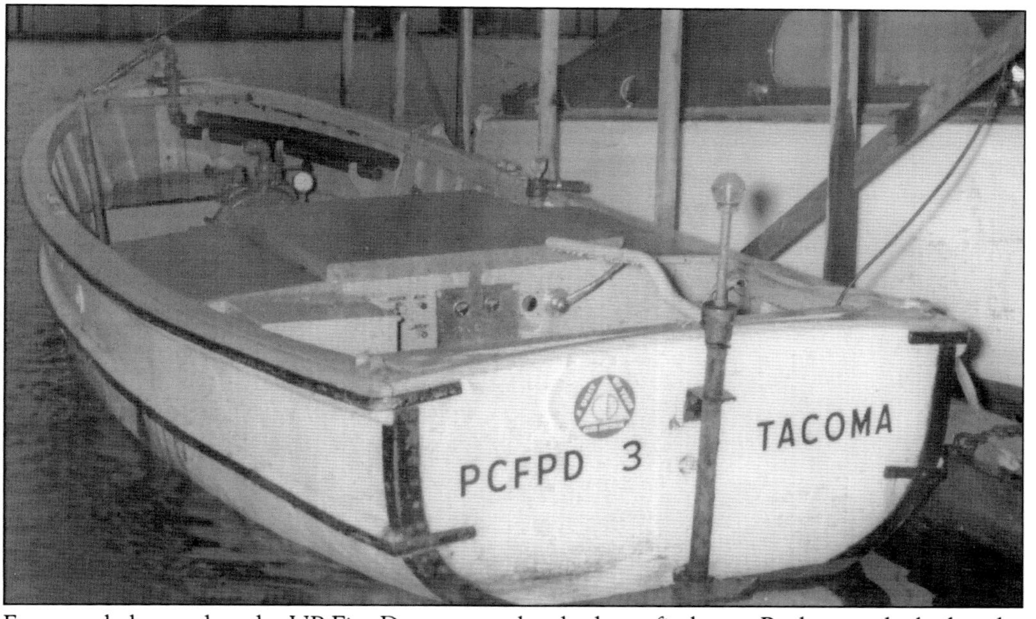

Few people know that the UP Fire Department has had two fireboats. Both were docked at the Day Island marina and serviced the marina area and the shoreline of Puget Sound in University Place. The small boats were easily maneuverable into areas that the bigger Tacoma fireboats could not access. The second boat, in the photograph below, was transformed into a fire boat by Bill Bush in 1975. Day Island can be seen in the background. It stayed in operation until 1990.

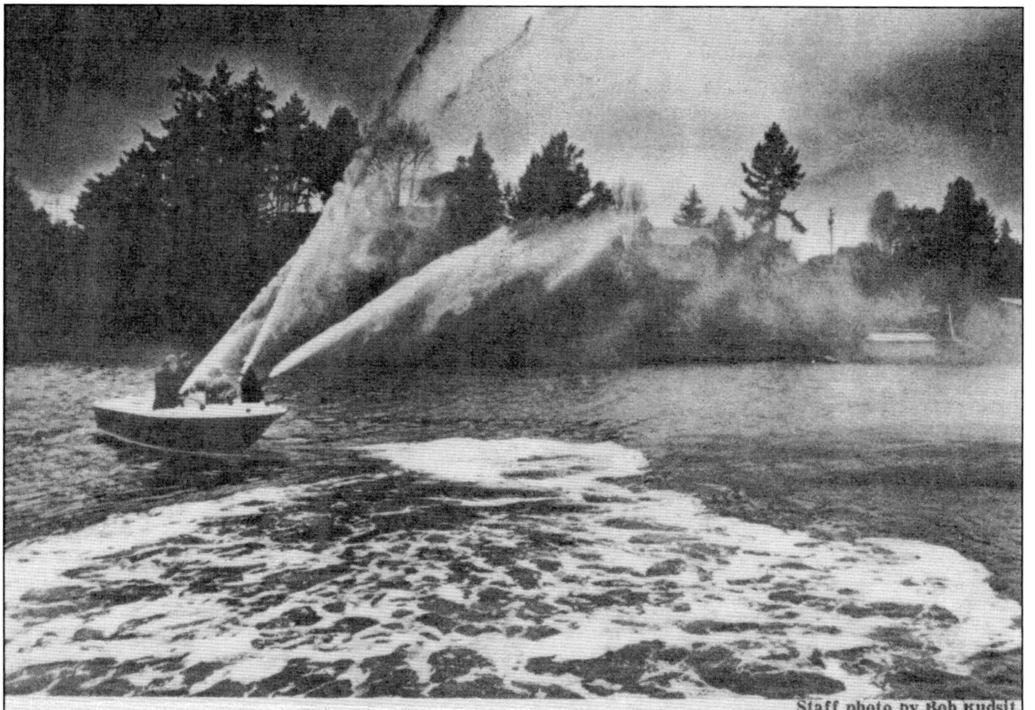

New University Place craft coughs up some saltwater

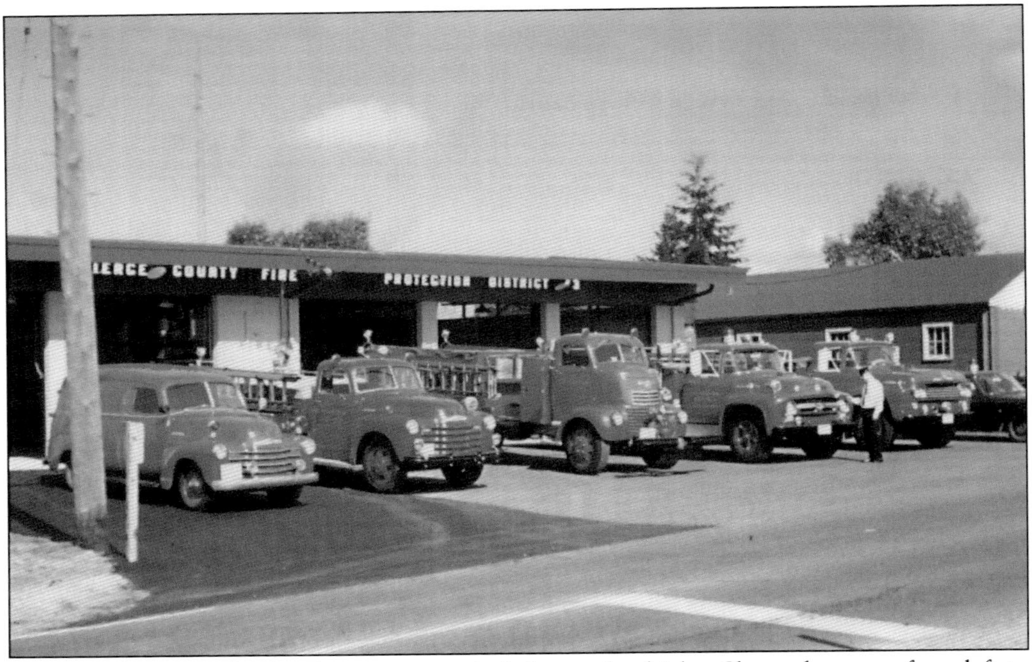

By the early 1960s, the fire department included several vehicles. Shown here are, from left to right, a 1948 Chevy panel truck, which served as an aide car (the department's first) and accessory vehicle; a 1948 Chevy; a 1942 GMC; a 1956 Ford; a 1960 Ford; and a 1963 Ford Fairlane, which served as the chief's car.

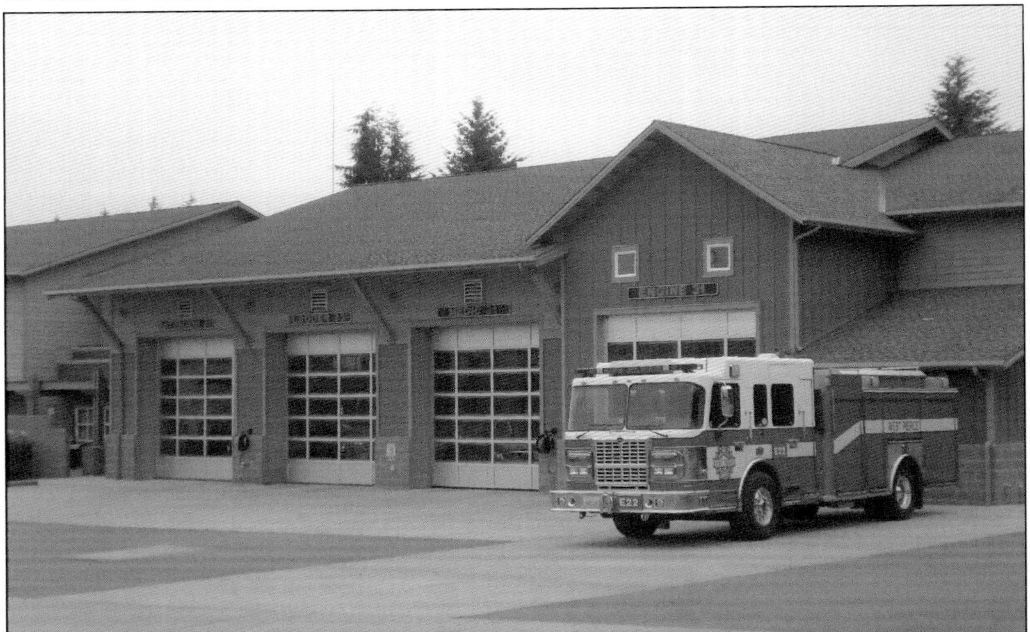

In 2003, the UP Fire Department moved into a beautiful new facility on Drexler Drive, behind the Town Center. The department still makes use of the station on Fortieth Street. The UPFD is now part of the West Pierce Fire District.

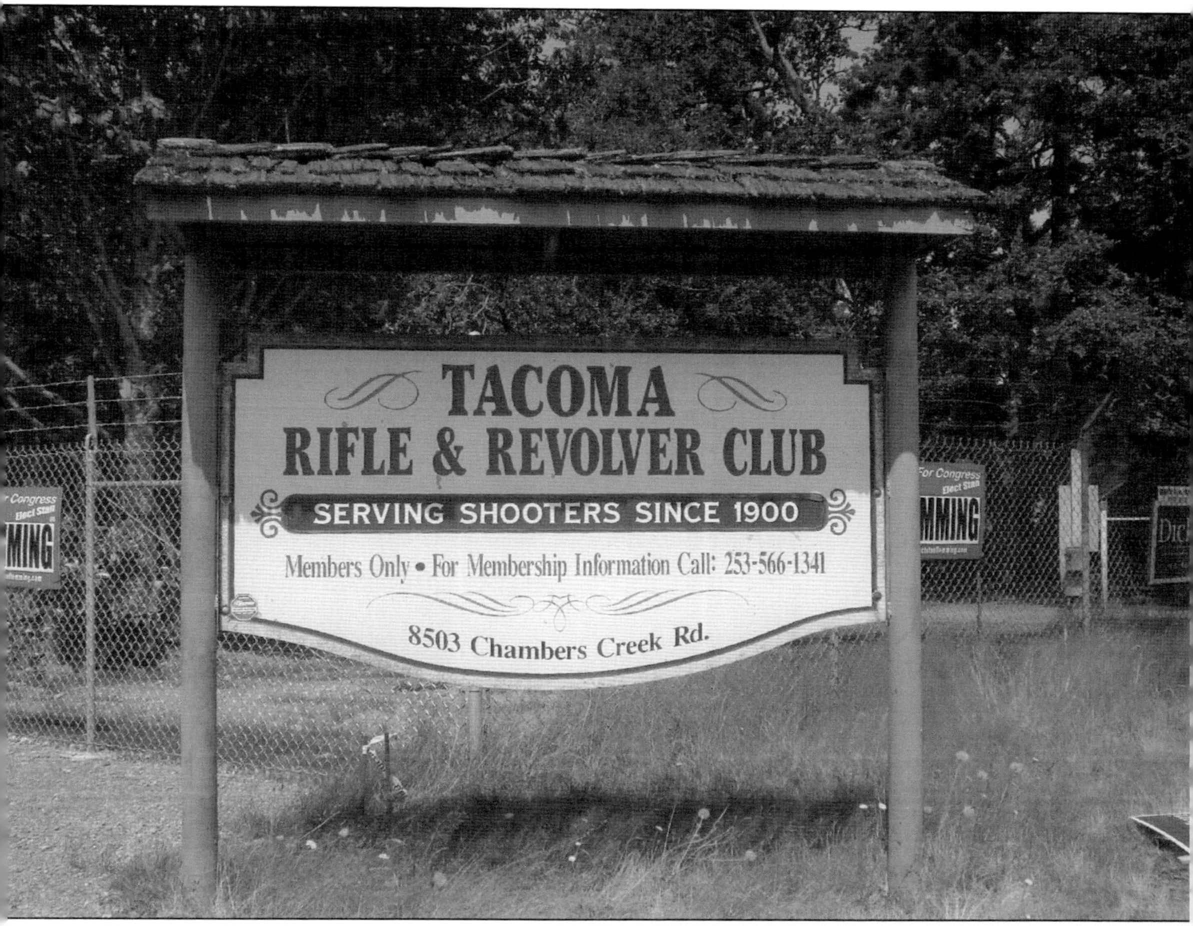

The Tacoma Rifle and Revolver Club has been at its location on the north side of Chamber Creek Road since 1908. As early as 1889, this site was used as a shooting range. In the early days, it was known as the Menlo Park Range and the Hornet Range. They merged in 1936 and became the Tacoma Rifle and Revolver Club. The club now occupies 70 acres, nestled between the Woodlake and Danbridge residential neighborhoods, and has over 1,000 members.

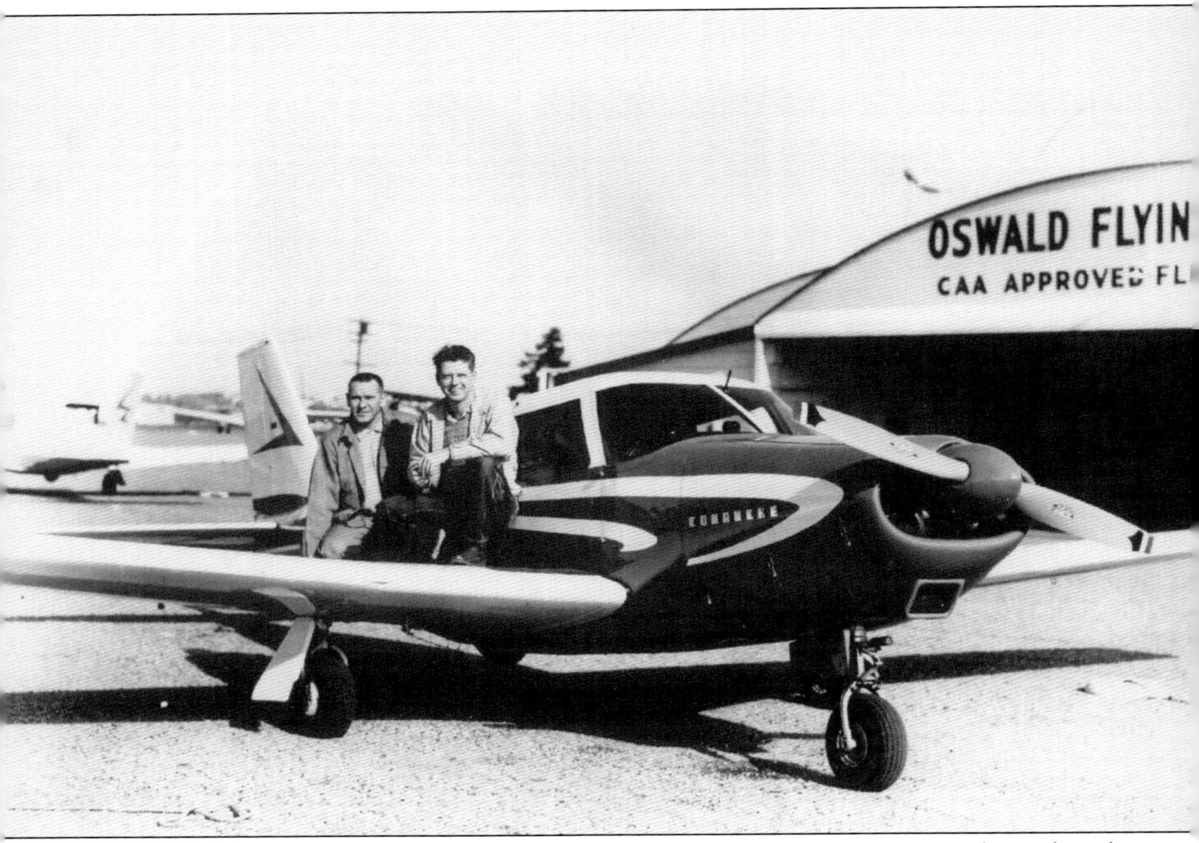

In the late 1940s, the Tacoma Airport was established in University Place. It was located on the west side of Sixty-seventh Avenue between Nineteenth and Twenty-seventh Streets. It was known locally as Oswald's Airport, after "Bud" Oswald, who operated the airport and ran a sales and flight instruction service. The airport was in operation until 1973. Many people will probably remember the Airport Café, later the Summer Sands, located across the street from the airport in Fircrest, where Columbia Bank is now located.

Five

Working, Eating, Playing, and Praying Together

By the 1950s, University Place was transforming from a rural, agricultural community to a very desirable suburb with great schools. Housing and business developments began to flourish, but no major factories or industries followed. The school district was the major employer. UP was becoming a bedroom community—most residents commuted to jobs elsewhere and came home to the quiet serenity of the neighborhood. Over the years, many restaurants and eating establishments have come and gone, leaving only memories. For those who have lived here for years, the likes of The Country Squire, The Huntsman, The Matterhorn, Berg's Tavern, Crazy Erik's, The Dairy Queen and Dairy Dell, The Hometown, A&W, KFC, Denny's, Pietro's Pizza, The Sea Galley, Mama Stortini's, Taco Time, Shari's, Captain Nemo's, and many others are well remembered. The only one that seems to have survived is the iconic Pine Cone on Twenty-seventh Street.

The community festival held every August has been going on since at least the 1950s, and added to that are the Duck Daze Parade and Garden and Antiques Show in the spring, the Apple Squeeze and summer concerts at the Curren Orchard, and the Christmas tree lighting in December.

The Parks and Recreation Department offers a full program of activities, from T-ball to baseball, soccer, flag football, and basketball for the area's youth, and many programs and outings for senior citizens. But no community would be complete without its places of worship. University Place was founded on a religious basis, with the Methodist Church trying to build a university here. The people who remained, and those moving in, continued to pursue and establish their various faith communities.

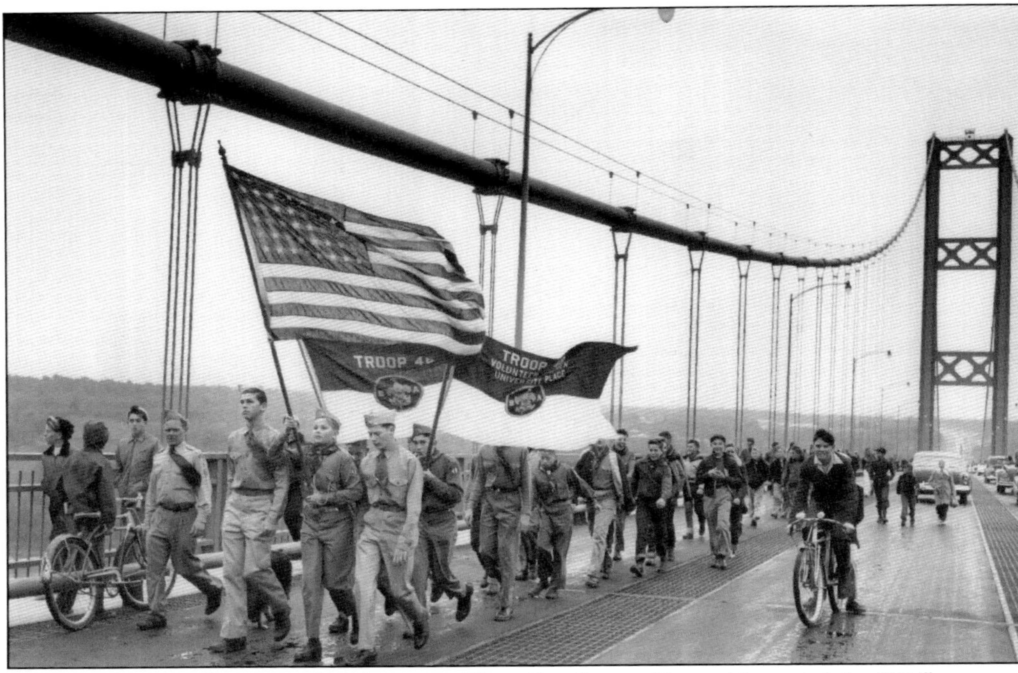

On Saturday, October 14, 1950, University Place Boy Scouts Troop 48 carried the US flag across the new Narrows Bridge as part of the dedication ceremony. This bridge replaced the infamous "Galloping Gertie," which collapsed in a windstorm on November 7, 1940, after being open only three months.

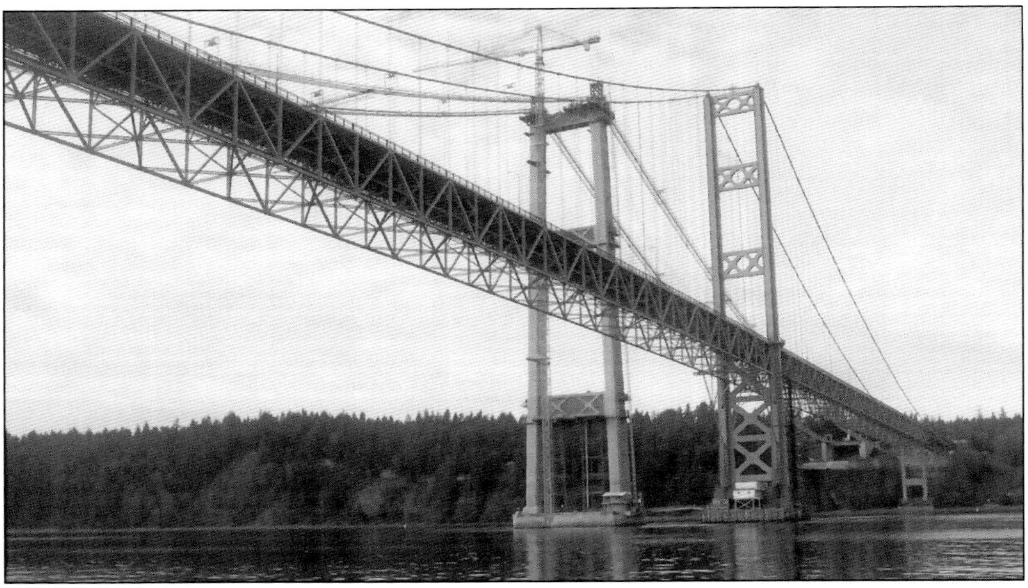

Although the Narrows Bridge is not in University Place, it is certainly visible to UP residents living near the water. When "Galloping Gertie" came down in 1940, George Curtis had the students outside at UP School watching as the inevitable happened. To ease traffic congestion on the 1950 bridge, a second Narrows Bridge was constructed under the watchful eye of UP residents. This bridge was completed in 2007.

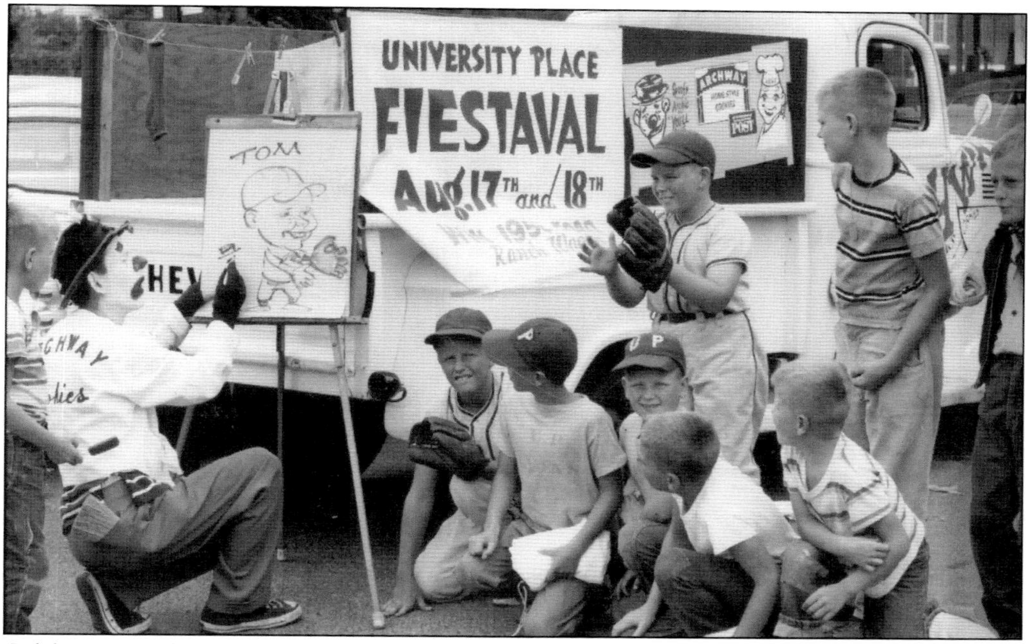

Celebrating and having fun together as family and neighbors has always been a part of living in UP. School carnivals and festivals abound, and each August the community has held its annual festival. Shown here is a "Fiestaval" in 1956. Spoofy, a clown cartoonist, does a caricature sketch of Tommy Nash, standing at center right. Hervie Martin is looking over Spoofy's shoulder. Others in the photograph are, from left to right, (kneeling) Bill Morton, Jimmy Piper, Gary Palmer, Dennis Martin, and Haze Martin; (standing) Nash, Mervin Martin, and Kirby West. To the right is the festival program cover from 1986.

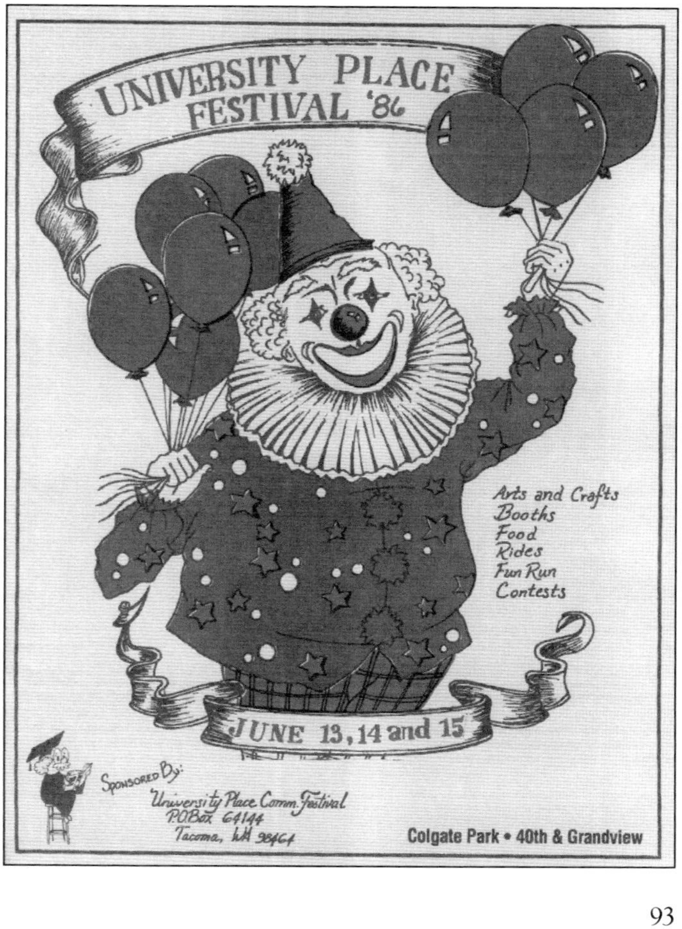

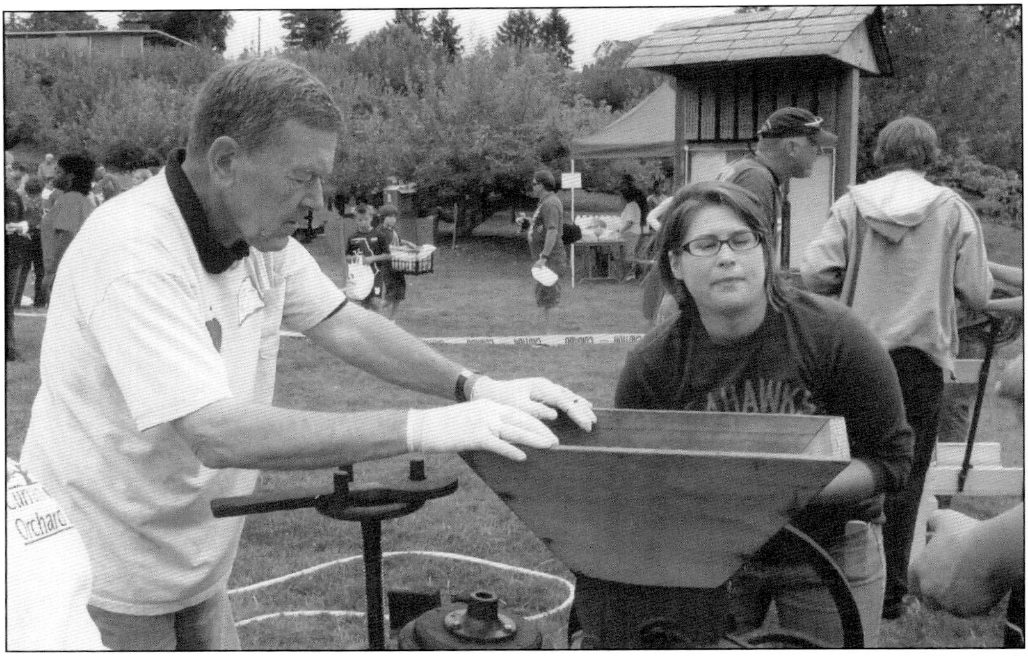

Each year, on the first Sunday in September, everyone is invited to the Curran Apple Orchard. Here, residents can pick apples (or buy some brought in from eastern Washington) and, with the help of volunteers, make fresh apple juice in an apple press. In the above photograph, Bill Barrett mans an antique 1874 press. The photograph below shows Kelly Wresley hand-cranking the press while Catherine Vandiver feeds in the apples. (Both, courtesy of Sally Barrett.)

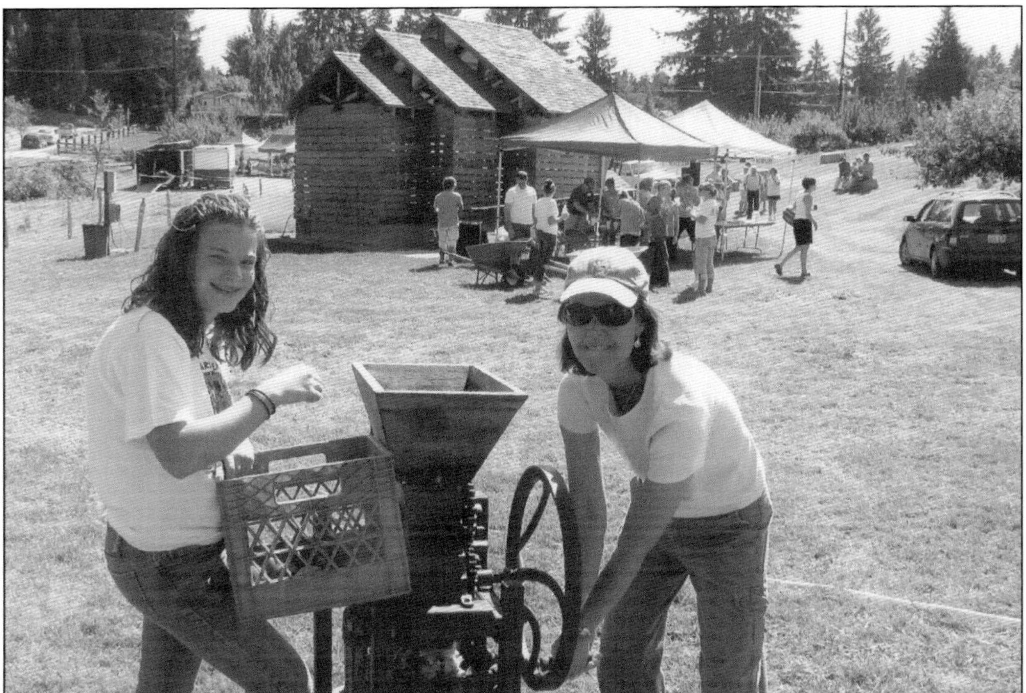

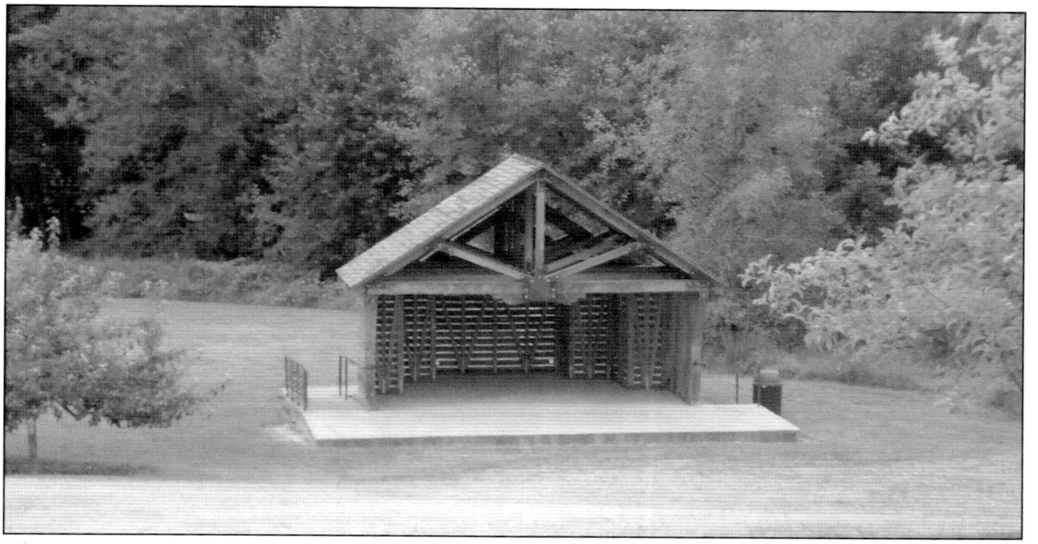

This stage was built by Curtis High School wood shop students as a community project. It is located in the Curran Apple Orchard and is used in the summertime for a community concert series sponsored by the city.

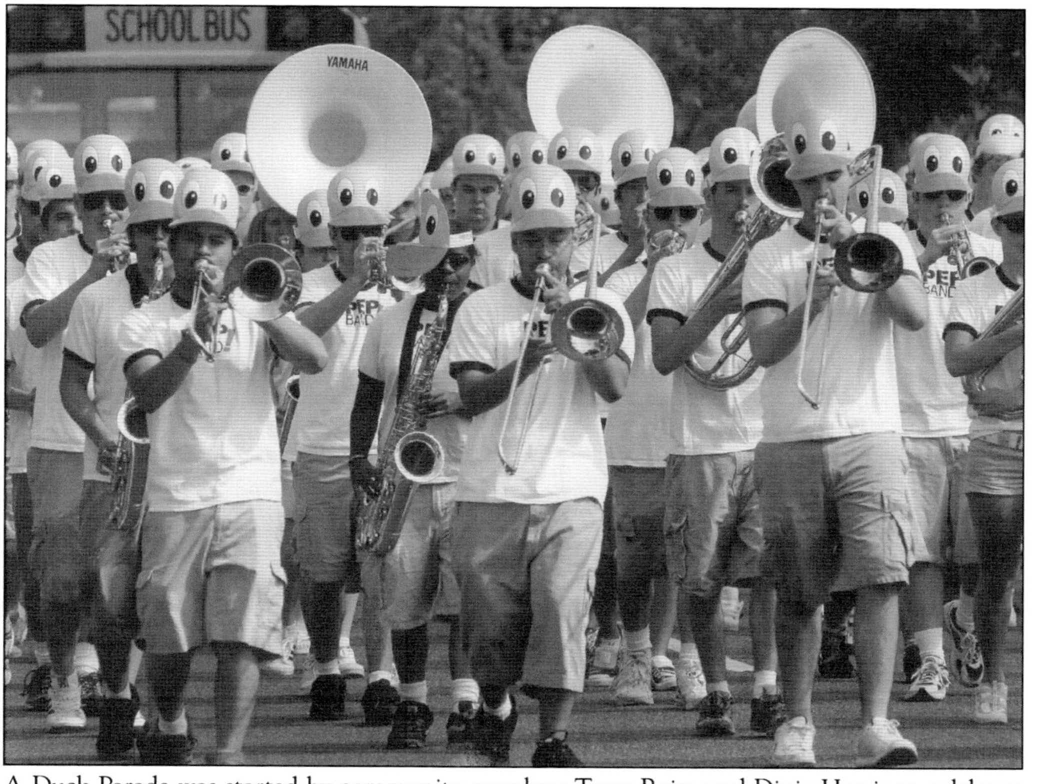

A Duck Parade was started by community members Terry Reim and Dixie Harris to celebrate the end of the long rainy season and to showcase all of the changes and improvements along Bridgeport Way between Twenty-seventh and Fortieth Streets. It ends with an antique car display, open house at the fire station, and booths throughout Windmill Village and Homestead Park.

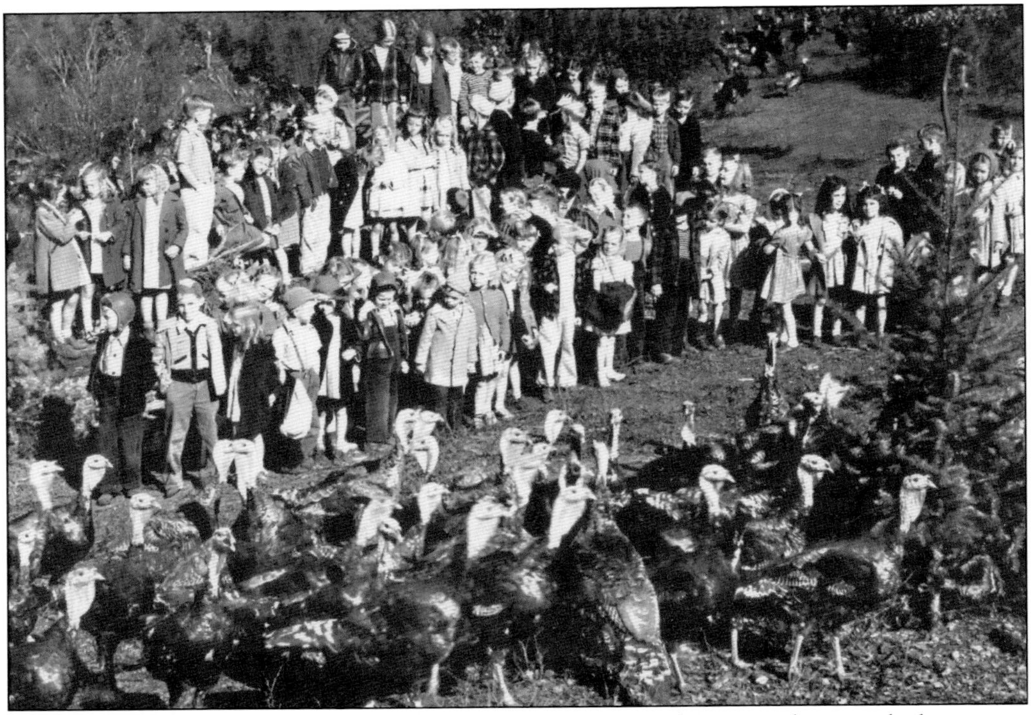

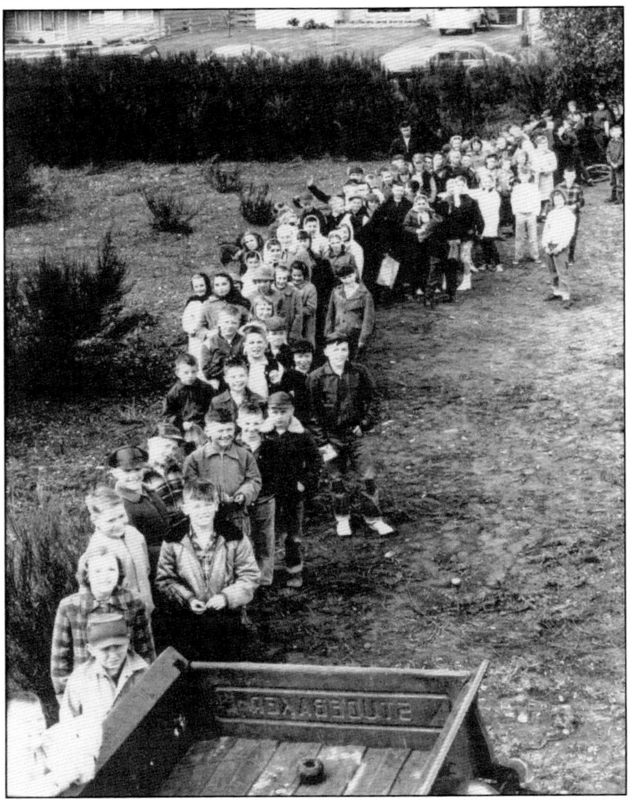

These two photographs have been in the collection of the UP Historical Society for several years, but nobody seems to know exactly what they depict, when they were taken, or the names of those shown. Can you help? Contact the author at uphistoryman@yahoo.com.

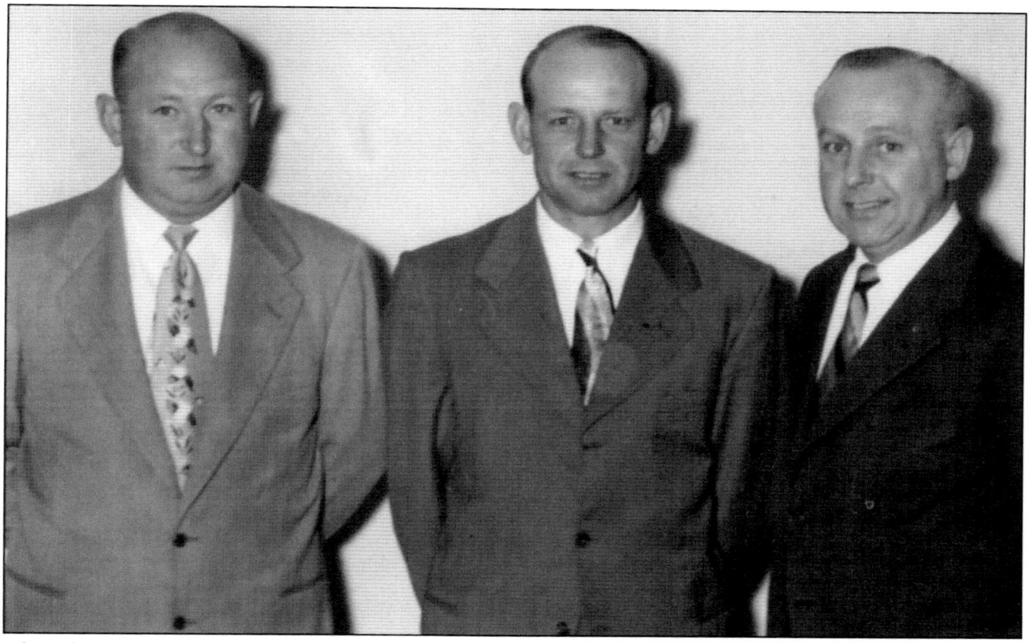

The Thomas brothers—Frank (left), Joe (center), and Al (right)—sons of Frank and Agnes, who opened the first grocery store in UP in the early 1900s, were responsible for the development of the first bona fide shopping center in University Place, located on family-owned property at the northeast corner of Twenty-seventh Street and Grandview Drive. The shopping center eventually included Samuelson's Apparel, a laundry facility, a nursery, a photography studio, a Dairy Queen, and a Washington State Department of Licensing location for testing and renewal of drivers' licenses.

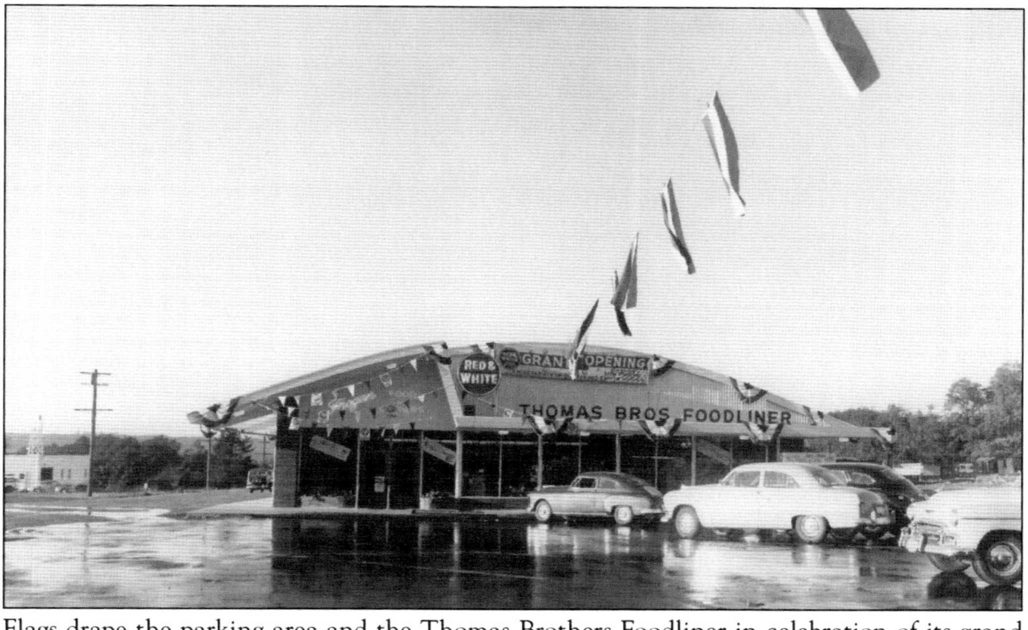

Flags drape the parking area and the Thomas Brothers Foodliner in celebration of its grand opening on September 13, 1950.

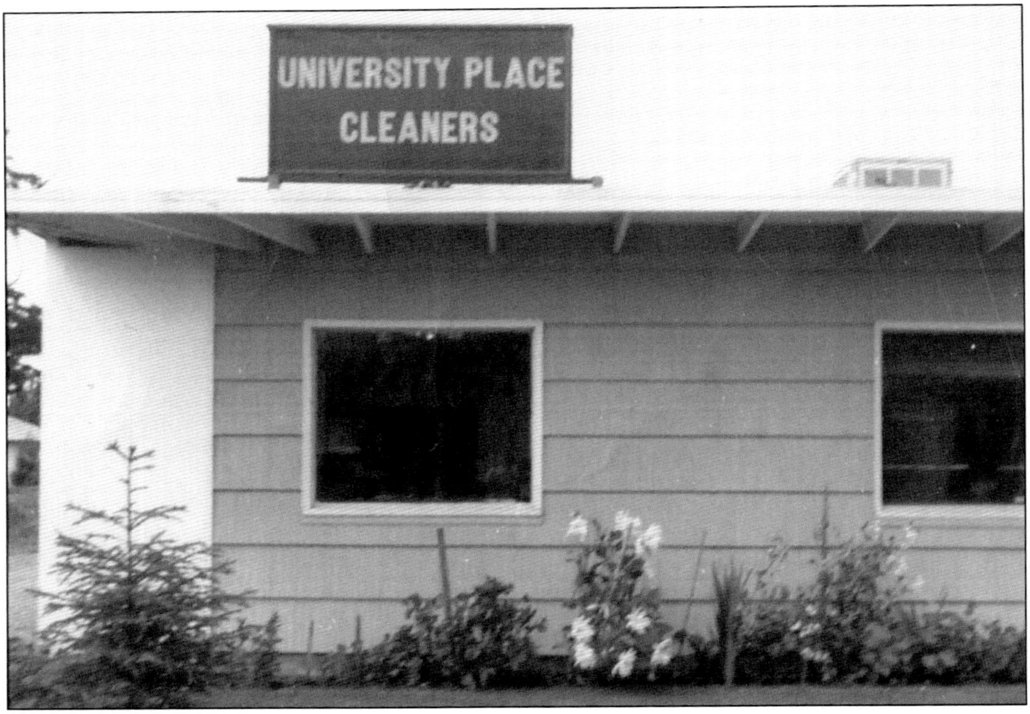

The UP Cleaners, near Thirty-seventh Street and Bridgeport Way, was used by generations of community residents between 1954 and 1987. It was owned and operated by Norman and Marie (Broback) Storset. They met in Portland in 1940, married in 1941, and moved back to Tacoma, where they both worked in the Brobacks' shipyard, Pacific Boat Building Company, during the war years. They opened UP Cleaners (above) in 1954 and can be seen below in front of the remodeled store in 1977. They retired in 1984 and turned over the business to Carmen and Terry Storset, who operated it for a few more years before it closed to make room for the Windmill Village development. (Above, courtesy of the Storset family; below, courtesy of the Broback family.)

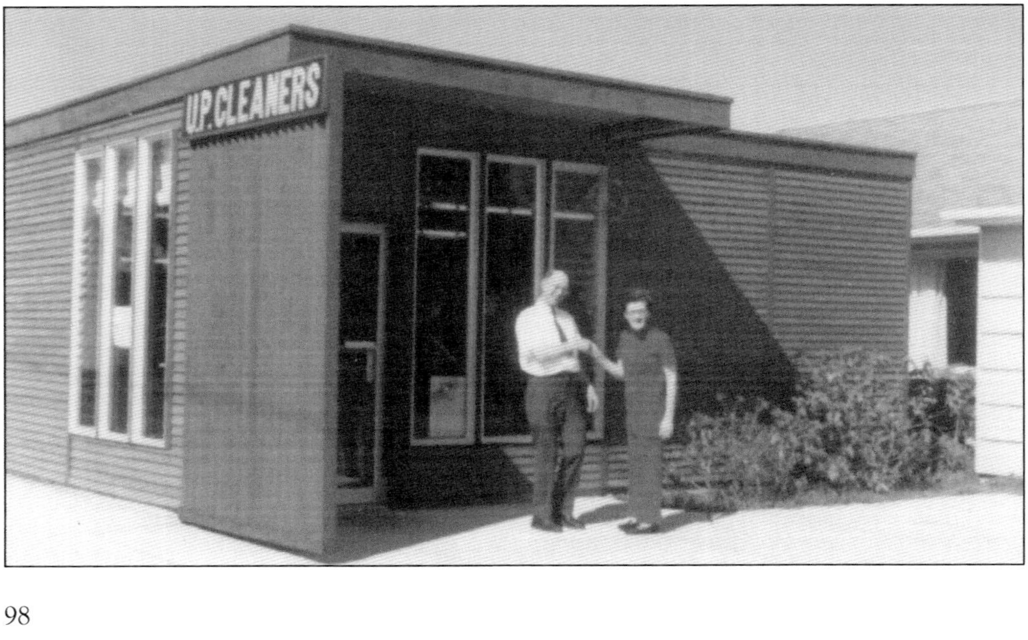

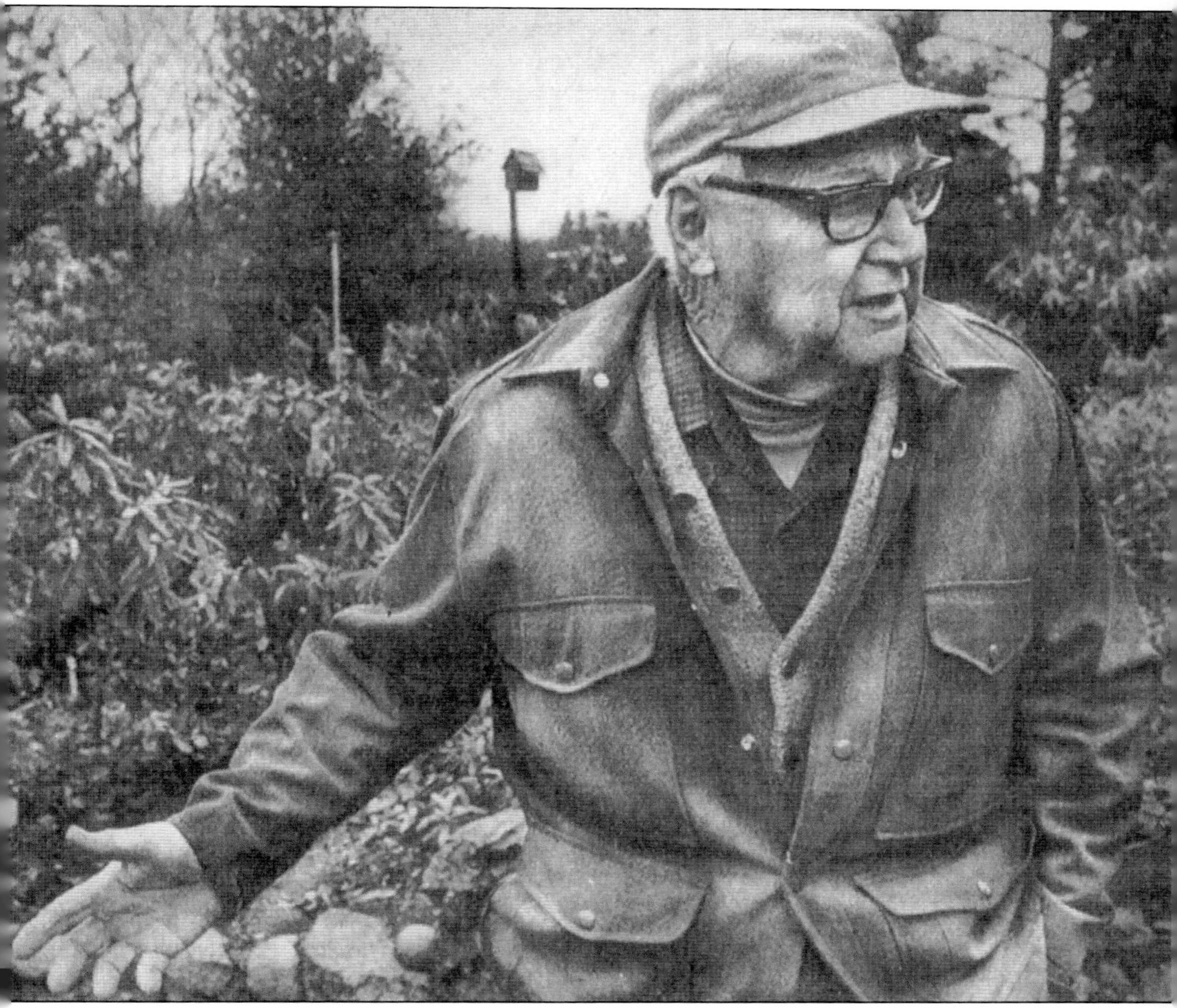

Almost directly across Bridgeport from UP Cleaners was a nursery owned by Hjelmar Larson. For over six decades, more than 25 of those years in UP, Hjelmar grew and hybridized rhododendrons. He had 64 new varieties registered, such as Golden Wedding, Rosy Dream, and Skookumchuck. His rhododendron seeds were sold worldwide. Regarding where to live, Hjelmar once stated, "If it grows rhododendrons, it's a good place to live. It's a good place for man. If it doesn't grow rhododendrons, get out of there." Evidently, University Place was a good place to grow them.

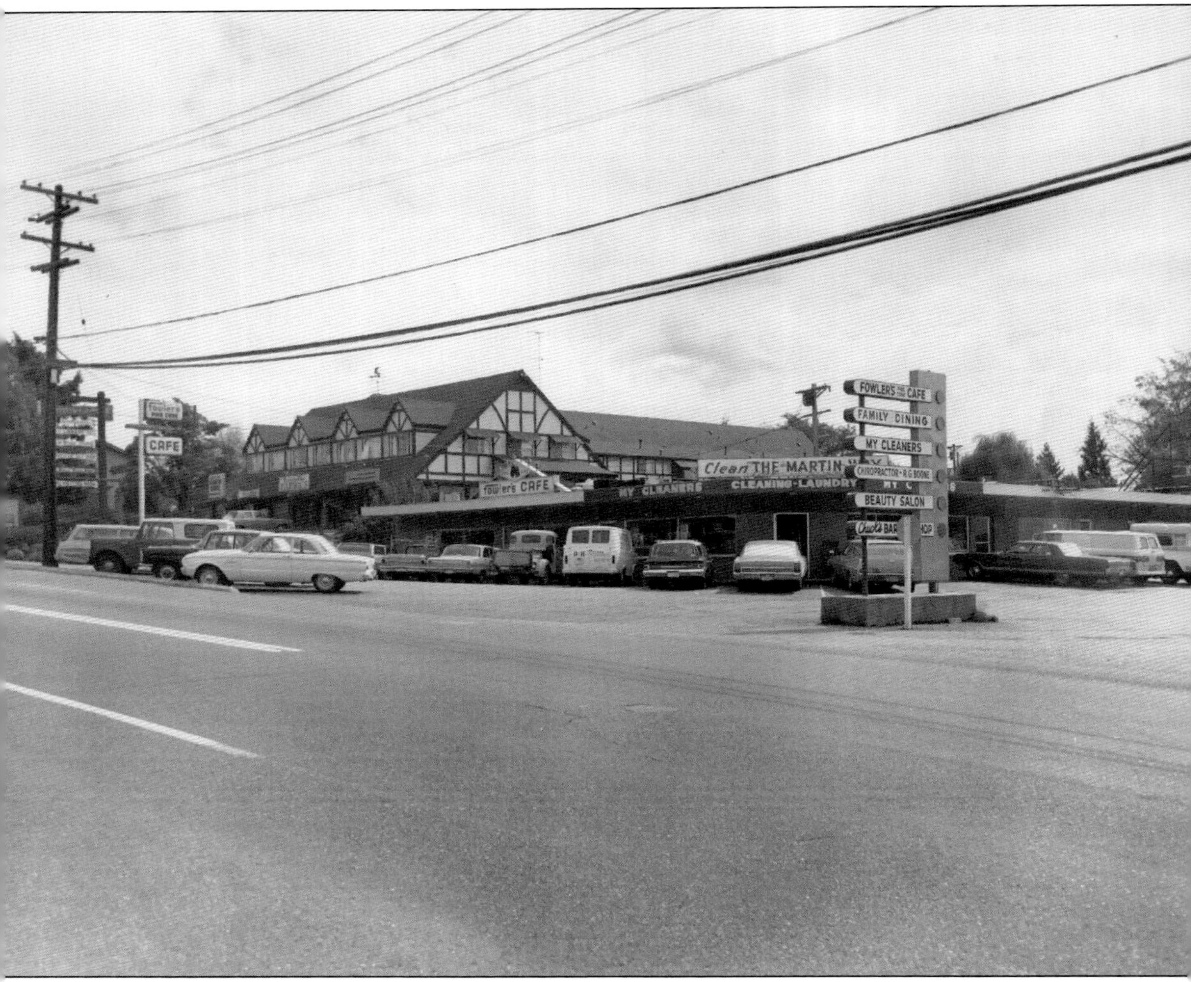

Farther up Twenty-seventh Street from the Thomases' Shopping Center was this complex, developed in the mid-1950s and early 1960s. The low, flat building in front was owned by Al Trosper. It housed the Pine Cone Café, My Cleaners, Chuck's Barber Shop, a beauty shop, a dentist office, and a chiropractic office. Trosper had a sheet-metal shop in the back of the building. He also had several other business ventures in UP. In the background is the Prestige Center, developed by the Van Buskirks in 1963. It included many businesses on the lower level and apartments on the second floor. (Courtesy of Juanita Fowler Bjork.)

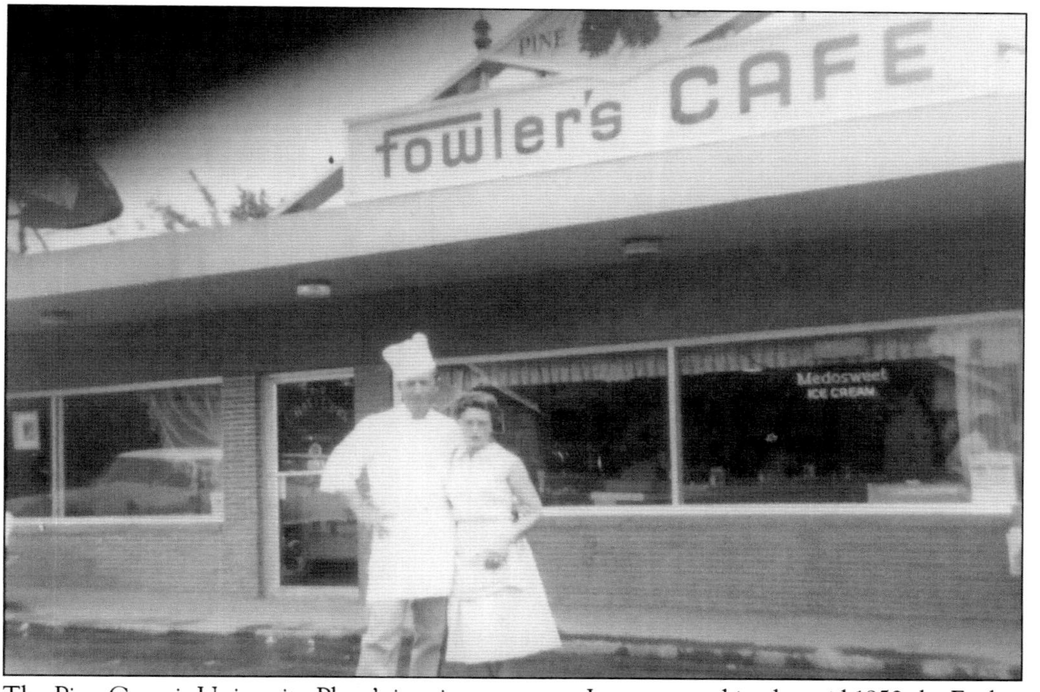

The Pine Cone is University Place's iconic restaurant. It was started in the mid-1950s by Evelyn Bergstrom and Ethel Bodecker, who came up with the name from the pine cone motif that graced the original dinner plates. In 1958, Art and Juanita Fowler acquired the Pine Cone and turned it into a UP institution. With its counter dining and Naugahyde booths, it became UP's version of a diner. Although larger today, with more dining area, the Pine Cone retains much of its 1960s flavor under its current owner, Steve Warp. The above photograph shows the Fowlers in front of their new enterprise in 1958. The photograph below shows them hard at work meeting customers' orders. Art ran the kitchen, and Juanita ran the front. The Fowlers sold their interest in the Pine Cone in 1972. (Both, courtesy of Juanita Fowler Bjork.)

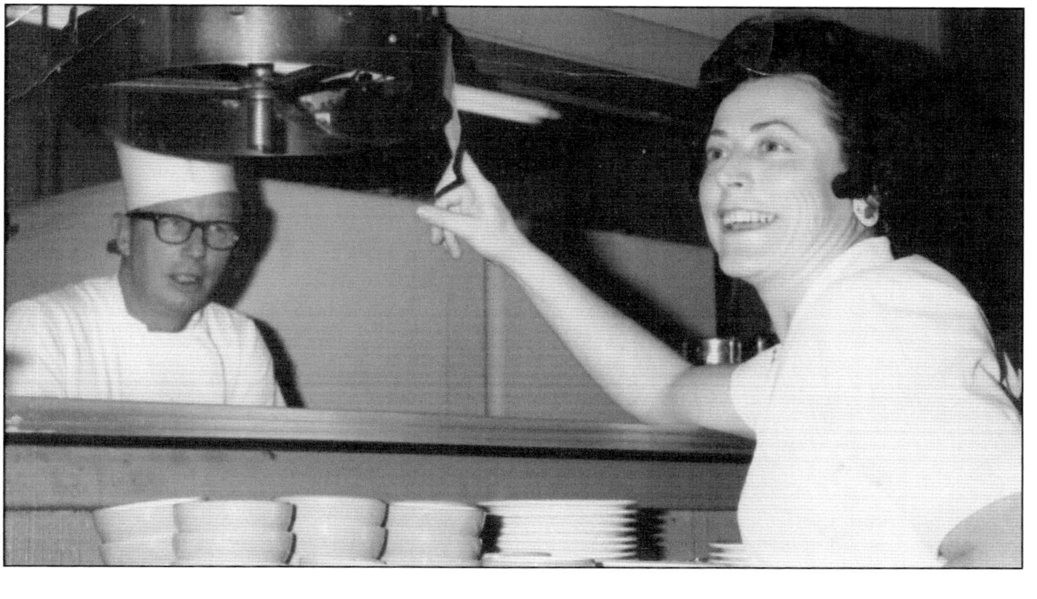

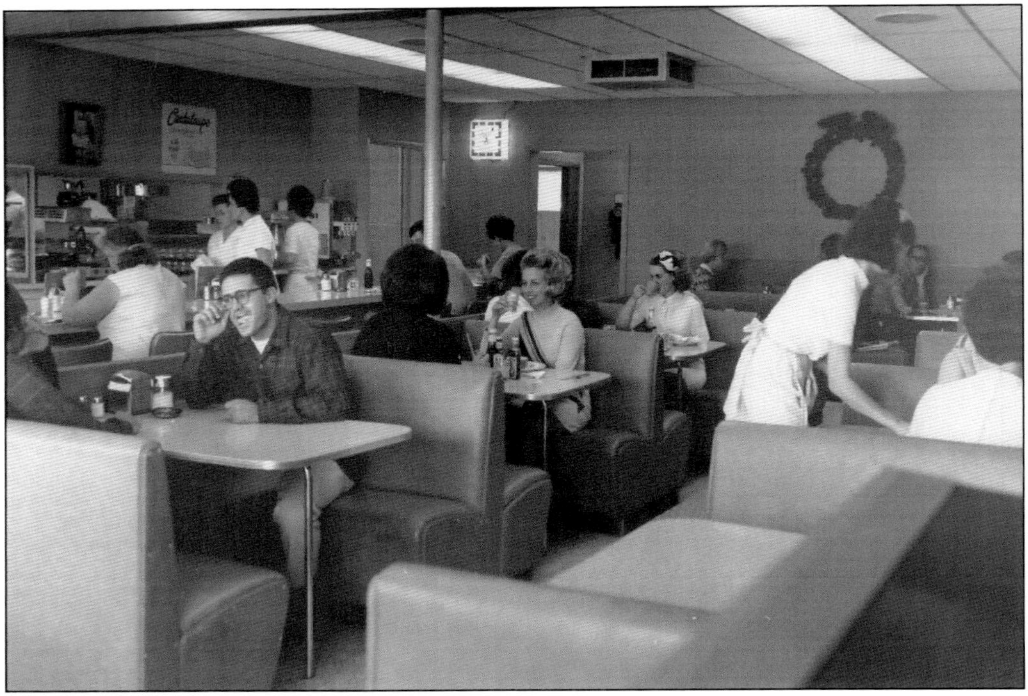

The inside decor and diner atmosphere of the Pine Cone is captured in this 1960s photograph. It was a great place to come for a cup of coffee, a piece of homemade pie, or a simple meal—or just to meet friends and neighbors. (Courtesy of Jaunita Fowler Bjork.)

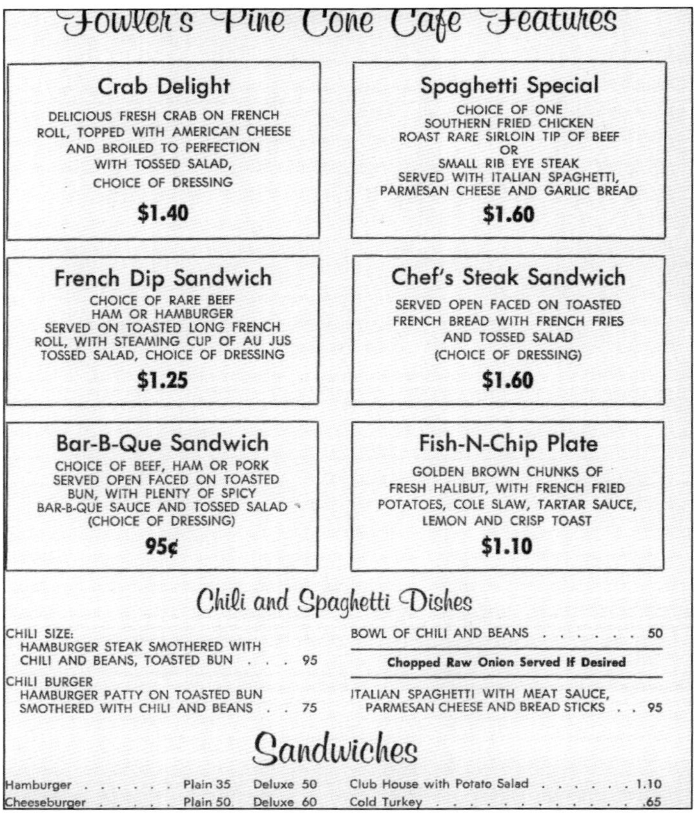

Fowler's Pine Cone Cafe Features

Crab Delight
DELICIOUS FRESH CRAB ON FRENCH ROLL, TOPPED WITH AMERICAN CHEESE AND BROILED TO PERFECTION WITH TOSSED SALAD, CHOICE OF DRESSING
$1.40

Spaghetti Special
CHOICE OF ONE
SOUTHERN FRIED CHICKEN
ROAST RARE SIRLOIN TIP OF BEEF
OR
SMALL RIB EYE STEAK
SERVED WITH ITALIAN SPAGHETTI, PARMESAN CHEESE AND GARLIC BREAD
$1.60

French Dip Sandwich
CHOICE OF RARE BEEF HAM OR HAMBURGER SERVED ON TOASTED LONG FRENCH ROLL, WITH STEAMING CUP OF AU JUS TOSSED SALAD, CHOICE OF DRESSING
$1.25

Chef's Steak Sandwich
SERVED OPEN FACED ON TOASTED FRENCH BREAD WITH FRENCH FRIES AND TOSSED SALAD (CHOICE OF DRESSING)
$1.60

Bar-B-Que Sandwich
CHOICE OF BEEF, HAM OR PORK SERVED OPEN FACED ON TOASTED BUN, WITH PLENTY OF SPICY BAR-B-QUE SAUCE AND TOSSED SALAD (CHOICE OF DRESSING)
95¢

Fish-N-Chip Plate
GOLDEN BROWN CHUNKS OF FRESH HALIBUT, WITH FRENCH FRIED POTATOES, COLE SLAW, TARTAR SAUCE, LEMON AND CRISP TOAST
$1.10

Chili and Spaghetti Dishes

CHILI SIZE:
HAMBURGER STEAK SMOTHERED WITH CHILI AND BEANS, TOASTED BUN . . . 95

CHILI BURGER
HAMBURGER PATTY ON TOASTED BUN SMOTHERED WITH CHILI AND BEANS . . 75

BOWL OF CHILI AND BEANS 50

Chopped Raw Onion Served If Desired

ITALIAN SPAGHETTI WITH MEAT SAUCE, PARMESAN CHEESE AND BREAD STICKS . . 95

Sandwiches

Hamburger . . . . . . Plain 35 Deluxe 50
Cheeseburger . . . . . Plain 50 Deluxe 60
Club House with Potato Salad 1.10
Cold Turkey 65

This 1972 menu from the Pine Cone captures the simple offerings and reasonable prices that made this UP's neighborhood restaurant. (Courtesy of Jaunita Fowler Bjork.)

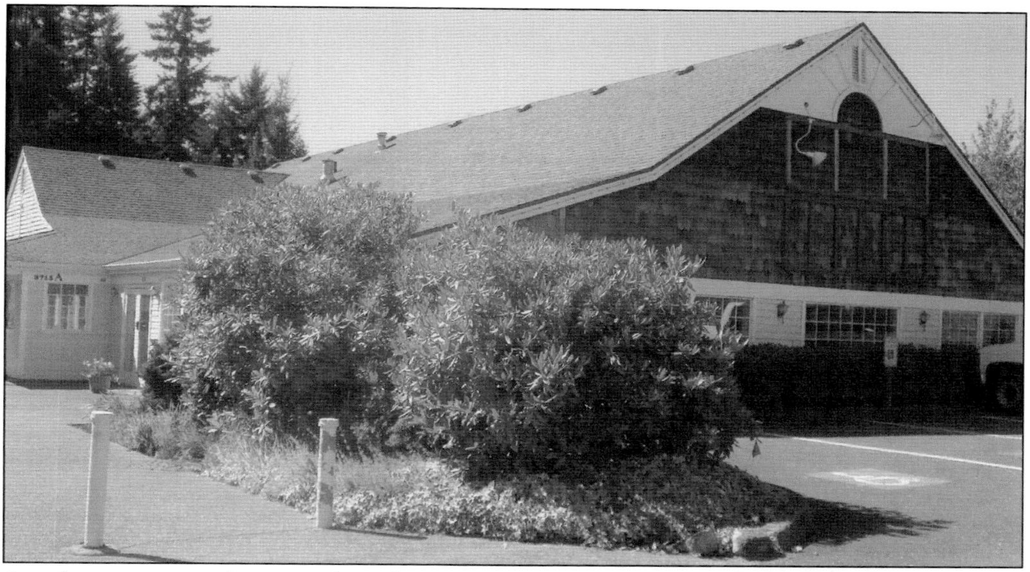

Another restaurant that gained quick community recognition and support was Mama Stortini's, located in the Windmill Village near Thirty-seventh Street and Bridgeport Way. It was started in the 1990s by Joe Stortini, a former teacher at Mount Tahoma High School, state senator, county commissioner, and county executive. Mama Stortini's soon became a UP favorite. Anyone associated with Curtis High School activities will certainly remember banquets catered with Mama Stortini's spaghetti. The establishment was forced to close in 2007 to make room for the Town Center project. Joe is extremely proud of his association with Bob Lucey and the UP Children's Fund, which was established to help the families of young cancer victims Mark George and Sarah Shuckhart. Over a quarter of a million dollars was raised. Joe now owns and operates Joeseppi's Italian Restaurant on North Twenty-first Street in Tacoma. The above photograph shows the building that once housed Mama Stortini's. It remains empty, awaiting the Town Center development. At right, Joe begins preparing spaghetti sauce. (Right, courtesy of Joe Stortini.)

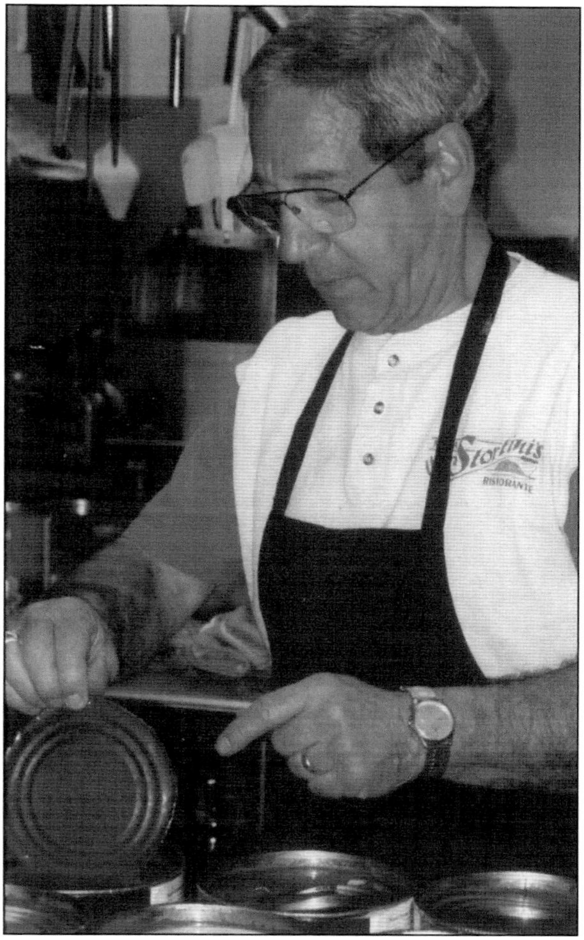

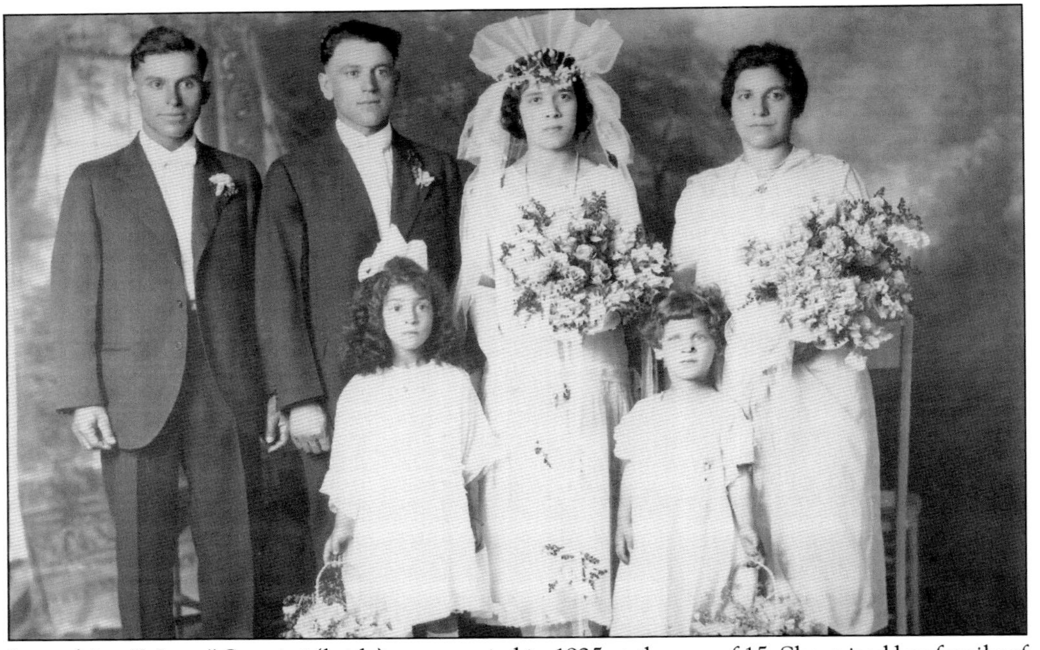

Joesephine "Mama" Stortini (bride) was married in 1925 at the age of 15. She raised her family of five children in the Hilltop area of Tacoma on South Hosmer Street. In honor of her outstanding Italian recipes, Joe opened Mama Stortini's in University Place. (Courtesy of Joe Stortini.)

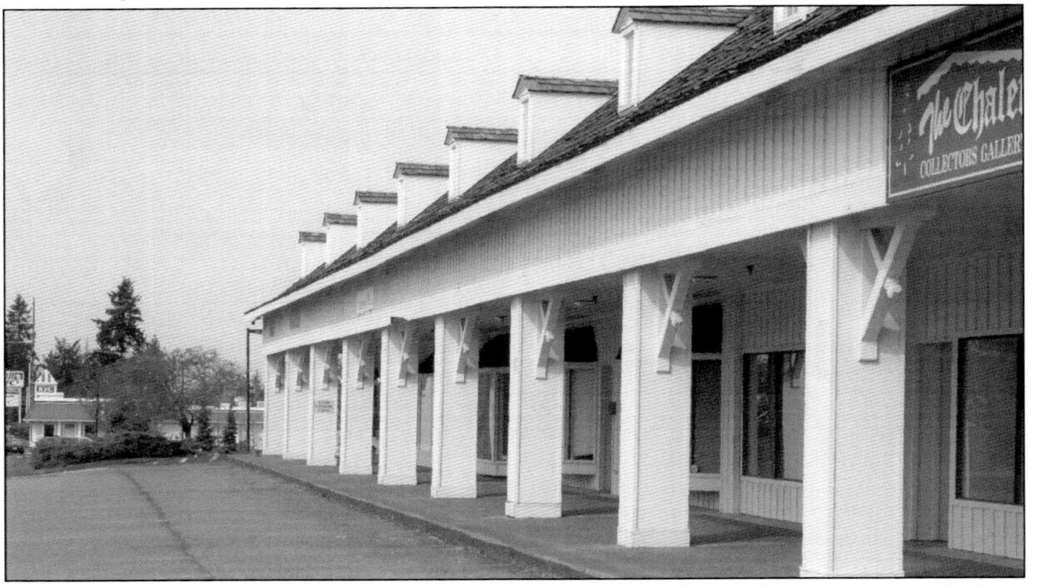

Another shopping development located next to the Windmill Village on Bridgeport was called the Clocktower Square. It was the home of several businesses, including The Chalet, Pierce's Jewelry, and a post office. The development, however, was never very successful. In this photograph, a KFC can be seen in the background. Roundtable Pizza and Denny's, along with a newly built UP Library, occupied the surrounding property. All of these were torn down to make room for the Town Center, which is still a work in progress. (Courtesy of the Tacoma Public Library, Northwest Room, Richards Studio Collection.)

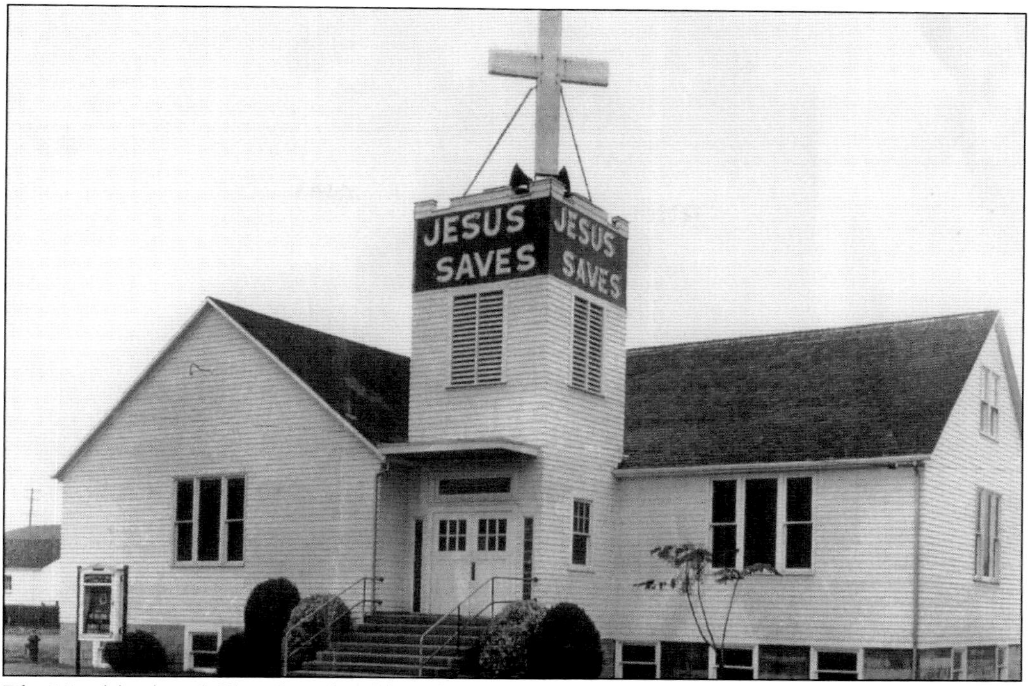

The Neighborhood Church is the oldest church in University Place, dating back almost 100 years. Its Sunday school began in the vacated Lemon's Beach School in 1919. Under the oversight of the Lelands, Konsmos, Nelsons, Gulicksons, and Jacksons, this Pentecostal Sunday school continued to grow. In 1937, the congregation bought a home on Twenty-ninth Street and Mountain View Avenue. The house was demolished, and the first phase of the church was built. In 1943, it was officially chartered as the University Place Assembly of God. As the congregation continued to grow, the need to relocate became necessary, and the church (now known as The Neighborhood Church) moved to its present location at Twenty-eighth Street and Bridgeport Way in 1961. The original 1937 church is shown above. It was purchased by a Baptist church and continues as a place of worship today. (Above, courtesy of Inez Leland Glass.)

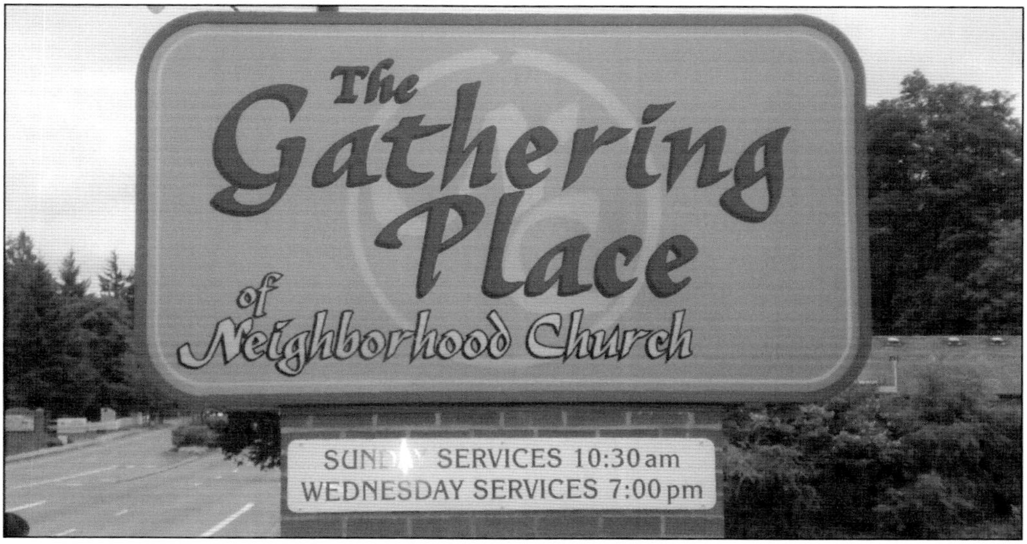

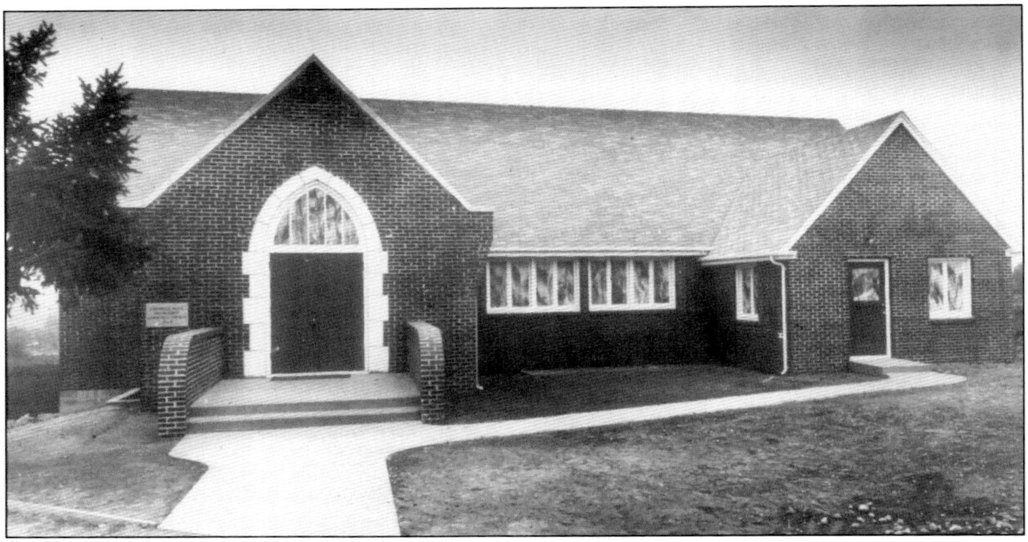

The early days of the University Place Presbyterian Church date back to the 1920s when First Presbyterian Church of Tacoma started a number of mission Sunday schools in "outlying areas" of the city. One of these Sunday schools was held in the clubhouse on Day Island in 1927. In the late 1930s, the Sunday school was moved to the old tomato shed on Grandview Drive and was called Wayside Chapel. From there, it moved to the auditorium of UP School in 1941 when the newly formed University Place Fire Department took over the tomato shed. In 1943, the congregation officially organized into the University Place Presbyterian Community Church (UPPCC). Property was purchased on the northwest corner of Twenty-seventh Street and Sunset Drive. The first church was built in 1949. As the UP community's population began to explode in the 1950s, so did the size of UPPCC's congregation. In 1955, two worship services, at 8:30 and 11:00 a.m., began. By the end of 1956, plans for building a new sanctuary began. Ground breaking took place in March 1959 (below), and the new building was dedicated a year later. UPPCC continues to be a major center of worship and community service. (Both, courtesy of UP Presbyterian Church.)

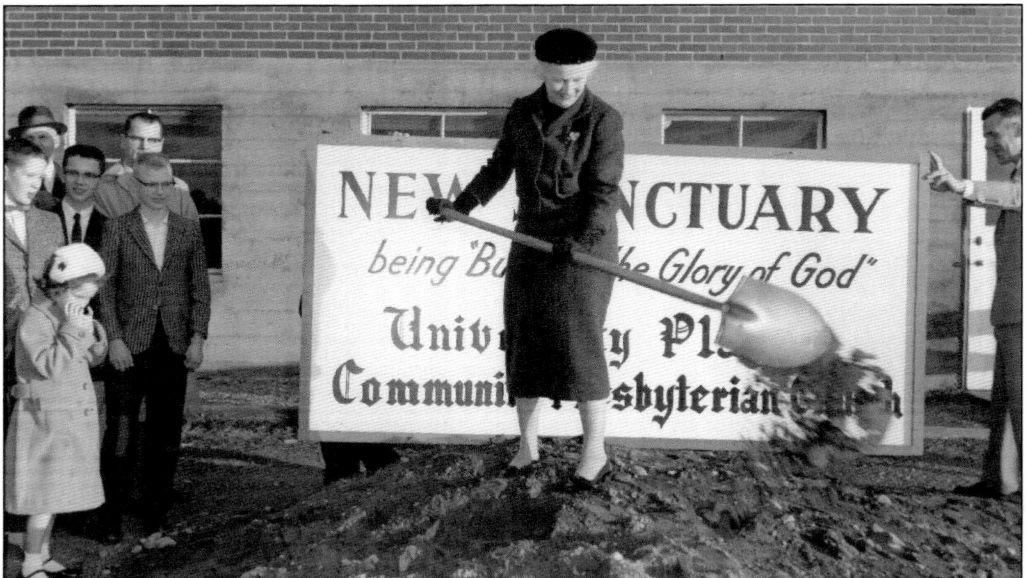

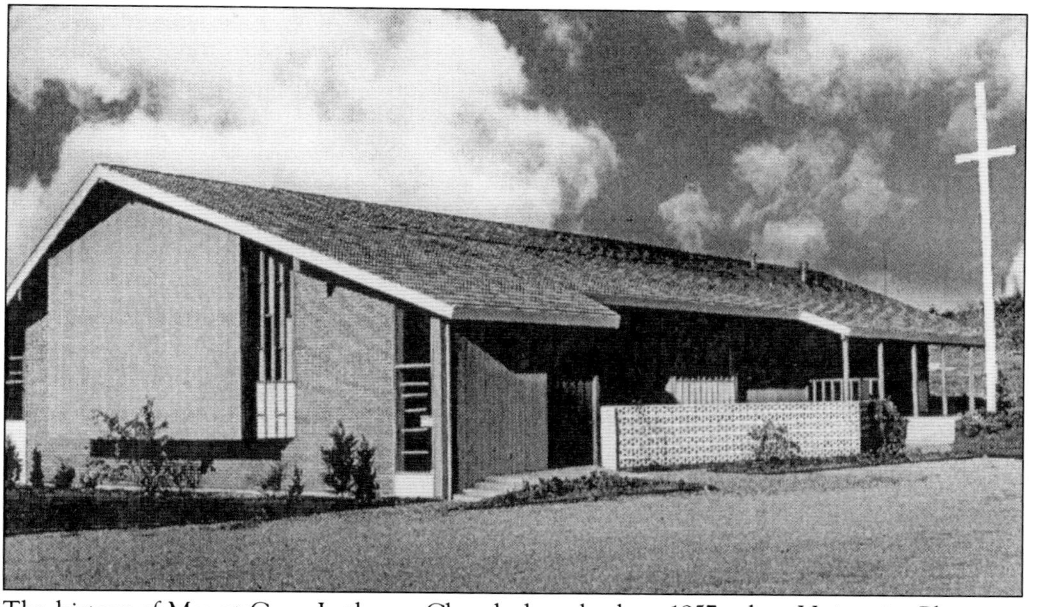

The history of Mount Cross Lutheran Church dates back to 1957, when University Place was assigned as a field mission of the Augustian Lutheran Church by the National Lutheran Council. By late 1958, the new church and Sunday school were formed, and worship services began at the Masonic Lodge on Grandview Drive. In 1959, property was purchased across from the junior high school on Fortieth Street. Construction of the new church was completed in September 1960, and Mount Cross Lutheran Church attained self-sustaining status. (Both, courtesy of Mount Cross Lutheran Church.)

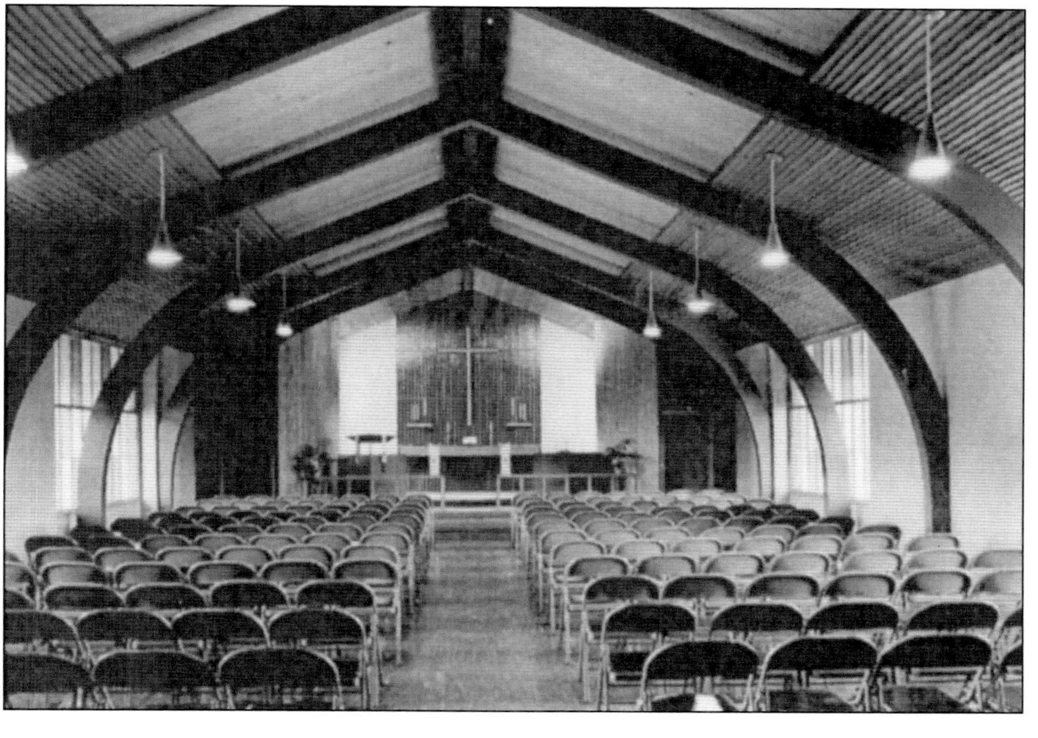

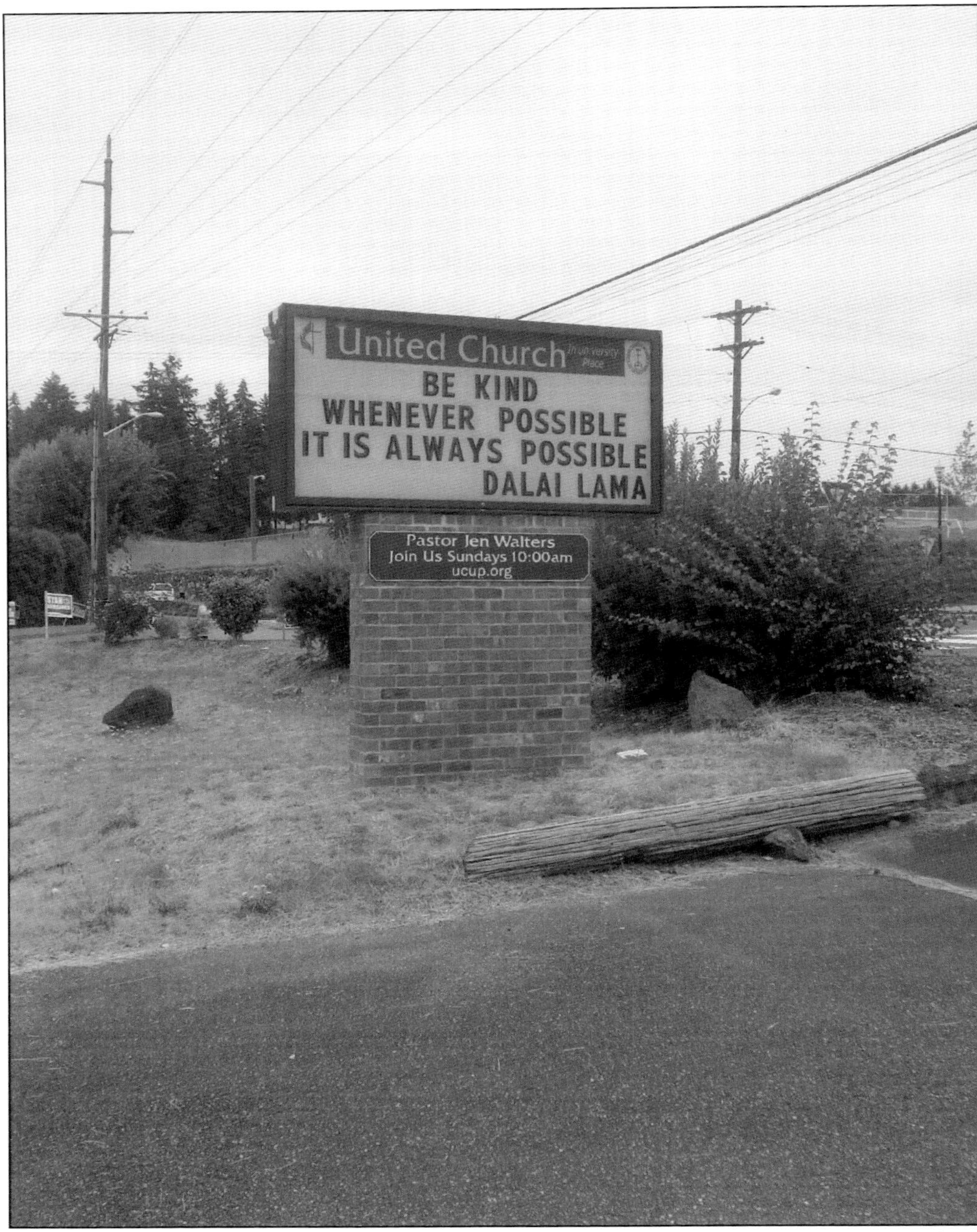

The United Church In University Place came into being in 1970 through the merger of two smaller churches, the Mayflower United Church and Aldersgate United Methodist Church. The two churches had been holding separate services since the early 1960s. The property of the Mayflower Church, on Fortieth Street and Grandview Drive, was retained, and the Aldersgate property was sold to fund additions to the new church. The United Church started the latchkey program, now sponsored by the school district, and has long been the home of Narrows Co-op Nursery School. The church's sign, with its ever-present and constantly changing inspirational messages, greets drivers as they pass along Grandview Drive.

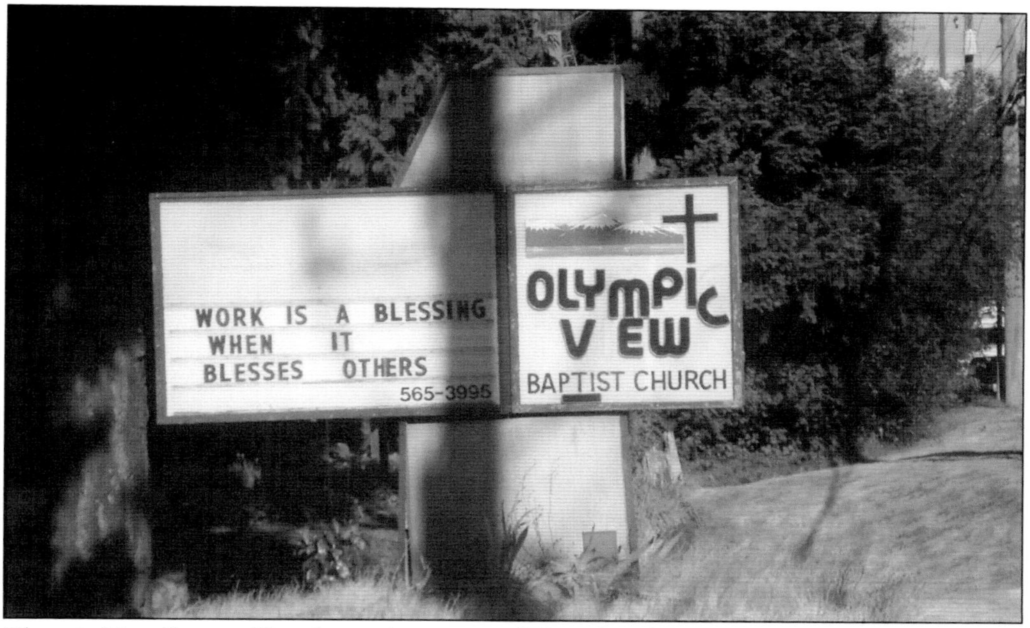

Olympic View Baptist Church, on the corner of Elwood and Cirque Drive, came into being in 1972. It started as a Bible study group that was praying about the possibility of starting a church in University Place. The group welcomed their first pastor, Leroy Shauer, that year, and he served the congregation for the next 10 years.

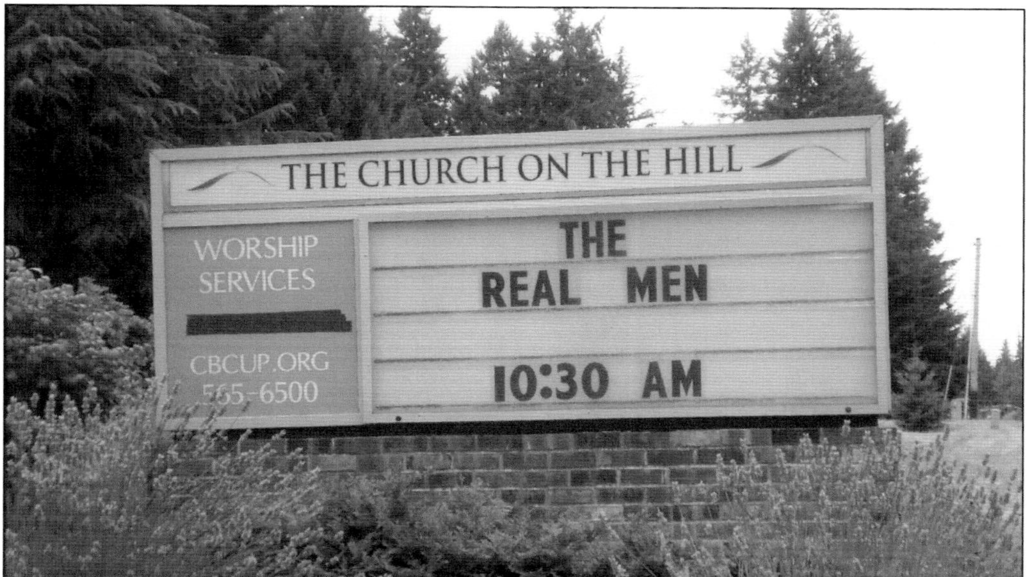

The Church On The Hill was first organized as the First Swedish Baptist Church of Tacoma in 1893. It was initially located at South Twelfth and J Streets. Its name was officially changed to Central Baptist in 1935, and the congregation moved to a new location at Eleventh and Grant Streets in 1950. In 1969, the church bought five acres of land on the corner of Sixty-seventh Avenue and Cirque Drive and another 11.5 acres in 1976. Construction of The Church On The Hill began in 1978, and the new facility was dedicated on November 18, 1979.

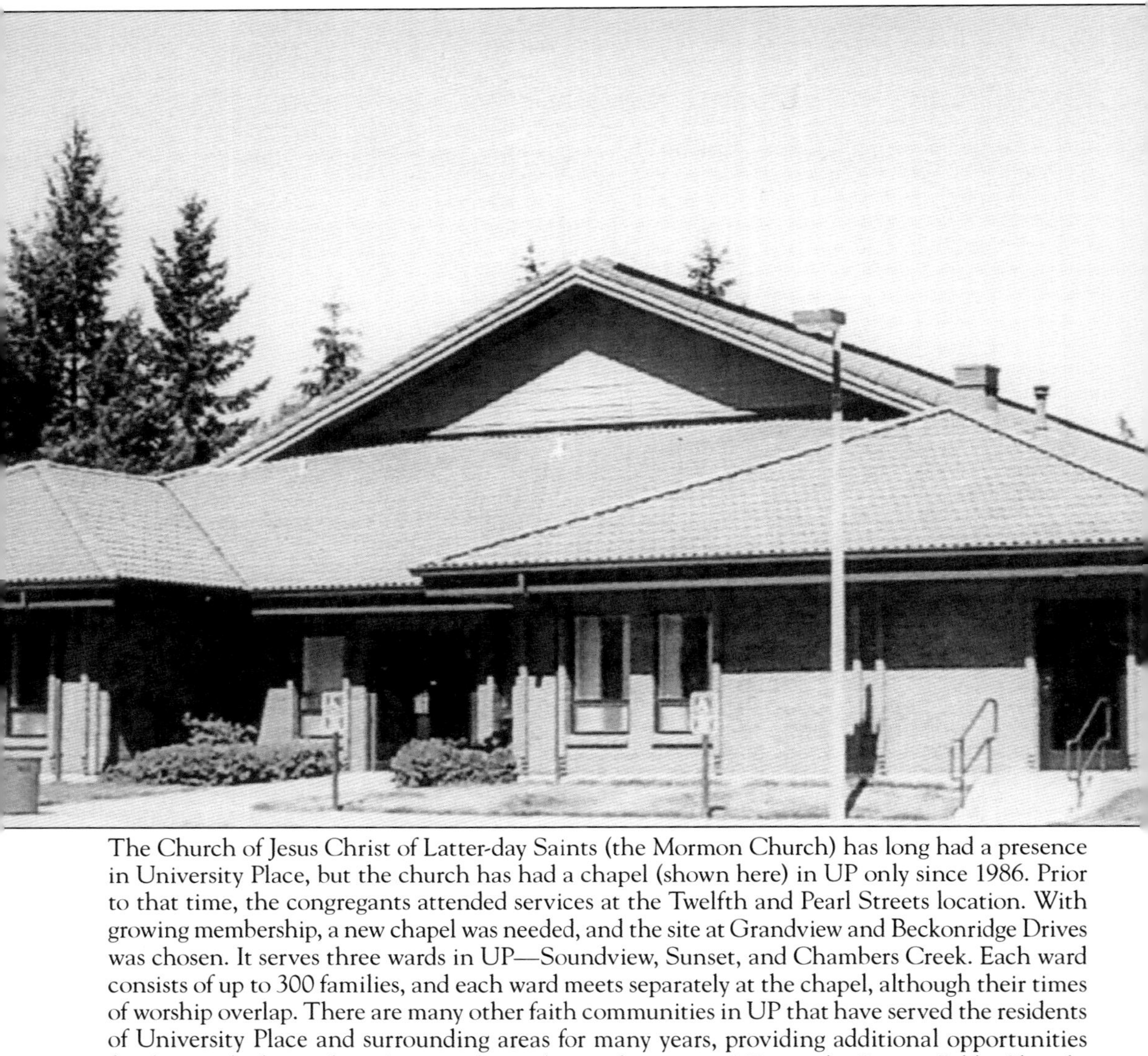

The Church of Jesus Christ of Latter-day Saints (the Mormon Church) has long had a presence in University Place, but the church has had a chapel (shown here) in UP only since 1986. Prior to that time, the congregants attended services at the Twelfth and Pearl Streets location. With growing membership, a new chapel was needed, and the site at Grandview and Beckonridge Drives was chosen. It serves three wards in UP—Soundview, Sunset, and Chambers Creek. Each ward consists of up to 300 families, and each ward meets separately at the chapel, although their times of worship overlap. There are many other faith communities in UP that have served the residents of University Place and surrounding areas for many years, providing additional opportunities for diverse faith worship. Among these places of prayer in UP are the Sunset Bible Church, Hope Community Church, Providence Reformed Baptist, Dae Joong Church, Community of Christ Church, Northwest Independent Church Extension, Pacific Community Church, Tacoma Foursquare Church, and the Islamic Center of Tacoma. (Courtesy of Andy Ward.)

Six

To Be or Not to Be . . . A City

In a period of 150 years, University Place has risen from a wilderness to a developed community exceeding 31,000 residents. This growth, mostly coming after World War II when the rush to suburbia began, created the need for change as rapid as the population growth. For many years, the school district and community were nearly synonymous, and residents often looked to the school board to make community decisions. When the population doubled from 5,000 to 10,000 between 1952 and 1962, the school district could barely keep up its educational responsibilities, much less deal with community issues. There were many improvement clubs and lots of volunteers, but nobody had real authority to make binding, legal decisions for University Place. That is when talk of incorporating as a city began in 1962, and the rhetoric was not always nice. Those that wanted to retain the independent status of UP clashed sharply with those that sought cityhood. The biggest fear among residents was that the school district would be absorbed by Tacoma School District if UP was annexed by Tacoma. An election was held, and the incorporation petition failed, but bitter feelings remained, and some pockets of UP still threatened to annex to Tacoma or Fircrest. That the community remained intact speaks highly to the inner pride residents still had in being a part of University Place. A community council was formed in early 1963 to help mend the wounds and to begin dealing with issues like police protection, traffic safety, library, parks, sewers, and community activities. It did not hurt that Curtis High School sports teams were becoming powerhouses in the Seamount League. The community survived, but it would be another three decades and a new generation of citizens before the idea of incorporation would make a comeback. By that time, Pierce County had discontinued comprehensive planning for UP in favor of focusing on a countywide growth management plan. UP Water Company could not keep up with growth and was taken over by Tacoma Public Utilities, and the school district (supported by the fire department and SOUP) petitioned Pierce County to cease granting building permits for housing developments or apartment complexes until a plan for orderly development was drafted. Under the new Pierce County Comprehensive Plan of Development in the early 1990s, UP would be designated as an "Urban Growth Area," which mandated that urban government services be provided by cities. This left University Place with few options. It would either become a city itself, or risk being annexed by neighboring cities. Many meetings were held throughout the community, and the issue was put before the voters in November 1994. Incorporation passed overwhelmingly, and UP elected its first city council on April 25, 1995.

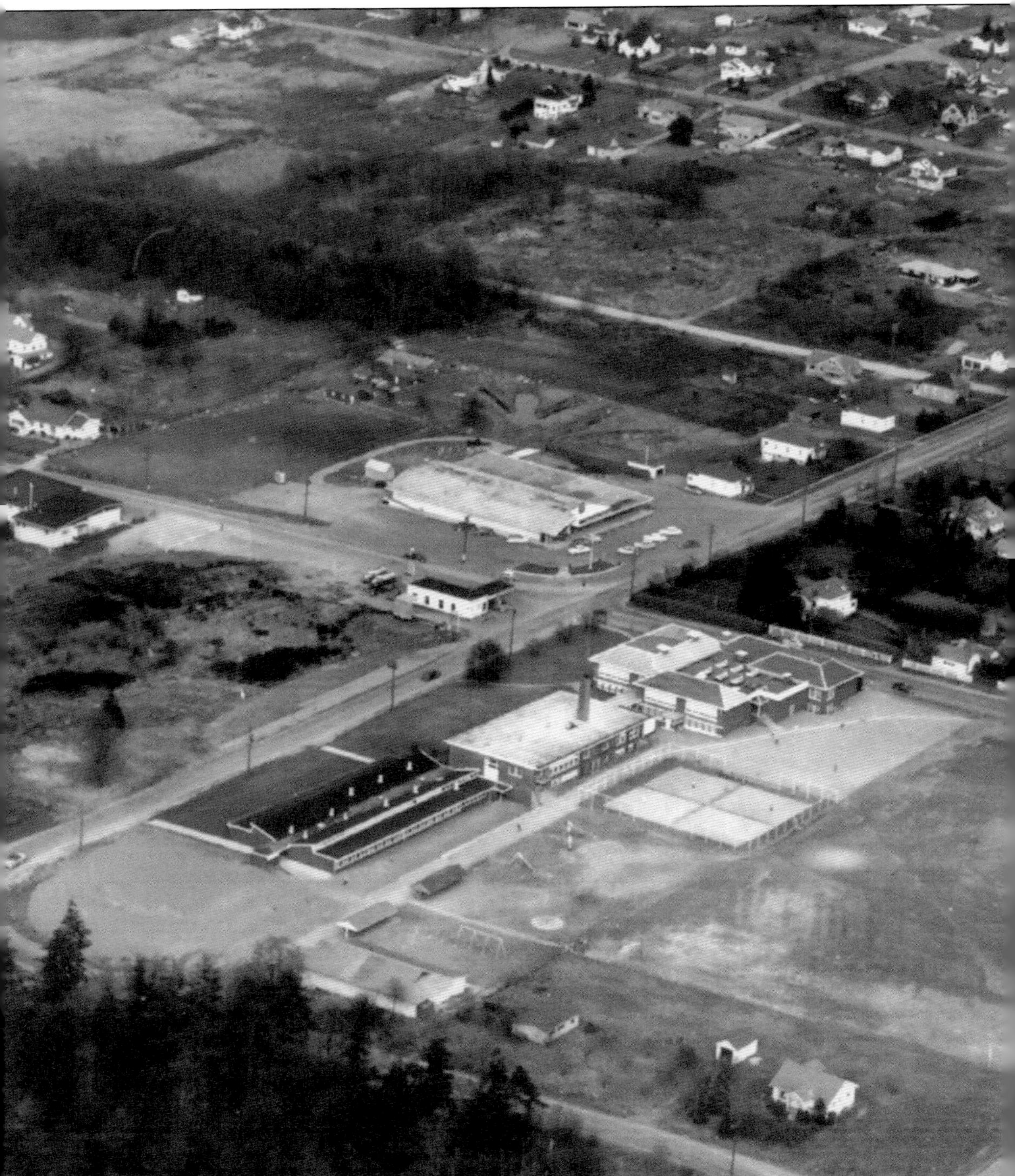

University Place began to grow rapidly in the 1950s. This 1955 photograph shows the development along the Twenty-seventh Street corridor (running diagonally through the center of the photograph), which was the core of UP at the time. As stated in the Comprehensive Plan for University Place,

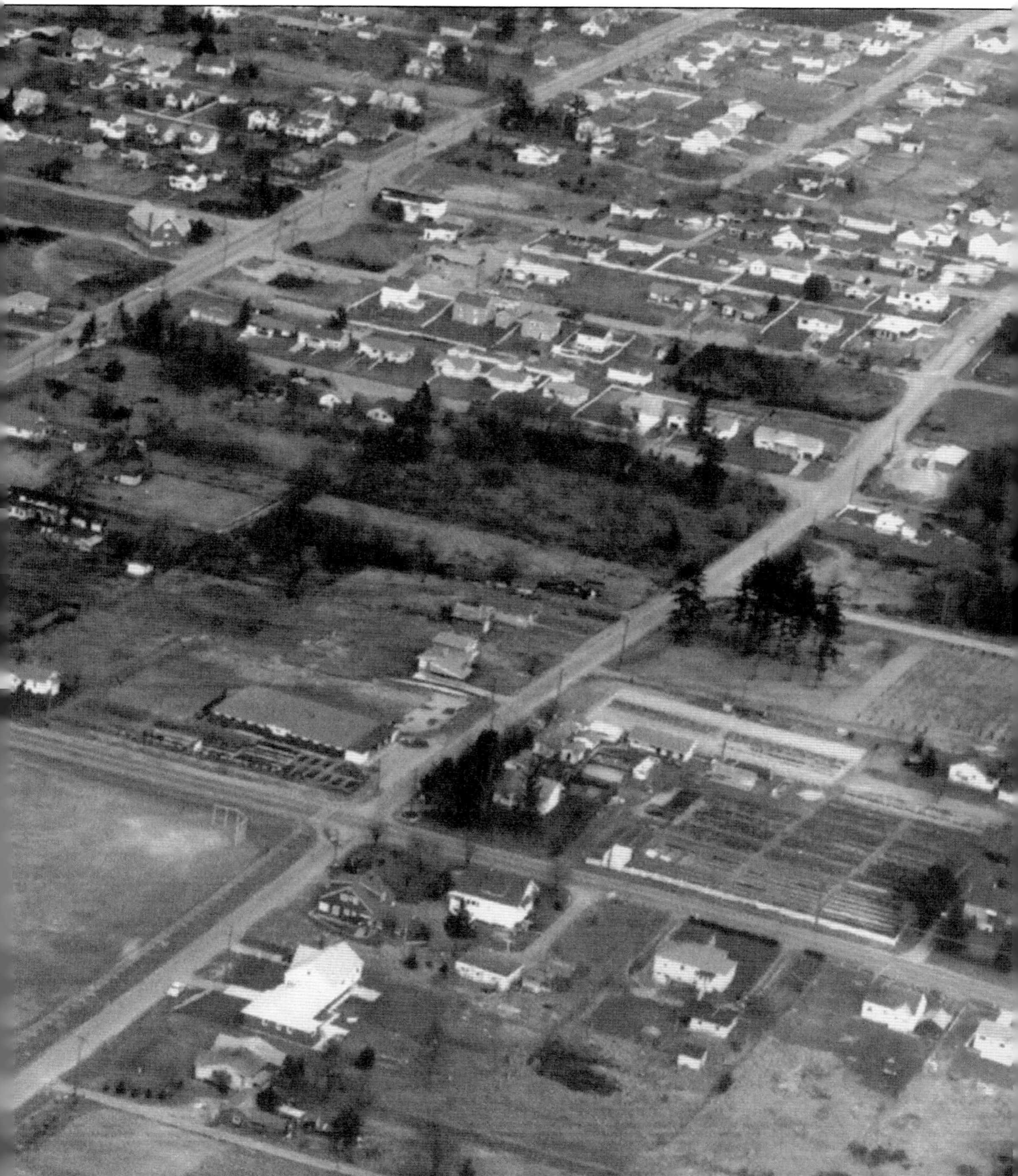

developed by the Pierce County Planning Commission in 1955, "University Place is a suburban frontier. Only fifteen percent of the potential building sites are built upon." The other 85 percent is mostly to the south and east of this picture.

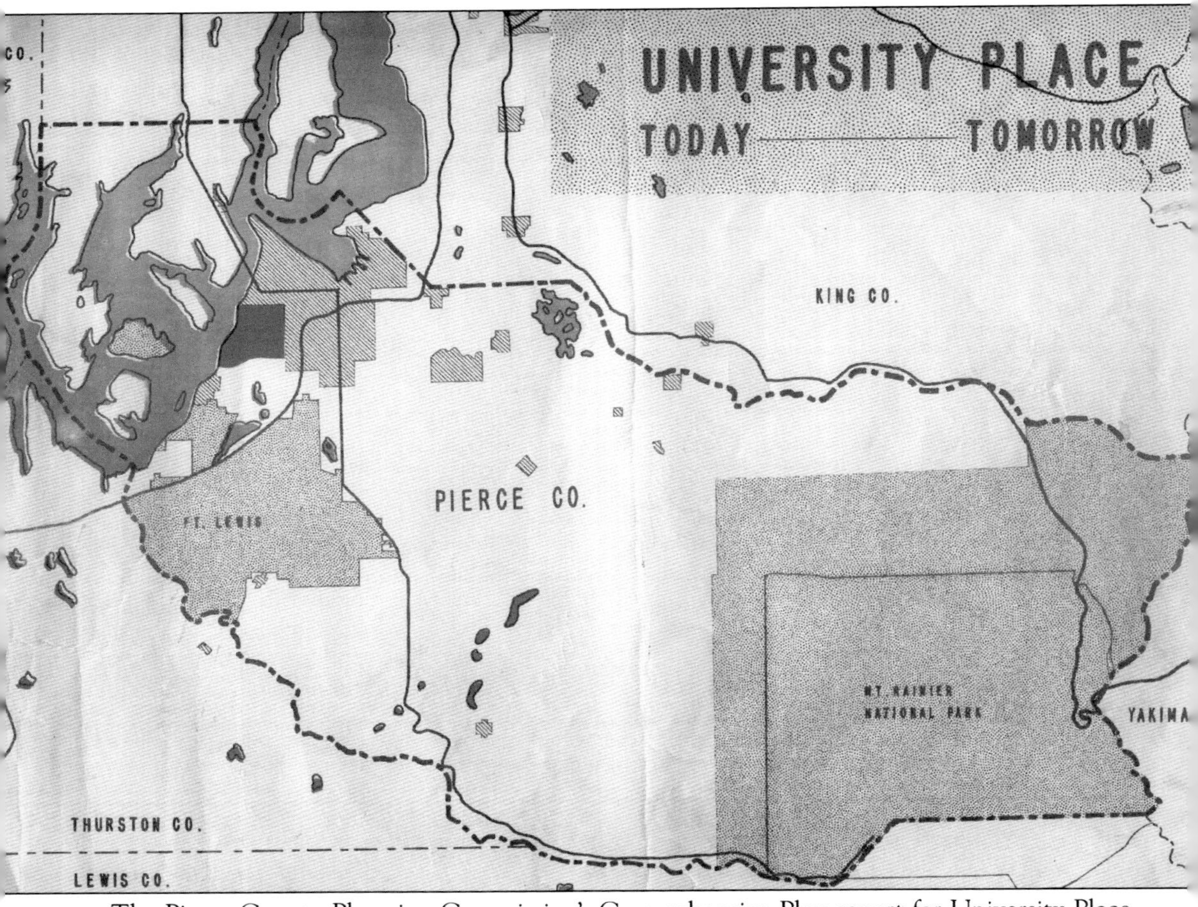

The Pierce County Planning Commission's Comprehensive Plan report for University Place in 1955 was the first real study of the community. Its analysis and predictions are remarkable: anticipating a population growth to over 30,000 (it was barely over 5,000 at the time), seeing the need for more schools and determining potential locations, a gradual moving of the business district from Twenty-seventh Street to Bridgeport Way, and even the developing of the Fred Meyer shopping center near Chambers Creek Road and Bridgeport Way.

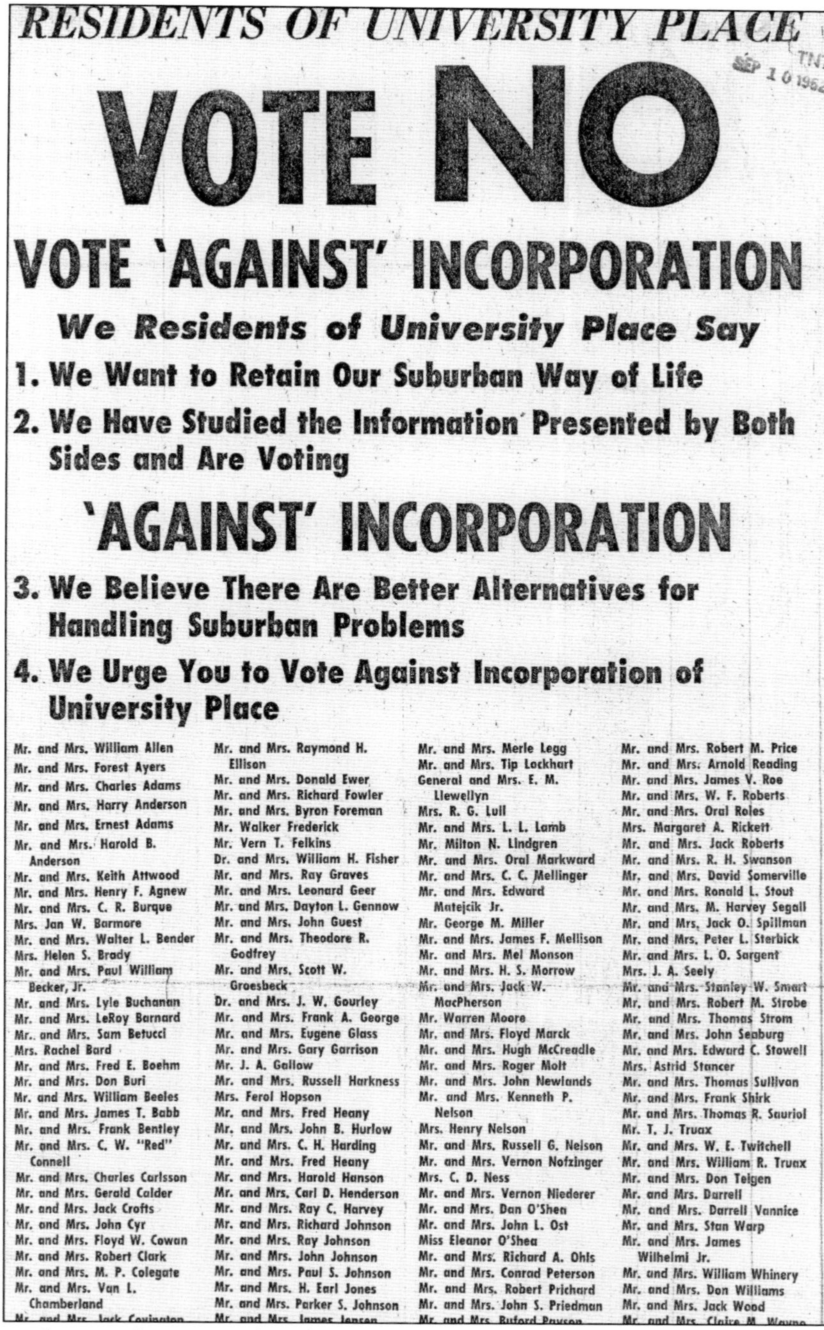

RESIDENTS OF UNIVERSITY PLACE

VOTE NO

VOTE 'AGAINST' INCORPORATION

We Residents of University Place Say

1. We Want to Retain Our Suburban Way of Life
2. We Have Studied the Information Presented by Both Sides and Are Voting

'AGAINST' INCORPORATION

3. We Believe There Are Better Alternatives for Handling Suburban Problems
4. We Urge You to Vote Against Incorporation of University Place

Mr. and Mrs. William Allen
Mr. and Mrs. Forest Ayers
Mr. and Mrs. Charles Adams
Mr. and Mrs. Harry Anderson
Mr. and Mrs. Ernest Adams
Mr. and Mrs. Harold B. Anderson
Mr. and Mrs. Keith Attwood
Mr. and Mrs. Henry F. Agnew
Mr. and Mrs. C. R. Burque
Mrs. Jan W. Barmore
Mr. and Mrs. Walter L. Bender
Mrs. Helen S. Brady
Mr. and Mrs. Paul William Becker, Jr.
Mr. and Mrs. Lyle Buchanan
Mr. and Mrs. LeRoy Barnard
Mr. and Mrs. Sam Betucci
Mrs. Rachel Bard
Mr. and Mrs. Fred E. Boehm
Mr. and Mrs. Don Buri
Mr. and Mrs. William Beeles
Mr. and Mrs. James T. Babb
Mr. and Mrs. Frank Bentley
Mr. and Mrs. C. W. "Red" Connell
Mr. and Mrs. Charles Carlsson
Mr. and Mrs. Gerald Calder
Mr. and Mrs. Jack Crofts
Mr. and Mrs. John Cyr
Mr. and Mrs. Floyd W. Cowan
Mr. and Mrs. Robert Clark
Mr. and Mrs. M. P. Colegate
Mr. and Mrs. Van L. Chamberland
Mr. and Mrs. Jack Covington
Mr. and Mrs. Raymond H. Ellison
Mr. and Mrs. Donald Ewer
Mr. and Mrs. Richard Fowler
Mr. and Mrs. Byron Foreman
Mr. Walker Frederick
Mr. Vern T. Felkins
Dr. and Mrs. William H. Fisher
Mr. and Mrs. Ray Graves
Mr. and Mrs. Leonard Geer
Mr. and Mrs. Dayton L. Gennow
Mr. and Mrs. John Guest
Mr. and Mrs. Theodore R. Godfrey
Mr. and Mrs. Scott W. Groesbeck
Dr. and Mrs. J. W. Gourley
Mr. and Mrs. Frank A. George
Mr. and Mrs. Eugene Glass
Mr. and Mrs. Gary Garrison
Mr. J. A. Gallow
Mr. and Mrs. Russell Harkness
Mrs. Ferol Hopson
Mr. and Mrs. Fred Heany
Mr. and Mrs. John B. Hurlow
Mr. and Mrs. C. H. Harding
Mr. and Mrs. Fred Heany
Mr. and Mrs. Harold Hanson
Mr. and Mrs. Carl D. Henderson
Mr. and Mrs. Ray C. Harvey
Mr. and Mrs. Richard Johnson
Mr. and Mrs. Ray Johnson
Mr. and Mrs. John Johnson
Mr. and Mrs. Paul S. Johnson
Mr. and Mrs. H. Earl Jones
Mr. and Mrs. Parker S. Johnson
Mr. and Mrs. James Jensen
Mr. and Mrs. Merle Legg
Mr. and Mrs. Tip Lockhart
General and Mrs. E. M. Llewellyn
Mrs. R. G. Lull
Mr. and Mrs. L. L. Lamb
Mr. Milton N. Lindgren
Mr. and Mrs. Oral Markward
Mr. and Mrs. C. C. Mellinger
Mr. and Mrs. Edward Matejcik Jr.
Mr. George M. Miller
Mr. and Mrs. James F. Mellison
Mr. and Mrs. Mel Monson
Mr. and Mrs. H. S. Morrow
Mr. and Mrs. Jack W. MacPherson
Mr. Warren Moore
Mr. and Mrs. Floyd Marck
Mr. and Mrs. Hugh McCreadle
Mr. and Mrs. Roger Molt
Mr. and Mrs. John Newlands
Mr. and Mrs. Kenneth P. Nelson
Mrs. Henry Nelson
Mr. and Mrs. Russell G. Nelson
Mr. and Mrs. Vernon Nofzinger
Mrs. C. D. Ness
Mr. and Mrs. Vernon Niederer
Mr. and Mrs. Dan O'Shen
Mr. and Mrs. John L. Ost
Miss Eleanor O'Shea
Mr. and Mrs. Richard A. Ohls
Mr. and Mrs. Conrad Peterson
Mr. and Mrs. Robert Prichard
Mr. and Mrs. John S. Priedman
Mr. and Mrs. Buford Payson
Mr. and Mrs. Robert M. Price
Mr. and Mrs. Arnold Reading
Mr. and Mrs. James V. Roe
Mr. and Mrs. W. F. Roberts
Mr. and Mrs. Oral Roles
Mrs. Margaret A. Rickett
Mr. and Mrs. Jack Roberts
Mr. and Mrs. R. H. Swanson
Mr. and Mrs. David Somerville
Mr. and Mrs. Ronald L. Stout
Mr. and Mrs. M. Harvey Segall
Mr. and Mrs. Jack O. Spillman
Mr. and Mrs. Peter L. Sterbick
Mr. and Mrs. L. O. Sargent
Mrs. J. A. Seely
Mr. and Mrs. Stanley W. Smart
Mr. and Mrs. Robert M. Strobe
Mr. and Mrs. Thomas Strom
Mr. and Mrs. John Seaburg
Mr. and Mrs. Edward C. Stowell
Mrs. Astrid Stancer
Mr. and Mrs. Thomas Sullivan
Mr. and Mrs. Frank Shirk
Mr. and Mrs. Thomas R. Sauriol
Mr. T. J. Truax
Mr. and Mrs. W. E. Twitchell
Mr. and Mrs. William R. Truax
Mr. and Mrs. Don Teigen
Mr. and Mrs. Darrell
Mr. and Mrs. Darrell Vannice
Mr. and Mrs. Stan Warp
Mr. and Mrs. James Wilhelmi Jr.
Mr. and Mrs. William Whinery
Mr. and Mrs. Don Williams
Mr. and Mrs. Jack Wood
Mr. and Mrs. Claire M. Wayne

As stated in the introduction to this chapter, the first attempt at incorporating University Place into a city nearly tore the community apart. This full-page advertisement against incorporation was placed in the *Tacoma News Tribune* on September 10, 1962, just before the vote was taken. After the petition was defeated, a community council was formed to reconsolidate the community and try to deal with issues that led to the incorporation debate in the first place, which the school district had no authority to resolve.

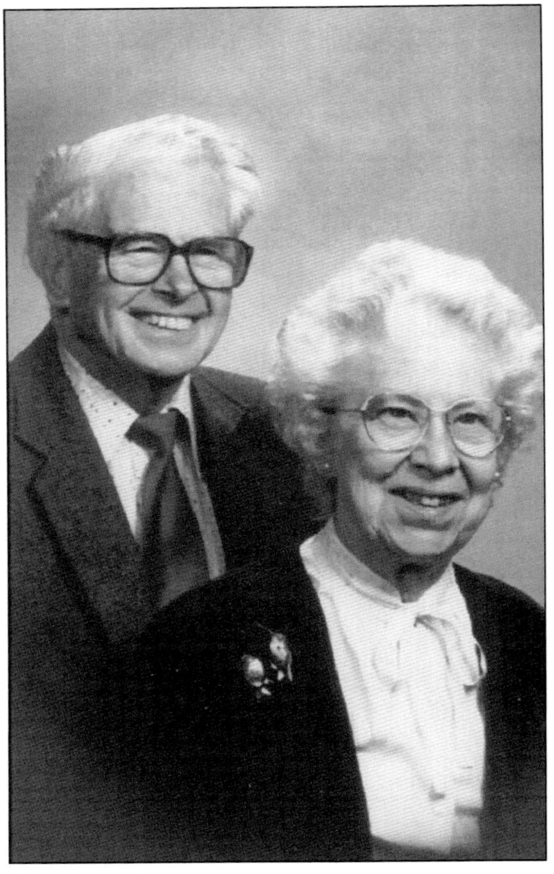

Two residents who had a great deal of impact on the community after moving here in the mid-1950s were George and Adriana Hess. George was a military doctor who, after being discharged, opened the first medical practice in University Place. He also served on the school board from 1962 to 1969, when he resigned to join the Peace Corps, returning to UP in 1972. His wife, Adriana, was even more involved in community life. She helped form the UP Community Council after the divisive incorporation effort of 1962. She incorporated the UP Parks and Recreation District in 1978 and served as a commissioner for 10 years. Adriana was a true environmentalist, intent on preserving open spaces, trees, and wetlands that were rapidly disappearing as UP grew. She founded SOUP (Save [later, Serve] Our University Place) to deal with those who were, from her perspective, abridging community rights for the sake of profit. When Adriana died in 1998, Morrison Pond, which she had purchased to protect this wetland, was donated by George to the City of University Place. It was named the Adriana Hess Wetland Park and Audubon Center. It is located on Morrison Avenue, south of Twenty-seventh Street.

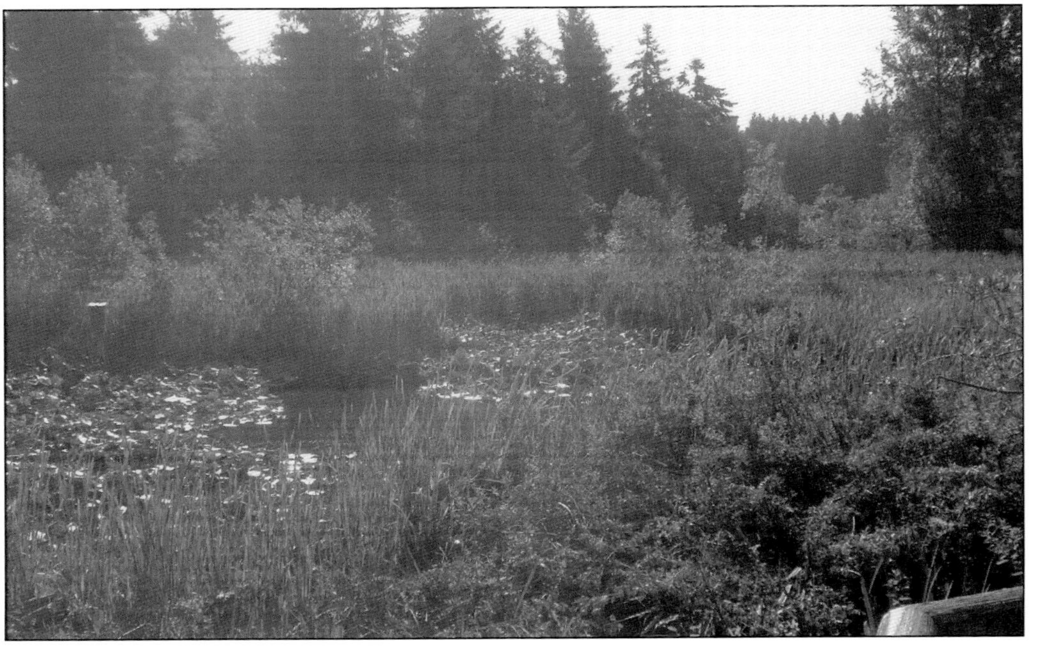

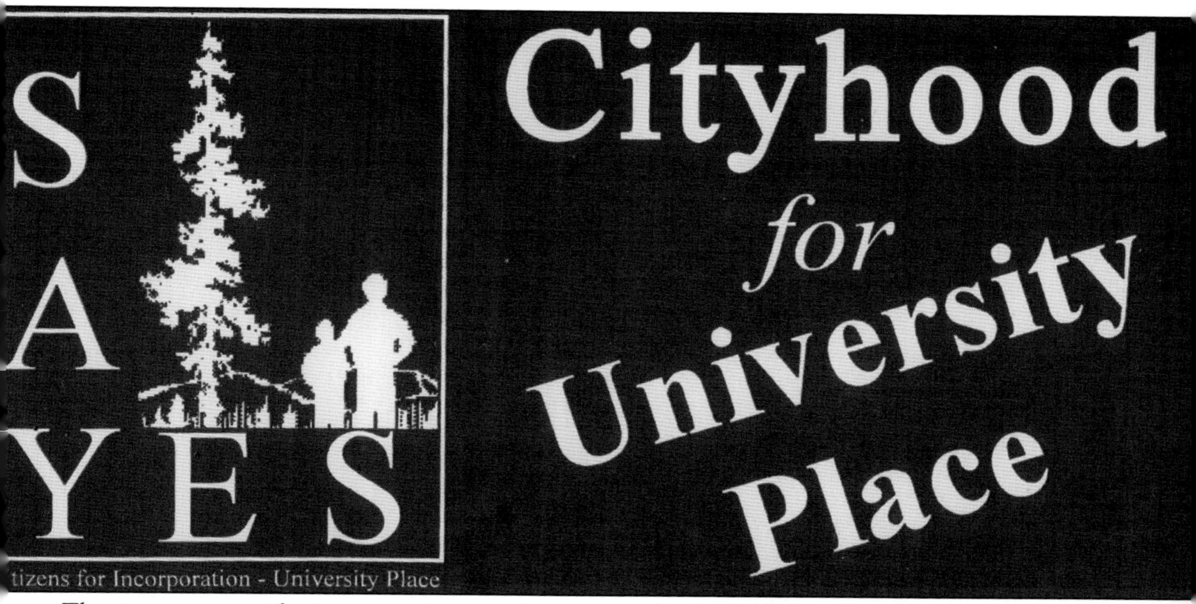

The time to reconsider incorporation as a city came in the early 1990s, when the Pierce County Council adopted the new Pierce County Plan of Development that would designate UP as an "Urban Growth Area," meaning that the government services must be provided by a city. So it was time to step up and become that entity or face the real possibility of being annexed, along with the school district, by Tacoma. Many community meetings were held to discuss the consequences and responsibilities that would come with cityhood. Finally, the election for incorporation was held on November 8, 1994. The resolution passed with over 80 percent of the vote. Ron Williams was selected to serve as interim mayor until a city council was elected on April 25, 1995. The date of official incorporation was August 31, 1995.

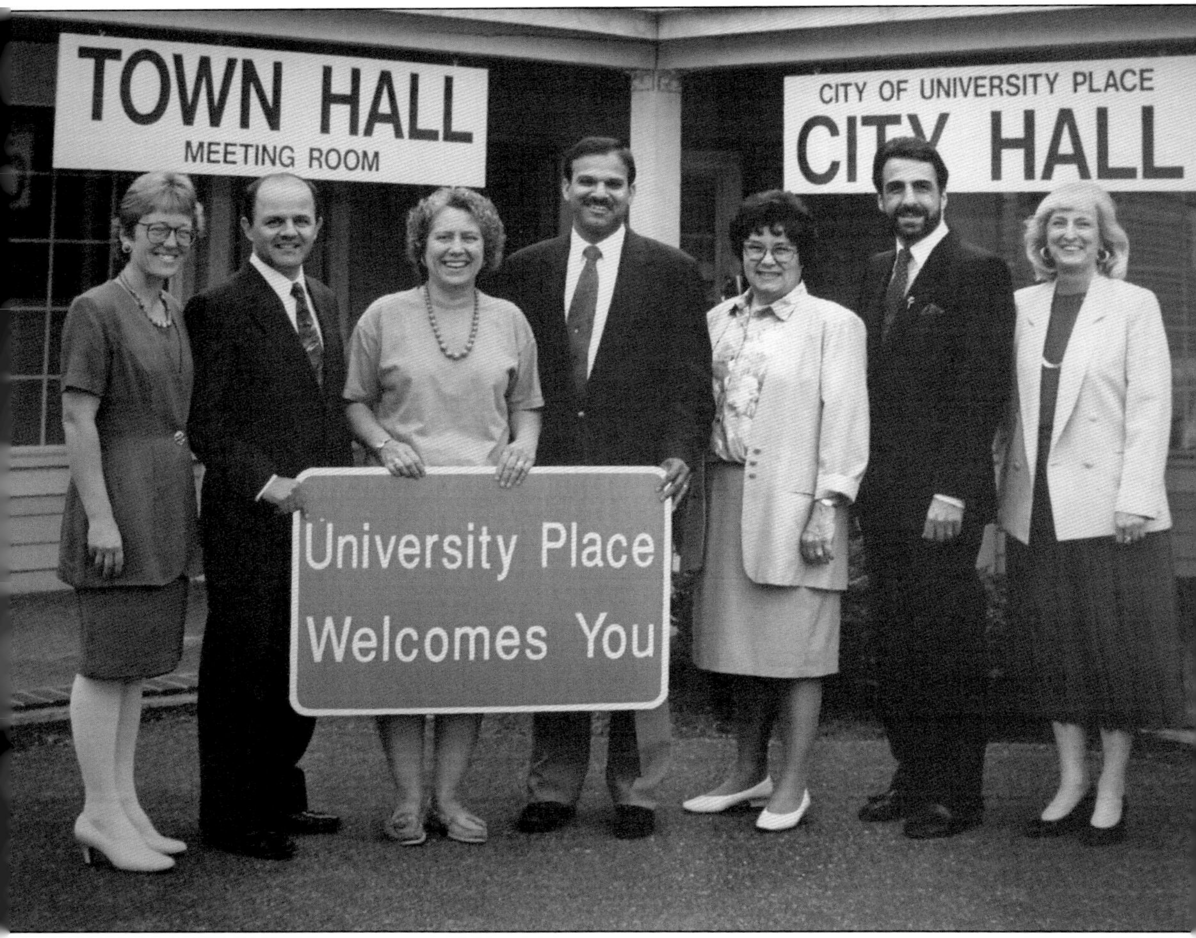

After voting to become a city, another election was necessary to select the persons who would comprise University Place's first city council. The election was held April 25, 1995. Smiling and standing outside the new city hall in Windmill Village (the old Broback farm) are, from left to right, Debbie Klosowski, Ron Williams, Jean Brooks, Stan Flemming, Linda Bird, Ken Grassi, and Lorna Smith. Flemming was selected to serve as the first mayor.

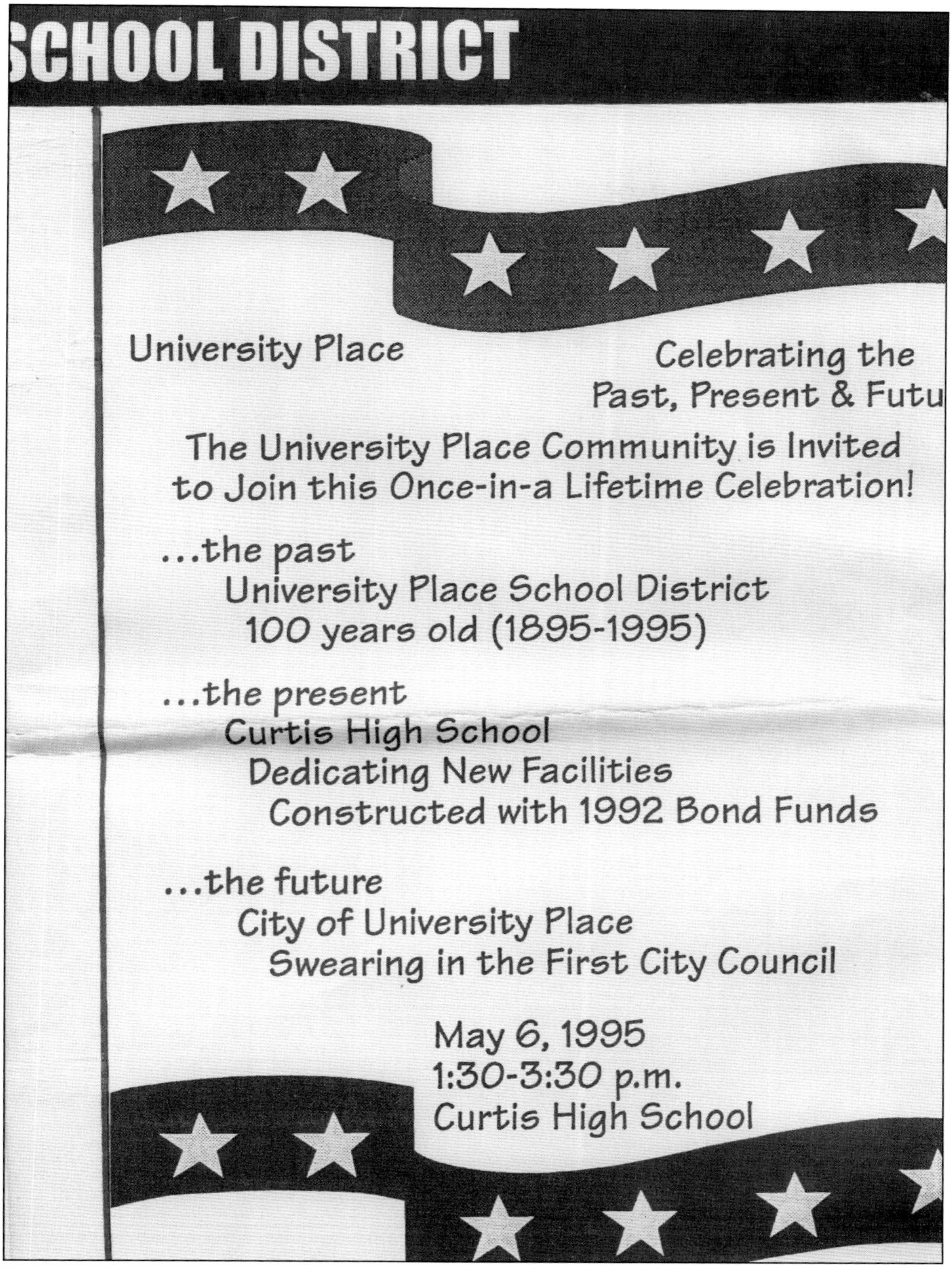

Bringing the past, present, and future together, the University Place School District sponsored a community celebration on May 6, 1995, to recognize 100 years of profound change and advancement. Among the announcements made at the celebration were: the school district was now 100 years old, new facilities at Curtis High School were ready for occupancy, and the first City of University Place Council would be sworn in.

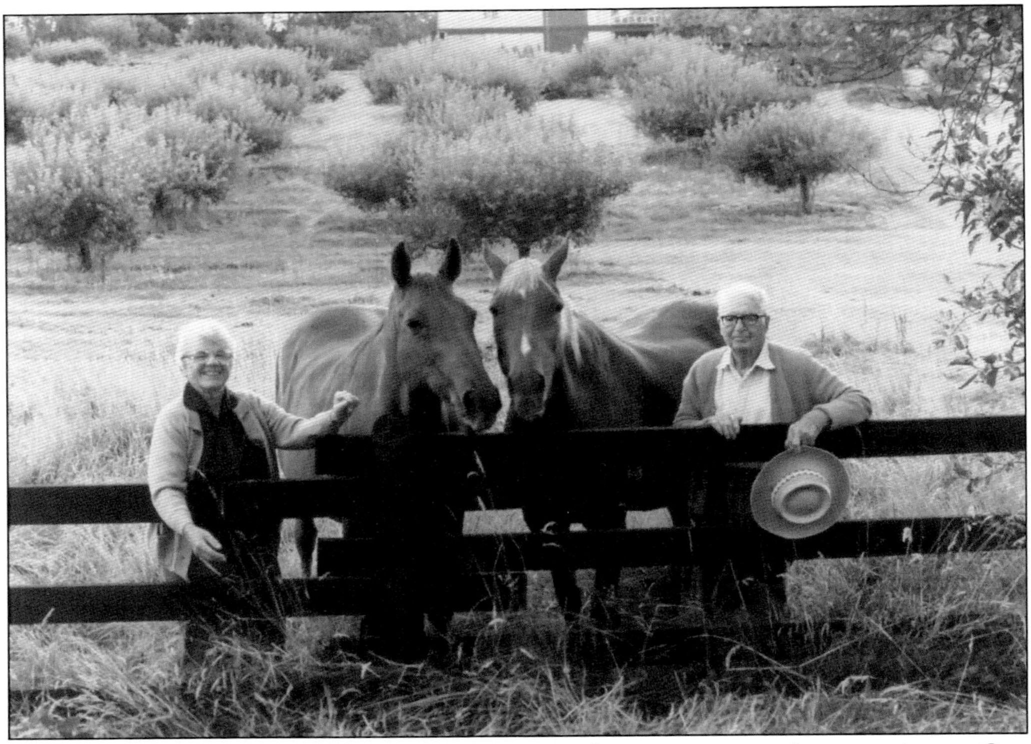

As a city, University Place could now acquire property for preservation and community use. One such purchase was of the apple orchard and home of Charles and Mary Curran. The Currans came to UP in the mid-1950s and built their Robert Price–designed home overlooking the orchard they planted and the pasture for their two horses. The orchard is now home to a summer concert series as well as the annual apple squeeze.

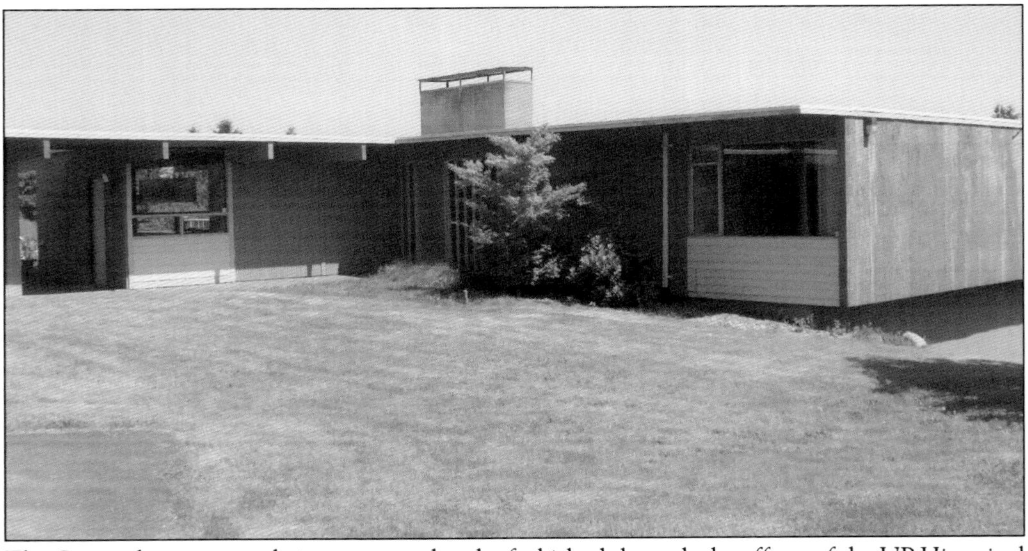

The Curran home is now being preserved and refurbished through the efforts of the UP Historical Society in the hope that it will become a community meeting place and perhaps a museum for University Place.

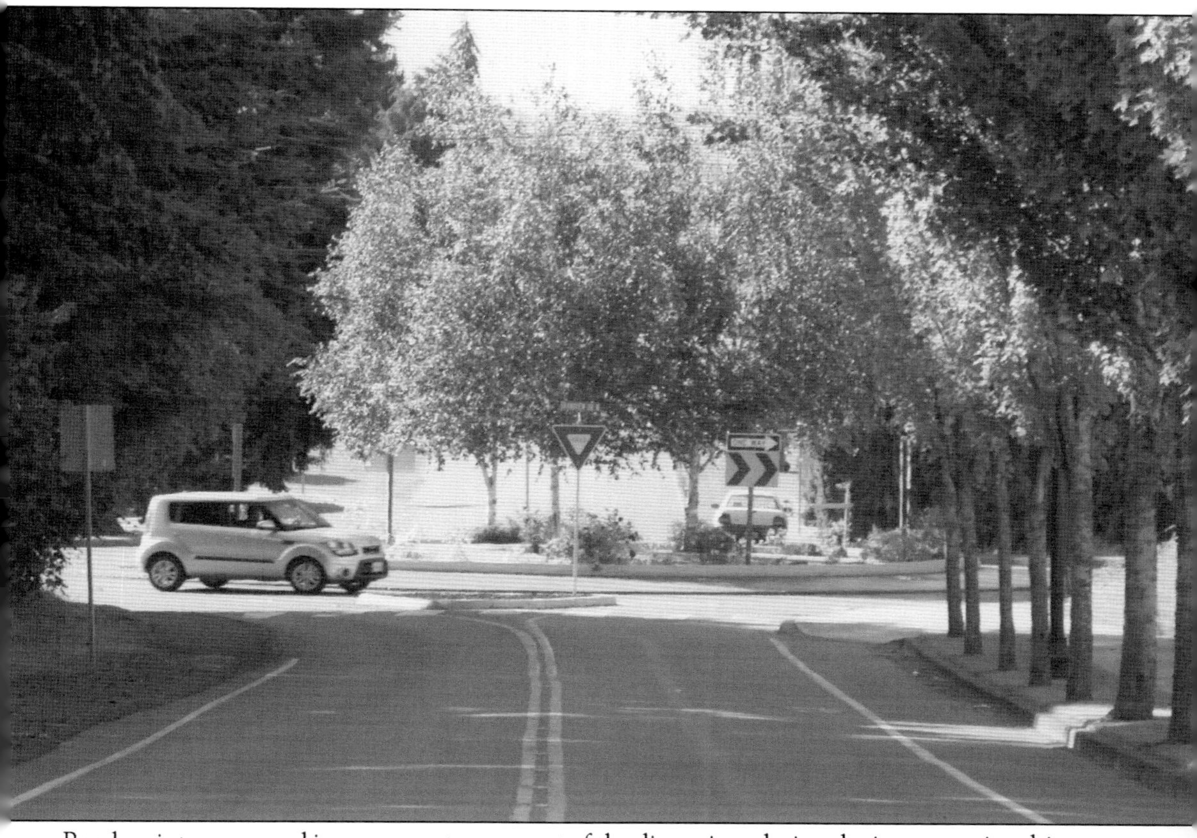

Road maintenance and improvements were part of the discussions during the incorporation drive. Discussion also included what could be done with the tax revenues that would be kept within UP instead of being spread throughout Pierce County. Many changes were made. Grandview Drive was transformed by sidewalks, streetlights, and roundabouts. Loved by some and hated by others, the roundabouts temper traffic flow without stop signs or traffic lights. The tree-lined street and median strips planted with shrubs and flowers make Grandview a beautiful drive almost any time of the year, and parking spaces invite drivers to stop and take a stroll along the pathway overlooking Chambers Bay Golf Course and Puget Sound, with the Olympic Mountains in the distance.

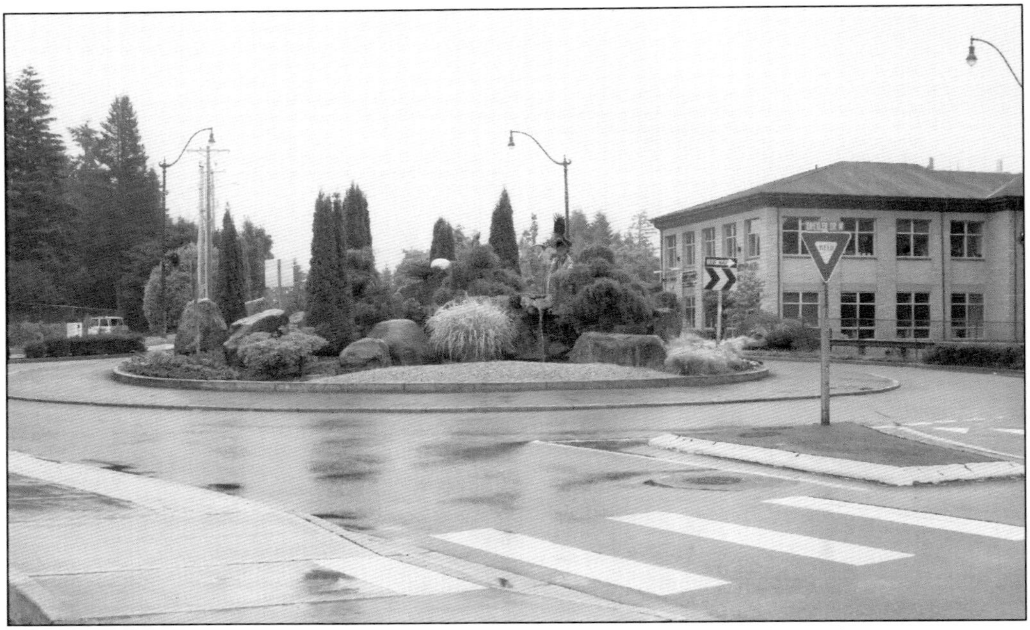

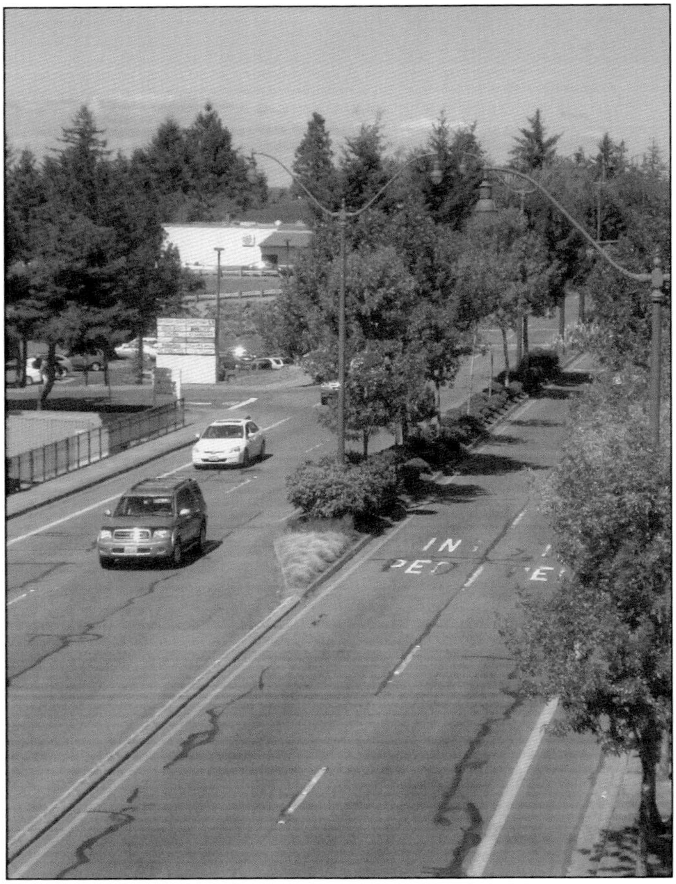

Road beautification was not confined to Grandview Drive. Sidewalks and streetlights have been installed along most major roads. A few more roundabouts were added on Fortieth Street (pictured above) near the center of UP and another at Cirque Drive and Alameda. Bridgeport Way (pictured at left), the main road through University Place, is now adorned with trees, flowers, and median strips with streetlights. The difference between the almost uncontrolled, unregulated growth along pre-city Bridgeport Way and its current status is remarkable.

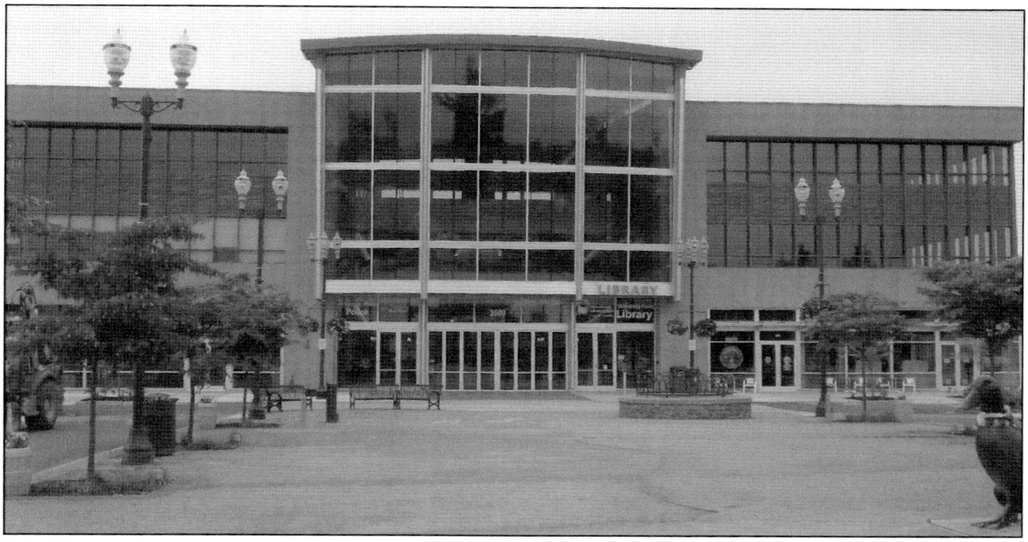

The Town Center project had its beginning in the minds of city visionaries as early at 2001. The dream was to create a nexus of commercial and living space that would become the center of community life and activity and also provide much-needed tax revenue for the city. Businesses already located in the Clockhouse Square and Windmill Village were given notice to move out. Even the new UP Library was torn down to make room for the project. The idea became controversial among residents and city council members. By the fall of 2007, only an underground parking garage was evident. When the recession of 2008 hit, plans for a grand Town Center almost came to a standstill. The centerpiece building of Town Center (above) was finally completed in February 2011. The main building houses the UP Library, the UP Police Department, and the Frog and Kiwi Café. Below is the duck statue at Town Center, placed in memory of the UP businessman, civic leader, and cofounder of Duck Daze, Terry Reim.

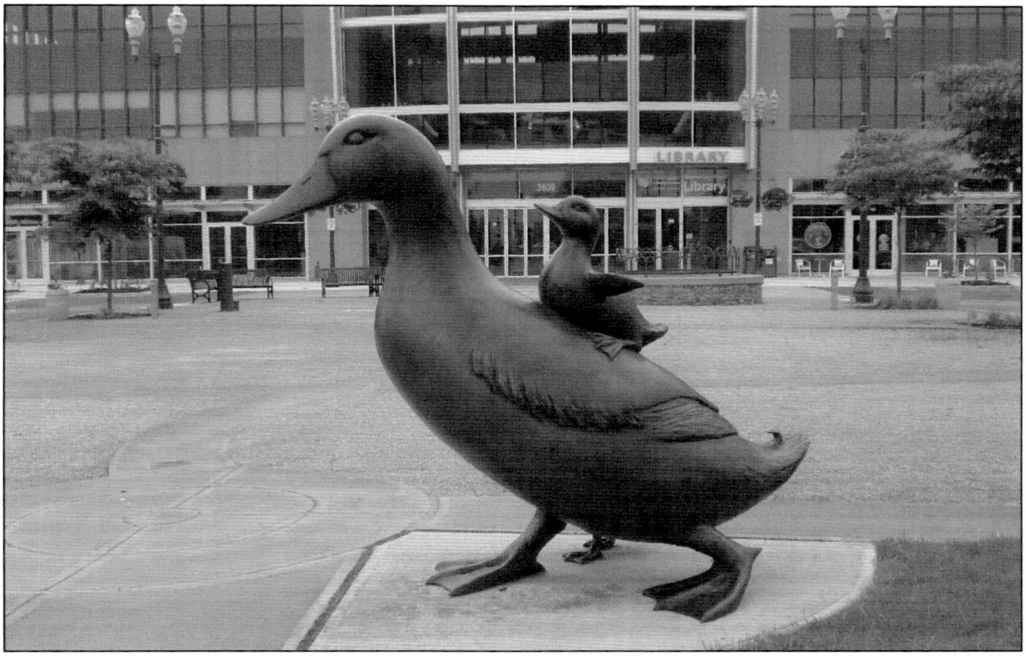

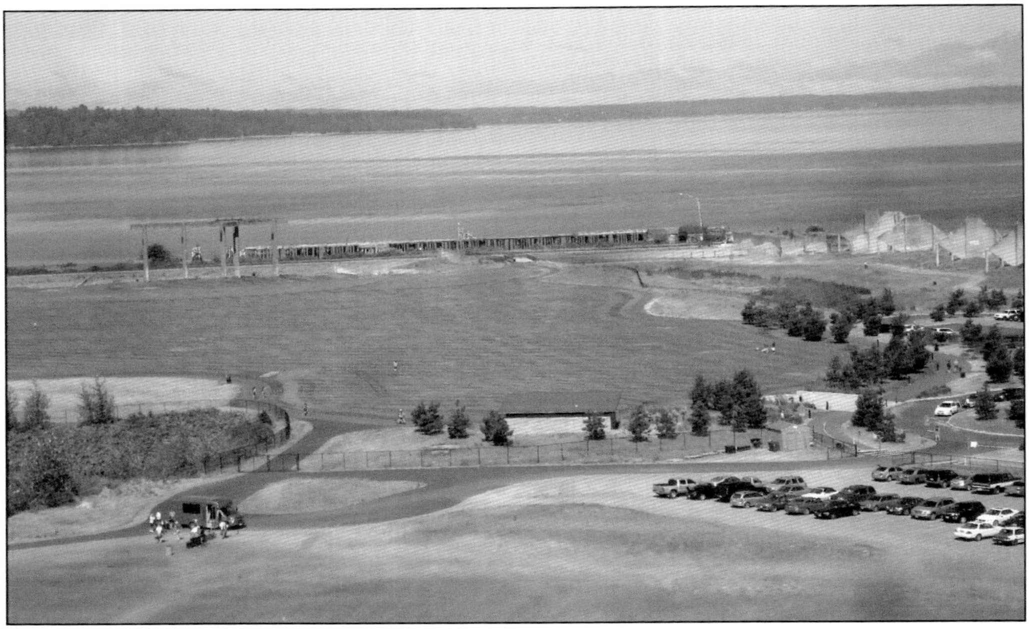

The development of the Chambers Creek Properties by Pierce County is another work-in-progress that has already resulted in tremendous benefits to the community. The Central Meadow of the former sand and gravel pit is in constant use for picnicking, sunbathing, kite-flying, strolling, and sporting activities.

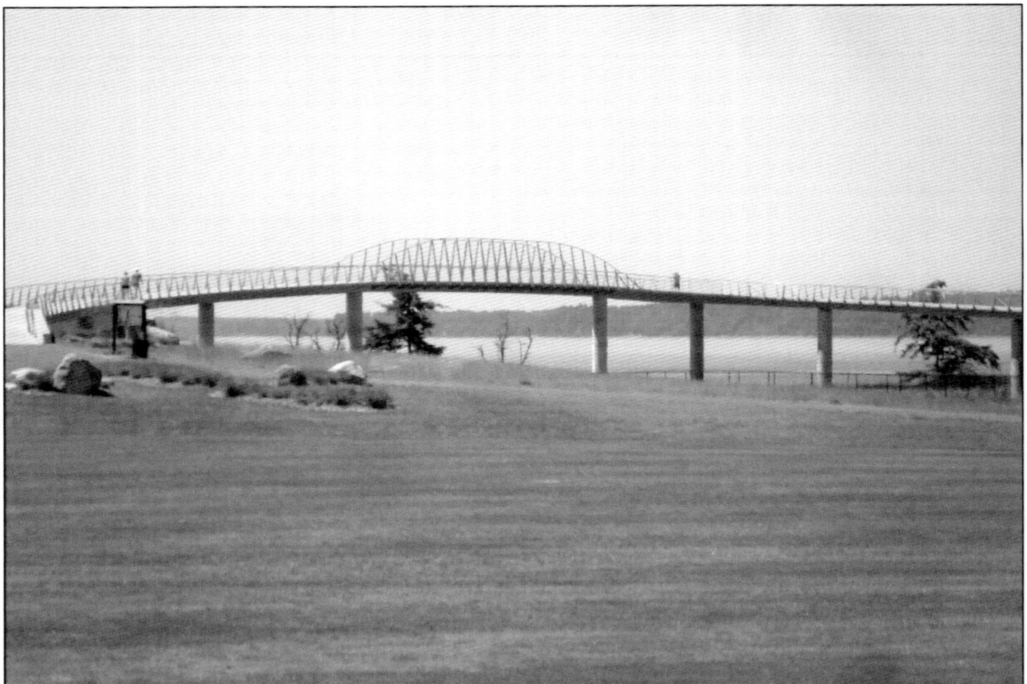

The Bridge to the Sound was opened in September 2010, and for the first time in over 100 years, residents have direct access to two miles of beach along the shore of Puget Sound.

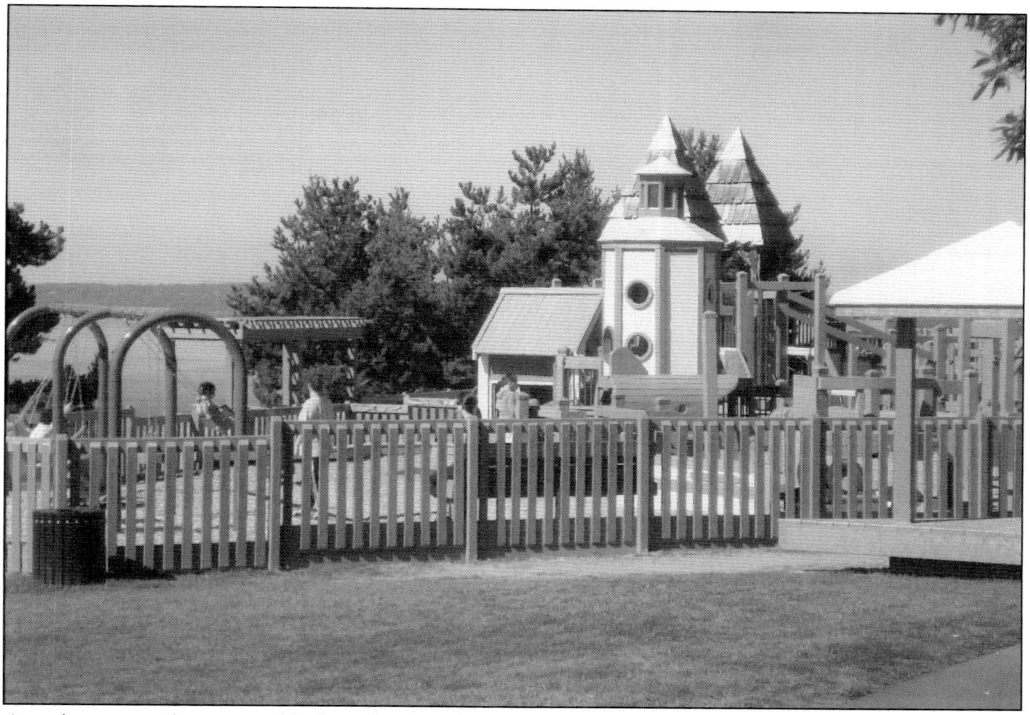

Another asset that was added to the North Meadow of the Chambers Creek Properties is this beautiful playground, dubbed The Playground-By-The Sound. Through a community-wide online effort, this playground was awarded a grant from Pepsi-Cola. Hundreds of volunteers showed up to put it all together.

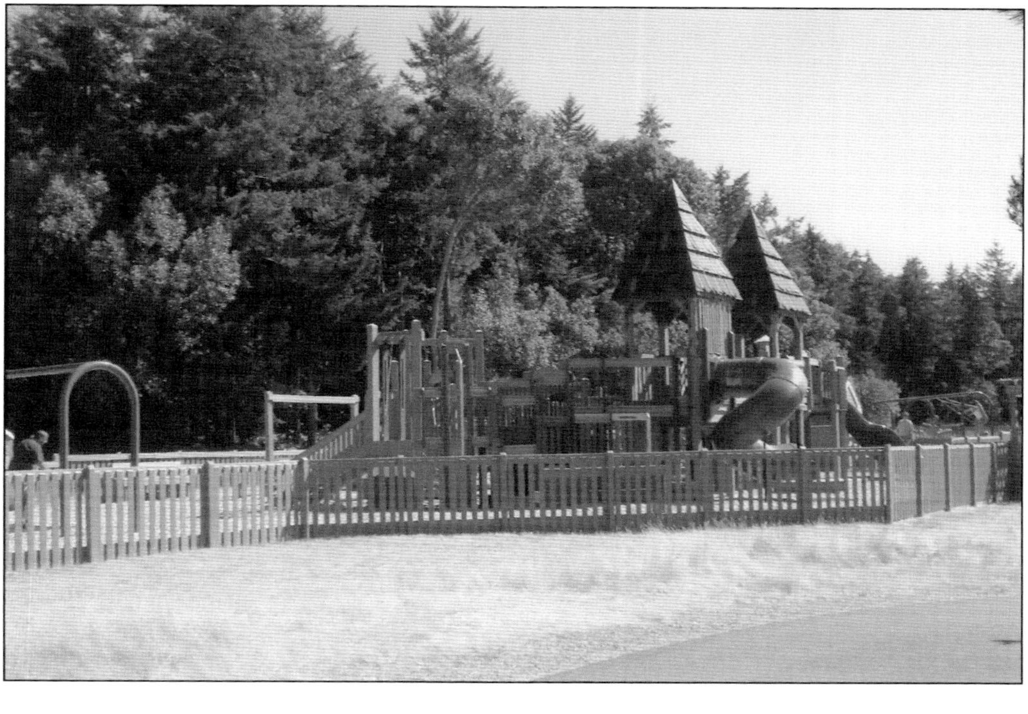

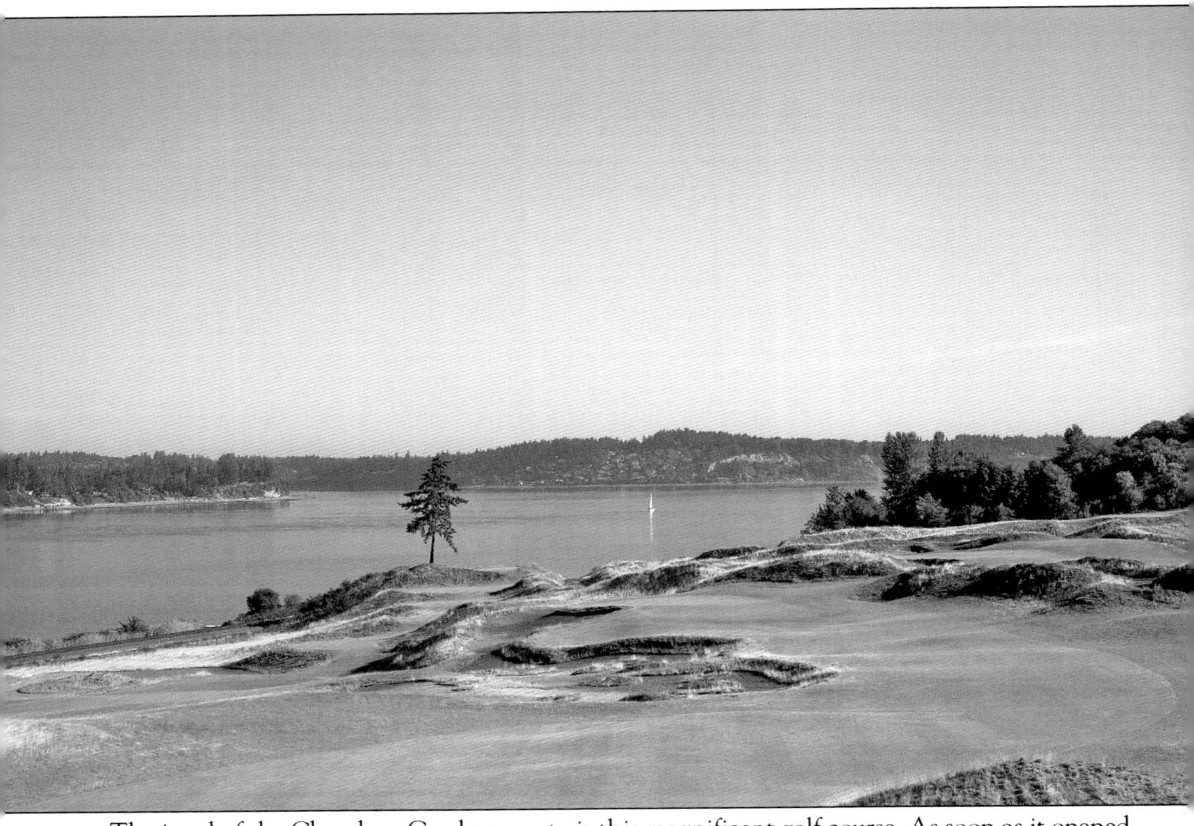

The jewel of the Chambers Creek property is this magnificent golf course. As soon as it opened in 2007, Chambers Bay Golf Course was recognized nationally as a premier golf course and one of the best in the country. It hosted the US Amateur Golf Tournament in August 2010 and will be the site of the US Open Golf Championship in June 2015. (Photograph by Martin Miller; courtesy of Jamie Fay, Chambers Bay Golf Course.)

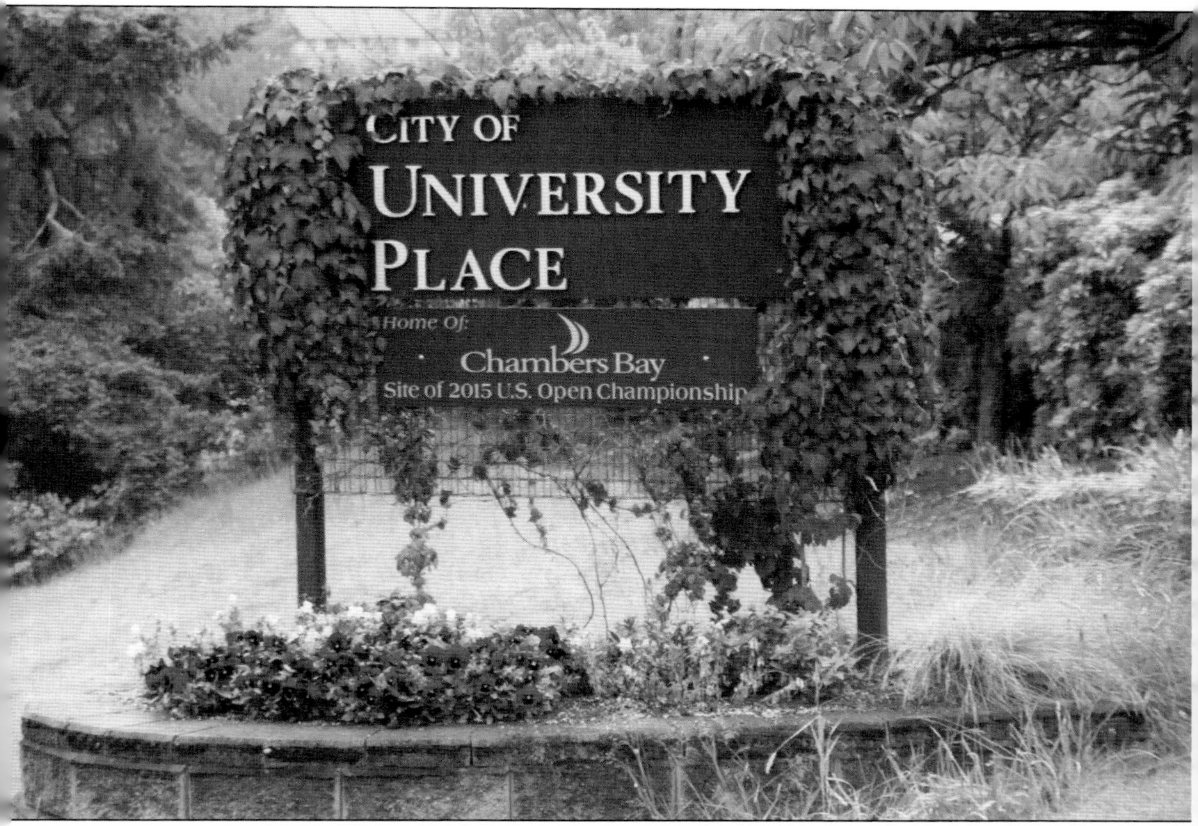

Welcome, EVERYONE, to THE University Place.

AUTHOR'S NOTE

As I come to the end of writing this book on the history of University Place, I cannot help feeling excited and relieved, but also anxious, about what I may have left out and/or errors I may have made. I discovered early on that it is much easier to teach history than to write it. It is incredibly difficult to research what is not recorded somewhere. I encourage all of you to write your own personal histories and share them. If you, as readers of this book, have knowledge of any UP families or buildings, please write their stories and gather any pictures you may have and submit them to me at uphistoryman@yahoo.com. I will make sure they become a part of the UP Historical Society records.

What is not preserved is soon lost forever. I will end this book with my favorite quote by Arthur O'Shaughnessy: "Each age is a dream that is dying, or one that is coming to birth." University Place of today was built on the dreams, aspirations, and imaginations of those who came before us. It is now up to all of us to pursue our own goals and dreams and continue to make University Place and our world an even better place to live.

—Arne Handeland
August 31, 2012